W9-BBU-705

BLUFFTON COLLEGE
THE TRUTH MAKES FREE
SEAL
BLUFFTON, ALLEN COUNTY, OHIO

Carlos de Alvear

MAN OF REVOLUTION

Museo Nacional, Buenos Aires *John Vanderlyn*

CARLOS DE ALVEAR
(about 1844)

CARLOS DE ALVEAR
MAN OF REVOLUTION

The Diplomatic Career of Argentina's First Minister to the United States

By THOMAS B. DAVIS, Jr.

19  55

Duke University Press, Durham, N. C.

Cambridge University Press, London, N.W. 1, England
Library of Congress Catalogue Number: 55-6526

Printed in the United States of America by
The Seeman Printery, Inc., Durham, N. C.

PREFACE

Argentines have praised General Carlos de Alvear often and widely for his military victories in the War for Independence and in the War against Brazil. But his countrymen have known little about his long diplomatic career—intermittently from 1824 to 1852—in the United States. And with good reason: during the dictatorship of Rosas no mention of Alvear or any other public official could appear in the public press except in the most casual manner. The General died in the United States shortly after the overthrow of Rosas, and in Argentina the ensuing decades of constitutional government centered in domestic development. The nation sought to forget the hated Rosas administration, and so the documents on foreign relations during the dictatorship have remained in the archives undisturbed except for the occasional perusal of some special scholar and the periodic investigation of government officials in the Ministry.

But the men who shaped national policy did not forget the experience of Alvear. They read his dispatches that covered more than a quarter of a century, accepted his conclusions, and put their nation on guard. The General had discovered that the country of Monroe and Adams no longer posed as the friend and protector of his nation: it evaded settlement of the Falkland Islands problem; it ignored the plight of his country as it faced European intervention. Repeatedly he declared, in dispatches so carefully read in Buenos Aires, that the United States had determined to conquer all Latin America. This ill-founded prophecy never came to pass, but Argentines learned to look askance at the northern republic in the decades that followed—even to our own time. The beginning of the century-old Argentine indifference to the policies of the United States is to be found in some part in the diplomatic correspondence of General Carlos de Alvear.

It is the purpose of this study to detail the issues that gave rise to this traditional antipathy. Alvear first voiced this suspicion consistently; he first cited the history of the United States to prove that his country should hold suspect the great republic to the North, and in desperation he advised his countrymen to organize a southern bloc that might counter the rising power of the North Americans.

In discussing a problem relating to the Western Hemisphere, the propriety of using the term "American" inevitably presents itself. Certain historians in the United States have abjured the word except for designating the people of the New World as distinguished from those of other lands. Those writers ignore long and popular usage in the New World as well as the Old, in South America as well as in North America, which has applied that name to the United States and its people. Many Latin Americans seem to prefer the term "North Americans," but this euphemism conceivably could give grounds for objection to Mexicans and Canadians. In short, there is no satisfactory substitute in the English language for the word "American" when referring to those things related to the United States—nothing akin even to the artificial Spanish term *Estadounidense*. Pleading the inadequacies of the English language, I have not sought an evasion.

Problems of translation often proved vexing. Where Spanish word order or punctuation did not agree, when literally translated, with English usage, I have not hesitated to change the phrasing in order to retain the clarity of the original idea. Particularly must one exercise generosity toward the mechanics of General Alvear's composition.

No person completes a historical study alone, and I have received my full share of assistance. In a seminar with Professor Samuel Flagg Bemis, Sterling Professor of Diplomatic History and International Relations at Yale University, I first became acquainted with General Alvear. Besides securing for me the loan of photographic materials which the Library of

Congress obtained from the Archivo General de la Nacion in Buenos Aires, Professor Bemis provided me with useful introductions when I studied there in the summer of 1941. Frequently I have drawn heavily upon his time and knowledge, and for these privileges I am particularly grateful.

To the Division of Cultural Relations of the Department of State I am indebted for an opportunity to complete my research in Buenos Aires. While in that city the officials of the Archivo General generously aided me in a survey of their materials. Señor Carlos Mallie greatly assisted me by transcribing certain almost illegible portions of Alvear's penmanship. I shall always remember with gratitude two Argentine scholars, Señor Marío Belgrano and Señor Rolando Dorcas Berro, whose advice guided me through the maze of official archival collections in Buenos Aires. I am under especial obligation to Señor Abelard Arenas Fraga, chief of the Archivo del Ministro de Relaciones Exteriores y Culto. He extended to me particular courtesies and assisted materially in the prompt completion of my work in his department. I should not fail to mention the assistance of the staff of the Yale University Library, of the Library of Congress, and of the National Archives in Washington. I am under more than ordinary obligation to my wife for her patience both as auditor and as proofreader and for her reserve, which has been equal to most occasions. That my work still possesses imperfections is my own inevitable responsibility.

T. B. D.

Port Chester, New York.

TABLE OF CONTENTS

Carlos de Alvear

MAN OF REVOLUTION

I

ALVEAR AND THE SPANISH-AMERICAN WAR FOR INDEPENDENCE

> Ferocious Artigas was popular, not only in the Banda Oriental [Uruguay], but also in the rest of our country. So was Quiroga. . . . Artigas was the first among us who took advantage of the brutish imbecility of the lower classes, and he made them serve him in the enslavement of the upper classes while he exercised power without any check beyond that of his brutish will. And I gave to this barbarous system of Artigas all the opposition that I could, but unfortunately. . . .

Strong language. General Carlos de Alvear of Buenos Aires—like many another general since—was penning his memoirs in 1852. But time and disease had overtaken him, and long exile in the United States had kept him so far away that what he said would not matter. In the mad rush of the war for independence against Spain, of domestic turmoil and of dictatorship in La Plata, the General had lost his fortune, his political career, and even his family. Lost all but his pride and his fierce hatred of the enemy who first drove him from public life. No other defeat hurt so badly as that one: spared that defeat the other misfortunes might never have happened. And so he dipped his pen in gall as he recollected those days half a lifetime ago and half a world away.

So quietly had the General lived in New York City that even the newsmen had forgotten that he was almost the dean of the diplomatic corps. For fourteen years he had represented Argentina—then rigorously governed by Dictator Rosas. And probably nobody then living knew that President Monroe had once given him audience years and years ago. That event made a great impression upon him, and he had never forgotten how the President had graciously acknowledged certain untoward events by saying, "We are both men of revolution."

The ailing Minister had met his share of famous men and he called himself the equal of any. He outsmarted George Canning once, so he said. On another occasion he won over the great Simón Bolívar. San Martín he introduced to Buenos Aires when that leader was ready to enlist in the cause of liberty; and long before San Martín had crossed the Andes General Alvear had overwhelmed the Spanish citadel of Montevideo. For this first triumph of the Argentine revolution Buenos Aires had struck off a special medal in honor of the victory. At formal diplomatic dinners he used to wear that badge of honor, but the great New York fire of 1845 had swept away the last token of past glories.

Only his memories remained—memories of the days when he won his first military commission as an *alférez* in the Spanish army of liberation against Napoleon. They had fought hard in those days. They won, and Carlos de Alvear was not unknown in the army. Those were the glorious days—a fatherland to redeem from a foreign soldiery, and then the call to create a new country in the New World. He had served in all this, and not as one of the least, but as a leader.

Ever since Artigas defeated him in Uruguay, misfortune had been his companion; to leave his family hostage for his behavior, and to die alone, unknown, in exile. The General's memoirs never got beyond "the triumph of Artigas. . . ." Artigas . . . Quiroga . . . Rosas . . . His record on the first two was clear, but Rosas had bested him, tricked him into doing his will, then exiled him. Now a revolution from the north where Alvear often marched had overthrown Rosas himself. That revolution Alvear had missed, and the victors found his protestations of loyalty among the Dictator's papers. Artigas . . . Quiroga . . . He had the grace to omit Rosas. Some things a man cannot bring himself to write.

If he had really attempted a systematic account of his life (which he never did), General Alvear would have begun with the distant days on the Argentine-Brazilian frontier where he was born. In the little settlement of San Angel de la Guardia on October 26, 1789, his parents had presented their first-born son, Carlos Antonio José de Alvear, for baptism with due ceremony of the Church and of the times.[1] For eleven more years the Alvears lived in this border town of Missiones while young Carlos enjoyed an open and unschooled life. With his father absent on official surveys that would establish the Spanish-Portugese boundary and his mother busy with her regularly increasing brood, the boy developed independence and petulance, qualities that were to bring both good and ill fortune.

The joint boundary commission never completed the survey of the whole La Plata-Brazilian line, and the Alvear family returned to Buenos Aires in 1800. A few years later the parents, with eight children, embarked in the ship *Mercedes* for Spain. Serious illness of the commander of the small convoy of four ships caused Don Diego, as the next ranking official, to transfer to the flagship, thus separating the father from his family. The mother, worn out by the misbehavior of her twelve-year-old son, soon asked that he be transferred to his father's ship and command. It proved to be a final separation.

The outline of the Spanish coast stood clearly revealed to the east in the early light of October 5, 1804. Simultaneously, Don Diego sighted four British men-of-war to the north. Unknown to members of the little fleet now within sight of home, Spain, as an ally of Napoleon, had incurred British hostility. Upon overhauling the convoy the British demanded its surrender. In the short and disastrous action which followed the failure to capitulate, the ship carrying the Alvear family received a broadside at her waterline and sank. When a search later showed that about fifty persons had been rescued from the *Mercedes* but that none of his family had survived, the horrified father and his son were taken with the remainder of the little Spanish fleet to Portsmouth.[2] There for a time they were held as prisoners.

The Peace of Amiens (1802-1803) won limited benefits for the prisoners. They were brought ashore, enjoyed more generous subsistence, and the commander, at least, received financial compensation for his losses. This sum, together with his claims for all personal goods destroyed, the English restored. The father and son, living comfortably on this amount, moved in the best society and they met, so the father reported, lords and ministers of the first rank. During this period the father enrolled young Carlos in a local school near London.[3] Perhaps this education during his formative years, together with the decent and honorable treatment accorded to him and his father, account for Alvear's lifelong respect and admiration for English institutions and, in part, explains the liberal ideas which he contributed to the Argentine Revolution.

Thus, Don Diego and his son lived well while their homeland was being subjected to increasing Napoleonic indignities. French troops in Spain had aroused a latent Spanish nationalism, and as Napoleon turned his attention to Russia, Spanish resistance arose. Eventually this opposition reached such dimensions that England would support it. She dispatched a small expeditionary force to the Peninsula and permitted the return of Spanish prisoners and refugees. Don Diego, with a new English wife, and the youth, Carlos, returned safely to Spain. The father and son promptly enrolled in the *Carbineros Reales*, a choice regiment hitherto reserved for nobility. The *Junta* of Cádiz awarded Don Diego a captaincy. His son took place in the ranks and gained his father's approbation for bravery in action.

During the Peninsular War, Don Diego was transferred from the artillery to the position of Commandant of Cádiz and Governor of the Island of León. In the meantime, young Carlos received a commission as *alférez*, a rank equivalent to lieutenant. He participated bravely in the battles of Talavera, Yébenes, and Ciudad Real y Vitoria. "In all the battles," Don Diego wrote to a friend in Buenos Aires, "Carlos has carried himself with great valor and generosity in such a manner that he is honored and liked not only by his own troops but by the whole army."[4] Soon thereafter the proud father obtained the transfer of his son to a quiet post on the Island of León. There Carlos de Alvear's worthy contribution to the Spanish fight for freedom reached an unheroic conclusion.

Safe within the walls his father's influence had fashioned, the young *alférez* spent his hours off duty observing the political course of the *Junta* of Cádiz and hearing from afar the progress of Spanish and English arms against the French invaders. Then there came a lull in the war. While Napoleon was turning his attention toward Russia, both the invaders and defenders south of the Pyrenees stopped as if for breath. Cessation of active warfare brought more idleness to the restless Carlos. His service to Spain, which was only a stepmother to him, no longer seemed necessary. Both the exiled Ferdinand and his aging father, King Carlos IV, rested beyond his care if not beyond his knowledge. The Spanish monarchy could have meant nothing personal to the creole *carbinero*. Carlos de Alvear needed a new cause or a new country.

While yet in the service of Spain he heard the call of his native countrymen. Already prisoners from the revolted Spanish-American colonies had begun to trickle into Cádiz. Don Carlos knew some of the men from Buenos Aires and to them he gave such assistance as he could. For some he eased the terms of imprisonment and for others he managed to secure release. Imprisoned friends from the Plata region meant more than monarchs imprisoned in France, especially when these friends from his own land were preaching the liberal doctrines for which Carlos thought that he had been fighting in Spain.[5] In Cádiz, too, Alvear first encountered colonial soldiers like himself who discreetly talked of revolution for their homelands. They organized themselves into a secret order through which they could exchange information without fear of Spanish authorities. From their meetings he received his first accurate reports of colonial events. Their stories probably stirred memories of his childhood. This revolutionary group called itself the *Sociedad de Lautaro*, and eventually grew to a membership of forty. Among its members the *alférez* met other future leaders of the independence party—such men as José de San Martín and José Miguel Carrera. In later life Alvear somewhat dubiously represented himself as the center of this group.[6]

Soon the Cádiz group resolved to leave for Buenos Aires and to take up the burdens of revolution. They envisaged a period of secret plotting to overthrow an objectionable person here or there and after that a national triumph in the New

World.[7] Don Diego sympathized with his son's zeal and determination. In order that he should return without delay to his native land the father agreed to settle on the young man a part of his patrimony. Don Carlos received, in all, 230,000 reales, some of it in cash, and the rest he collected in London and in Buenos Aires. Fortified by such comfortable sums, he arranged passage to London for all his companions who needed it. In January, 1812, an impressive company embarked on the British ship *George Canning* for Buenos Aires.[8]

The *George Canning* slowly worked its way up-river to the Buenos Aires waterfront on March 9, 1812. And on that day disembarked men who would profoundly influence the Revolution.[9] At first Alvear outshone his companions. His handsome features, his military and political talent, his good family traditions, and his abundance of money soon won the favor of people who counted most in the small city.

Within a week after their arrival Alvear and San Martín offered their military services to the patriots. Both were accepted at once with their Spanish ranks. Since San Martín outranked other officers in the city,[10] he assumed control of a new military force of mounted grenadiers and appointed Alvear second in command. United in spirit and zeal, the two men quickly secured enlistments for their unit; the recruits, subjected to rigorous drill, soon formed a company exceptional for its fine spirit and ability.

For only a few months, however, did Alvear willingly concentrate on problems of the drill field. As a matter of fact, his military training had been neither extensive nor thorough. His real interest lay in politics. He devoted himself more to public affairs, and soon his attendance at maneuvers ceased altogether. It was San Martín who gave his whole attention to the new corps, and as this body increased in size and importance, its commander inevitably became a man of prominence.

The newly arrived revolutionists had found the civil administration of La Plata racked with internal dissension and uncertain of its powers. They found a people not profoundly revolutionary: an embryonic nation without a military or political policy and without consciousness of its lack, apparently; and with public life almost completely dominated by the capital city. A triumvirate appointed by the revolutionary *Junta* was attempting to provide a national administration when the *George Canning* brought its passengers into the city. During the summer of 1812 it failed in all endeavors to conduct a military campaign or to bring about the election of a representative assembly.[11] Many feared for the safety of the city itself.

Alvear plunged with zest into this conflict of governing agencies and attempted assemblies. A "Patriotic Society," organized with the consent of the revolutionary government in January, 1812, had quickly changed from an advisory agency of the administration into an opposition group. Alvear soon dominated this society and used it to accomplish his own ends. The newly arrived "generals in perspective" converted the political group into a secret lodge which they named "The Lautaro" in memory of their dreaming, Cádiz days.[12] Within a remarkably short time the lodge was directing the government itself. It agitated for centralization of executive power in one person and found eager seconds in the easy tasks of criticism. From various channels—military, political, and provincial—opposition gathered and flowed into the Lautaro. The lodge called secret meetings; it drafted plans, and within a few days it had overthrown the incompetent triumvirate.[13]

National development proceeded rapidly thereafter. Promptly the new triumvirs summoned a Constituent Assembly which confirmed separation from Spain but not from allegiance to Ferdinand VII, and established a civil administration. To this body Alvear was easily elected, soon becoming its president. The Assembly decreed that its deputies owed allegiance to the nation first of all. Other measures provided for the creation of a national entity to replace Spanish authority. In memory of the first revolt against the mother country, the Assembly decreed May 25 a national holiday and ordered masses to be celebrated for those who had died in the national cause. New currency carrying the present Argentine seal replaced Spanish coinage. Alvear introduced a measure to provide for the gradual abolition of slavery.[14]

Unquestionably the Assembly by such laws as these was effecting a revolution, and unquestionably Carlos de Alvear was a leader in the work. His military ambitions had lapsed: abandoning the Grenadiers, he now devoted himself to civilian leadership. In the realm of politics, though still young enough to be called "the boy" by his opponents, he exercised real talent, and through his aggressive program persuaded influential men to support the new measures. As President of the Constituent Assembly he warned of evils induced by divided responsibility. He cited the frequent conflicts of authority in the Spanish revolutionary *juntas*, and as an example of good organization he referred to the "North American republicans." The invigorated Assembly united the nation and centralized its power, but at the expense of increased personal influence (*personalismo*) in government.

This program of centralization eventually triumphed when the Assembly resolved to unify in a Supreme Director all public powers formerly held by a cabinet. Don Gervasio Posadas, an uncle of Alvear, was elected the first Supreme Director, while his nephew became Commander-in-Chief of La Plata forces, a position which made him responsible for the military progress of the revolution.[15]

Immediate military success under the new Constituent Assembly engendered a feeling of public security. San Martín and Belgrano were organizing forces in the northwest, and Alvear planned a campaign to gain control of the eastern side of the Plata Estuary—called the Banda Oriental—by capturing the royalist stronghold of Montevideo.[16] Seizure of this position was vital, for an enemy base so near the heart of La Plata menaced all armies which might march westward into Chile or Peru.

Montevideo had withstood the modest armies of Buenos Aires because it retained control of the sea. Since Buenos Aires possessed no sea power, the task of reducing the royalist city seemed insurmountable until Alvear sponsored the creation of a navy. Against great pessimism and much indifference he persisted until a small fleet of converted merchantmen was prepared to fight. Within a month Captain William Brown, the brave and skilful commander of the new "navy," drove royalist ships from the estuary and laid blockade to Montevideo. Alvear, after displacing General Rondeau as field commander, advanced by land, occupying military points along the way.[17] The rapidity with which he moved and laid siege to the city forced its surrender before his potential enemies within or without the fortifications could agree on a suitable course of action.[18]

The sunshine of victory lasted for weeks. The victors found such great stores of goods and military supplies that they required several months to transport them to Buenos Aires. The exulting Assembly rewarded its twenty-five-year-old commander with the title of Brigadier-General and ordered medals struck off in honor of the triumph.[19]

Sunny hours of public acclaims preceded the thunderstorm. With Montevideo liberated, Alvear prepared to move against José Artigas, the stubborn *gaucho* patriot who, while fighting the Spaniards, had refused to co-operate with the Buenos Aires government.[20] Reluctant to leave so powerful and rebellious a chieftain in the rear, the young commander invaded the northern hills of Uruguay in force, the more quickly to eliminate his enemy. Alvear's troops had advanced deep into the Oriental territory when word of revolts at home caused them to stop, and presently Artigas roundly defeated the forces from across the Plata.

As if to re-establish himself after this defeat, the conqueror of Montevideo won from Posadas the command of the Army of the North, then being gathered for a march across the Andes to aid the patriot forces of Peru. Rondeau, who had been awarded this post when removed from command before Montevideo, now felt himself sacrificed again to Alvear's vaulting ambition. The prospective commander had reached Córdoba on his way to join the army in Upper Peru when he heard that Rondeau and all the important officers in his staff had risen against him. On learning that the whole province had supported the revolt, Alvear did not attempt to join the army.[21]

Returning to Buenos Aires rather unheroically, the displaced commander faced a difficult situation. Even here opposition was growing. Some people resented his extreme youth.

Others disliked his imperious manner. His unconcealed military ambitions disturbed many citizens; the adoration of his followers offended still others. Artigas, promptly making common cause with Rondeau, defeated the forces of Buenos Aires that had been left in the Banda Oriental, and, invading Corrientes, killed his captured opponents with primitive torture. San Martín, collecting an army in Cuyo in preparation for his march over the Andes, paid no attention to these developments.

Now for a second time defeat on the frontier frightened the Assembly into approving another dictatorship. Posadas resigned on January 8, 1815, and the following day Alvear took the oath as Supreme Director. The new leader, only twenty-seven years old, tried to win the support of Artigas by appeasement. He surrendered to him the whole of the Banda Oriental, including Montevideo. The old *gaucho*, accepting these favors, promptly ordered his lieutenants to invade the upper provinces of Corrientes, Entreríos, and Santa Fé.

Alvear suffered equal failure in dealing with the contumacious northern army under Rondeau. The chieftains ignored all appeals in the name of brotherhood, sovereignty of the nation, respect for supreme authority, or fear of anarchy. Since it was known to be useless to appeal to San Martín, the desperate Supreme Director tried to displace him while the latter was preparing for his famous Andean march. But the whole province of Cuyo rallied to San Martín and ordered him to proceed with his work. The Director's envoys retired, and although San Martín did not interfere in La Plata politics he offered no help whatsoever.[22]

While events on the frontiers were becoming so desperate, Alvear sought to strengthen himself, at least on the home front. He ordered all Spaniards who had not declared allegiance to the United Provinces to be interned in Córdoba or other interior points. This Spanish exodus on six-day notice impressed many people as too harsh, and it embittered friends of the exiles. He secured passage of laws that virtually prohibited oral or written attacks on the government. Operating under Alvear's orders, a court martial ordered execution of a rebellious officer and public exposure of his body as a general warning. Civilians, temporarily cowed, believed that a similar fate awaited all those who opposed the Director.

Although the young leader pretended to ignore public opinion, he could not overlook the deficits in the Treasury. To raise funds he tried every expedient, even stay laws and expropriation of Church funds. All these frenzied efforts produced no real financial improvement; they served only to alienate the wealthy groups within the city.

Against such opposition the Director could not long retain his power. A revolt of his own troops, a force of 1,600 well-trained men under trusted officers, signaled the end. With his support dwindling everywhere, Alvear resigned as Supreme Director, but sought to retain command of an army with which to "protect" Buenos Aires from northern invaders, he said. But the city fathers did not wish the General to protect them. Nor did they wish to see his forces grow by further conscription. Yielding to a convenient street revolt, the Cabildo sanctioned withdrawal from the Assembly, thus seceding from the United Provinces. The city became, in theory at least, an independent unit. This action took place on April 15, 1815, and with it Alvear's place in the government of Buenos Aires came to an end.[23]

But the city, rid of its Director, was not rid of his army. The Cabildo raised a new force against its nominal defender. So ready were enlistments that within twenty-four hours barricades blocked every passage into the city. Any attempt to capture it would have demanded a greater sacrifice than the ex-Director could expect of his wavering forces. And so he was isolated. The muncipal authorities suspended all river traffic; they proclaimed him a criminal. At this critical juncture an Englishman serving as mediator bore to the proscribed leader the final terms: the Council would permit him, his family, and one other person free passage into exile. The General accepted these life-saving terms and the next day his small party embarked for Río de Janeiro.[24] In such a manner did Carlos de Alvear, shorn of his glory, end his career as a revolutionary statesman and soldier of the United Provinces.

. . . .

The years of exile bore heavily on the deposed Director. In Río de Janeiro many Spaniards and *Orientales* hated him for the capture of Montevideo. They even threatened his life. Because his financial resources proved inadequate for his family, he felt that injustice had been done by forcing them to share his exile.[25] Enemies circulated stories that he had escaped with the national treasury, and public acceptance of these tales hurt his pride. In some fit of anger or depression he wrote a long letter to the Spanish minister, Villalba, resident in Río de Janeiro, asking him to forward the enclosed *Memorial* to his King. This *Memorial*, written on August 23, 1815, completely repudiated the Revolution.

The exile began by reminding the King of his former services in the royal army and how, once Spain had been freed of invaders, he had returned to his homeland, only to find the country without an organized government. Since there existed no Spanish authority to which he could appeal, he had helped organize a local government to save the country from anarchy. Don Carlos insisted that he had taken control of the government only in order to lead it back to Spain.

After devious explanations of his revolutionary conduct, the fallen hero wrote of the sufferings that many subjects in the New World had endured for their sovereign. He cited his own exile as proof of willingness to suffer for the King. As this remarkable document reached an end, Alvear truckled for favor. He reiterated that always he had desired, after his opponents had been beaten, to return the provinces "to the domination of a sovereign who, alone, would be able to make them happy." He appended to the *Memorial* a letter to Villalba with a personal appeal:

> At least, I hope that, considering me a faithful vassal who sincerely reclaims the grace of Sovereign and hopes to merit it, Your Excellency will be pleased to recommend me to His Majesty before whom I shall present myself as soon as I can find safe transportation for my person and family.[26]

Nothing came of this petition and life in Río de Janeiro grew more difficult. Collapse of his party in Buenos Aires may have made him feel that he would never return to his native country again; secondary persecution by Spaniards in Río de Janeiro who had felt the weight of Alvear's hand in Buenos Aires may have been the last straw. At any rate, while popular hatred of him still raged in Buenos Aires, Alvear unwisely moved to Montevideo the better to harass and to overcome the government across the estuary.[27]

In the city which he had once entered as conqueror the exile found revolutionary backwash from Chile and Buenos Aires as well as refugees from Artigas. The discredited Chilean leader and companion of Cádiz, José Miguel Carrera, dominated this desperate jetsam that in turn fought Artigas, invaded the province of Buenos Aires, or sought alliances with chieftains of the northern provinces. The Chileans wished to overthrow the Buenos Aires government so that they could cross the Andes and return to Chile, where they hoped to displace San Martín and O'Higgins; Alvear wanted to capture Buenos Aires and make himself master of the city. Therefore, the two of them, working from the same base and using the same tactics, and at times joining forces, sought to capture the port. The union of former rebel leaders against persistently rebellious subjects evidently impressed the King of Spain. Although unanswered, Alvear's appeal to that monarch had been heard, presumably, in the highest quarters, for the Spanish Minister of Foreign Affairs advised the Viceroy of Peru to encourage the factions led by Carrera and Alvear.[28]

The Viceroy never received the instructions, for patriot forces in the Pacific intercepted the Spanish ships and read the incriminating document. Then Alvear's perfidy became known. Alternately he denied everything, or else claimed that he was trying to delude the King of Spain into revealing his plans for reconquest. In the meantime he renewed his efforts to overwhelm the Buenos Aires government. He rejoiced when the interim government of Pueyrredón met increasing opposition from rebellious northern and western frontiers. Sensing the rising power of the upper provinces, he determined that no campaign against the wealthy port should take place without his assistance. He rode to Santa Fé and there allied himself with Estanislao López, leader of a rabble whom aristocrats of

Buenos Aires habitually labeled *montoneros,* or heaps of rubbish. Alvear had often and correctly predicted that if the *montoneros* from the North should come into power, national confusion would follow, yet he unhesitatingly joined the northerners in hope of achieving a personal victory.

Indisputably this invasion brought national confusion. With the fall of Pueyrredón in 1819 all semblance of national government collapsed. Enmities as deep as life itself broke out. The internecine hatred of 1815 revived. Buenos Aires could not forgive its former idol for his association with Carrera, and no sooner did Alvear enter the city than he was forced to leave again. With a personal following of fifty to sixty exiled officials, he set up headquarters in an outlying town and alternately sent threatening notes to the city council and appeals to López for assistance. Once Alvear dared to slip into the city again on March 4, 1820, and to canvass his supporters secretly. When rumors of his presence reached the Cabildo, it promptly declared against him and put all citizens on their guard. He fled, still protected by furtive associates, for discovery would have meant certain death.[29]

By the end of July, López became convinced that he could neither overcome Buenos Aires nor force his unwelcome officers upon its citizens. Therefore, he ordered a general retirement before steadily increasing armies from the port. With this retreat Carrera and Alvear abandoned hope of controlling the city. The *Gaceta* proudly declared:

> The city of Buenos Aires has covered itself with glory and honor. More than 10,000 citizens, armed and supplied have remained for seventeen day in the best order. . . . It is necessary that Carrera should forget Buenos Aires forever, and that Alvear should give up the vain design of ruling this town.[30]

During the course of his retirement, López heard of a possible surprise attack upon a detachment of his troops stationed at the town of San Nicolás. He sent his discredited Director to notify the garrison and to organize resistance. For some reason, Alvear delayed that night along the road instead of completing the mission. The unwarned garrison was completely annihilated. López became so enraged at this faithlessness that he was on the point of shooting his confederate, but friends interceded. Instead he sent the disgraced adventurer to Montevideo for another period of exile.[31]

Neither Alvear's private letters nor his public proclamations give an adequate reason for his attempted return to public life after his treasonable appeal to the King of Spain. He may have been poor, homesick, or ambitious, but the strongest personal motives cannot condone his lack of a public program. To be sure, no one seemed to have a program in those unhappy days. The Argentines call 1820 "The Terrible Year." Twenty-four governments for the province of Buenos Aires alone during those twelve months justify the title. Alvear only made matters worse. He sought no justification for his invasion of 1820, but coolly observed, "If I had triumphed then, everything would have been forgotten like many other more serious things which sink into oblivion with the victory which sanctifies all things."[32]

After years of strife and political uncertainty the province of Buenos Aires finally assumed a temporary semblance of order under the leadership of General Martín Rodríguez, with Bernardino Rivadavia as his Secretary of Foreign Affairs. In a gesture of national unity, this administration passed a general amnesty law in 1822 for all political offenders. Under its terms the proscription against Alvear was eventually canceled. Considering his unpopular and violent three and one-half months as Supreme Director and his five years of counterrevolutionary activity, one wonders that he dared to return to Buenos Aires even after proclamation of the Act of Oblivion. But the new administration and the people themselves meant that past errors should be forgotten; they respected their pledged word. Rivadavia demonstrated his faith in Alvear's essential integrity by naming him in 1824 as minister to the United States where he would acknowledge the recognition of independence of the United Provinces made two years earlier and thus open official relations with the northern republic. This appointment provided Alvear with an opportunity to re-establish himself in the good opinion of his countrymen. At the same time it removed him from the fields of political conspiracy and military adventure.

II

ASSIGNMENT TO ENGLAND AND THE UNITED STATES: 1824

1. Interview with Canning

Complete anarchy temporarily destroyed by 1820 the last vestige of national government in La Plata. The provinces, having renounced allegiance to any unifying body, followed their local leaders. After recognizing this separation, the province of Buenos Aires organized its local administration and, in so far as it dared, assumed diplomatic representation in the name of the nation. Since this policy did not conflict with local desires, the back country acquiesced in the expression of authority, for none of these inland governments sought recognition abroad. Although a presumed unity existed along La Plata under the title of "United Provinces," the degree of cohesion would not bear close scrutiny.

At the very height of triumphant localism there appeared a reaction in favor of a truly national government. New leaders of the influential province of Buenos Aires, Martín Rodríguez and Bernardino Rivadavia, sought to win provincial allegiance at home while seeking recognition of national independence abroad. General Rodríguez was chosen as Governor. Rivadavia, as Secretary of Government and Foreign Affairs, proved the dominant member of the administration, for most of the reforms resulted from his initiative.

Rivadavia led the reaction in favor of nationalism. He sought ceaselessly to show his people that before they could expect recognition by the rest of the world they must establish a national organization free from perpetual discord and vengeance. He advocated the scrapping of old hatreds and supported the Law of Oblivion which would erase past political offenses. Thus he hoped to unite even the exiles in the creation of a new and worthy government. Enraged patriots who had escaped exile delivered impassioned protests: "It would be better to open the doors of jails in order to let the criminals run free than to support the Law of Oblivion."[1]

In the end Rivadavia won out: after the declaration of amnesty in November, 1821, political refugees including Carlos de Alvear came trooping back. This man, particularly, should have desired nothing so much as forgetfulness of his political errors. And for three years in quiet retirement he sought to repair his family fortune which had been ruined by revolution.

For his program Rivadavia won a sympathetic hearing from John Forbes, special agent of the United States, who sent to Washington lengthy and commendatory accounts of the new Secretary's honesty and fearlessness.[2] When the United States government urged Forbes to secure cancellation of privateering patents, he excused the minister for subsequent delay, saying that "the Herculean labor of cleaning the Augean stables . . . entirely occupies him by day and night."[3] Rivadavia himself frankly admitted the evils of which Forbes later complained and promised that at the first opportune moment he would discontinue the issue of patents. True to his word, he soon ordered the end of privateering and punished those who continued to operate under old papers. Forbes described to Secretary of State Adams the general consternation at the prospect of an honest government.[4]

Representatives of the United States continued to report the political issues facing the Rodríguez-Rivadavia administration. The letters of Forbes and of Caesar A. Rodney, the first minister of the United States to Buenos Aires, reveal a widespread desire for monarchy. This royalist sentiment, although discouraged by Rivadavia, continued among some political factions.[5] Persistence of monarchial rumors and the apparent readiness of European royalty to supply a king greatly disturbed republicans in Buenos Aires and became a source of concern to the United States.

Rumor of monarchy was only one of the menaces to the independence of the New World. The old scare of European intervention by force constantly endangered public peace. The French invasion of Spain in 1823 had made residents of Buenos Aires fearful lest they be the next victims of French prowess. Publication of a spurious treaty of Verona, consecrating the Holy Alliance of Europe to the suppression of revolution everywhere in the world, caused added alarm for safety of the new democracies.[6] Rivadavia particularly feared that France would supply Spain with her need for an expeditionary force. Rumors of another expedition headed out of Cádiz for Buenos Aires so distracted the administrator during the winter of 1824 that he determined to call a general assembly to plan resistance to the feared invasion. Revival of a royalist program and rumors of royalist intervention produced political repercussions which made the government seem insecure and republican effort futile.[7]

John M. Forbes, the American chargé, regretfully observed the rise of English and old Spanish influences in the government councils.[8] He noted a marked indifference to the United States, even though it had been the first and so far the only government outside the Latin-American states to welcome the United Provinces into the community of nations. It seemed that indifference for the United States had frozen into hostility. Reception of the first minister, Caesar A. Rodney, was a cold and formal affair. It elicited only the most apathetic newspaper comments. At the end of the year Secretary Manuel José García, in a long speech surveying important political events of 1823, did not even mention it. Despite the natural sympathy of the United States for the new nations and its early recognition of Latin-American independence, its national prestige had sunk to a flat zero. Meanwhile, agitation over the menacing power of the Holy Alliance distracted all who would try to think clearly, and turned all eyes to England.

The need of a new foreign mission became more pressing. Rivadavia desired definite information on European plans of intervention. He needed, or thought he needed, George Canning's friendship in order to block hostile European developments. He wanted to make a dignified bid for recognition of independence by England without appearance of servile requests. Since England had not recognized the Buenos Aires government, Rivadavia's agent could stay in England only in an unofficial capacity. Nevertheless, this agent could confer with all British officials who would receive him. As a screen for these projected *démarches* in the Old World, Rivadavia used a long overdue mission to the United States. He dispatched a minister to the Republic of the North for the purpose of initiating official relations between the two countries, but he sent him to his post by way of England.

The Minister of Foreign Affairs chose as unlikely a candidate as one could imagine. He named Carlos de Alvear as Minister Plenipotentiary. Attached to the mission was Alvear's boyhood companion of the first voyage to Spain and of the gentle captivity in England, Tomás de Iriarte, who held the post of secretary.[9]

It was a curious appointment. As Supreme Director young Alvear had been singularly unsuccessful. His handling of a diplomatic mission to Río de Janeiro during his short administration had revealed an irresponsible nature.[10] He was widely accused of attempting a betrayal of his country, and for a few years he and his secretary had actually made war on the Buenos Aires government. Their recently revived loyalty to Buenos Aires, even if sincere, was untried. Perhaps Rivadavia thought this a proper occasion to test Alvear's loyalty on a traveling mission the powers of which would be restricted to investigation and to formalities. Perhaps, also, if the Act of Oblivion meant forgetfulness of old errors, revolutionary sins should not be held against either the minister or the secretary.[11]

In La Plata political talent passed at a premium, and Rivadavia may have sensed the genuine capacity of the revolutionary refugee. Beyond doubt Alvear had the necessary energy to accomplish any reasonable task. If he retained his former audacity, lack of official credentials in England would not hinder him greatly. He could bear himself proudly in whatever circle. He had been a man of wealth; he had enjoyed prestige; and in the early phases of the Revolution he had displayed unmistakable talent. His military reputation might serve him well. To old soldiers he could talk of the victorious Peninsular campaign, and as conqueror of Montevideo he had enjoyed a well-publicized triumph. As a Brigadier-General and as a former Supreme Director of the country he would command respect. He knew England and Englishmen and, unhindered by barriers of language, he could move among social groups with ease. The elder Alvear had customarily returned to England for extended visits and was known personally to men highly placed in the government. No Argentine, Rivadavia apparently believed, was better qualified "to find some easy and unostensible way" of communicating with Canning.[12]

Although Alvear learned of his appointment in December, 1823, he did not receive his instructions until February 26, 1824. He found orders relating to both phases of his mission: those referring to his work in England, and those to guide his conduct in the United States.[13] From England he was to send back such news as he could gather, but everything was left to his prudence and discretion. Rivadavia directed him, if he deemed it wise, to seek an interview with Canning, but not to ask for dispatch of a minister or openly inquire about the possibilities of European intervention. He suggested that Alvear should begin by praising the moral standards of England and by declaring its remarkable government worthy of emulation.

> Make it sink into the mind of the minister that the City and the Provinces think more of England than any other European government because England is the most moral and illustrious country of Europe and ought to be the most beneficial to the new states, for the English conform best to the social order that the states know that they will have to achieve.

Publicly and privately he was to play upon this theme. Rivadavia further instructed the minister to declare that his government, knowing that the conduct of Great Britain would spontaneously work in favor of Buenos Aires, had sent no official diplomatic agent to London. He should state that his countrymen believed their main task should be the confirmation of independence and the development of natural resources. With these tasks well done, recognition would follow. Should opportunity afford, Rivadavia thought it worth while to present the claims of Buenos Aires to the Banda Oriental and to protest the repeated Brazilian invasions of that area after rejecting offers of peaceful settlement. He must make it clear that Buenos Aires would fight rather than surrender its claims.

In order to lay uneasy rumors in La Plata, Rivadavia ordered Alvear to neglect no opportunity to discover the attitude of the Spanish government toward its former colonies. Since Spain alone could never regain them, he was to make discreet inquiry on the likelihood of joint intervention by the Great Powers. No less important would be the real attitude of the English cabinet and English opinion on these same points. While in London the Minister should become acquainted with commissioners of other Spanish-American states who might be residing there and learn how their countries were preparing to meet the same problems. Rivadavia suggested that Alvear should limit his visit to fifty days, even if he had secured no interview with George Canning.[14]

While waiting for his instructions, Alvear set about preparations for the voyage. He fortified himself against any question of statistics or official acts by requesting the Secretary to supply complete files of the *Official Register*, *Statistical Register*, the *Sentinel*, the *Argos*, the *Argentine Bee*, and the *Record of Sessions*. Inexperienced administrators and revolutionary turmoil had wrought such havoc with reserve copies of official publications that numbers of some periodicals were missing, but Rivadavia ordered delivery of existing files, whether complete or not.[15]

Soon after receipt of his long-delayed instructions, the envoy departed for England, not without making known his dissatisfaction with his salary. The appointment carried a remuneration of 10,000 pesos per year for the minister and 2,500 pesos for the secretary. This allowance, he notified the Secretary of Treasury, was insufficient, and he asked for a greater sum in order that he might live in his accustomed style and in a manner worthy of a minister plenipotentiary.[16]

The Buenos Aires administration, in its message to the Fourth Legislature in May, 1824, reported the dispatch of the mission, but omitted all reference to the English detour. Briefly —and incorrectly—it reported:

> [Alvear] goes charged, also, with the duty of suggesting to the government of the United States how fitting it would be that to the two grand principles of abolition of privateering and of no European colonization in the territory of America, it should add this other one—that none of the new governments of this continent should change by violence its recognized limits at the time of emancipation.[17]

This declaration revealed that the administration heartily approved of the noncolonization paragraphs in President Monroe's famous declaration of December, 1823. The third principle, if established, would secure to Buenos Aires the territory of the Banda Oriental. But Rivadavia failed to speak frankly to the Legislature. Alvear's instructions especially stressed the unofficial English phase of the mission, and in some respects the Secretary laid as much store by what Alvear might accomplish in England as in the United States. As for the Banda Oriental, he had ordered the envoy to suggest both to England and to the United States that Brazil should observe the Spanish colonial boundary limits of 1810. But at the same time he was to make it clear that La Plata provinces intended to defend their rights to that area by force of arms. The instructions made no reference to additional principles which the United States might find it convenient to adopt. His summary of Alvear's purpose as presented to the Legislature was in its general tenor incorrect: Rivadavia sought approval for the mission by attributing to it instructions which he never gave.

Alvear arrived in Liverpool on June 5, 1824, after an eighty-four-day voyage. He promptly made the acquaintance of British merchants who gave a dinner in his honor. Both he and the merchants agreed on the mutual advantages of extensive trade relations between their countries; and the Englishmen, stimulated by the meeting, sent further petitions to Parliament requesting recognition of the Spanish-American countries. From Liverpool the envoy journeyed to Birmingham and then to London, in both cities encountering businessmen who drafted similar petitions. He reported to Rivadavia a generally favorable opinion toward the recognition of Latin-American republics; he heard that Canning in private interviews had declared his intention of recognizing Buenos Aires, Chile, and Colombia as soon as the fighting had ceased.[18] Welcome news of patriot victories in Peru, in the opinion of Alvear and the merchants, removed all reason for delay. He made sure that his personal accounts of Rivadavia were printed in the English press in order to convey to the Continent glowing reports of the stable administration on La Plata. As proof of favorable British commercial sentiment he reported the closing of negotiations for a loan of 3,000,000 *pesos fuertes* (hard money or gold, in contrast to paper issue).[19]

The minister neglected no opportunity to acquire accurate information on the possibility of another Spanish invasion of the former colonies. His dispatches from England, such as that of June 29, told of continued Spanish hostility, but declared that civil unrest would prevent any expedition leaving that country. French Ultra-Royalists were hoping to raise among their own sympathizers the necessary capital for a Spanish expedition, but their slender resources would prove inadequate. The restored King Ferdinand was trying to secure an English loan with which he would finance a small expedition to America. Since England demanded first that he should recognize the debts of the previous constitutional regime, there seemed little danger of an early attempt to subjugate the former colonies. Lord Liverpool, so he was informed, had prepared to break with Spanish conservatives by declaring that England considered herself free to adopt any policy she chose in reference to South America. He secured the text of the Polignac Memorandum and transmitted it without comment to Buenos Aires. At every turn England stood as the barrier to European intervention in Latin-America. According to all reports the continued hostility of a new French cabinet was due to insidious Russian influence. The European newspapers, which Alvear thought "moved by the corrosive poison of their sinister intentions," condemned English policy.[20] This potpourri of reports, conferences, and conversations was all good news to Buenos Aires.

Other Spanish-American emissaries whom the Argentine minister met in London corroborated this information. He spoke to these agents about his country's claim to the Banda Oriental, and reported that he had won their unqualified support on the issue. So strongly did Señor Michelena of Mexico feel about the matter that when the Brazilian minister broached the subject, the Mexican declared that his country would not recognize Brazilian action and would try to organize other American countries to wrest the territory from the monarchy. Feeling that he could not neglect such positive support, Alvear asked the representatives of Colombia and Mexico to exert diplomatic pressure on Brazil to return the seized territory. Reports of his attempts to create a bloc for enforcing national demands aroused the ministry at home. It seemed that he was about to make commitments which his government could not endorse. After arrival in the United States Alvear received instructions commending him for his zeal, but warning that he should make no authoritative replies because there had been a change of administration at home.[21]

Throughout his fifty-day visit in England, Alvear found the other representatives of the former Spanish colonies most cordial. They exchanged views on American and European affairs. The Peruvian Royalist, García del Río, allowed him to copy reports of two conferences he had secured with Prince Polignac of France. He also furnished a copy of a conference with Richard Rush, the American minister to England. Rush had disparaged the likelihood of external menace to the independence of the Spanish colonies: he had warned that the new countries should be alert to secret machinations within their own borders.[22]

Señor Hurtado of Colombia also opened his files to Alvear. He revealed that Spanish difficulties in raising forces for intervention had caused Austria to assist Spain, while the English were hostile to the whole program. Hurtado declared that in two conferences with Canning the English leader had shown that he favored New World interests by urging Portugal to recognize Brazilian independence at the price of some concession for the mother country. Canning, said Hurtado, hoped that

Portuguese recognition of Brazilian independence would point the painful but necessary way for Spain. Therefore the Colombian envoy believed that England had at heart the good interests of the New World, and so reported to Alvear.[23]

Alvear received so many favorable reports of English friendship that he believed recognition was simply a "matter of time and circumstance"—Canning's own words. He anxiously sought an interview with the Foreign Minister in order to remind him tactfully of La Plata's right to independence and elicit, perhaps, some indication of the date of English recognition. In Buenos Aires the British Consul-General had blandly assured Rivadavia that his envoy would have no difficulty in laying his information before the government,[24] but General Alvear was discovering that he represented an unwelcome cause which Canning did not wish to consider just then. The numbered days dropped away and he received no invitation to visit the great statesman. While preparing to resume his journey to the United States, he sent word of his plight to an English citizen, John Hullett, who had extensive business connections with Buenos Aires. The latter spoke to Canning in the General's behalf, asking that he be granted an early interview.[25]

On July 21, 1824, the day he had planned to leave London, Alvear unexpectedly received an appointment for noon the following day. Naturally he postponed his departure. And then one hour before the appointment a Foreign Office messenger delivered a list of eight questions to which Canning wished written answers by the time their conference should take place.[26]

Astonished by the short notice given him, Alvear interpreted the questionnaire as a means of securing unguarded statements, but so rapidly did he work that when he presented himself at the appointed time the answers were complete. Since he believed that Canning had sent the questions in order to trick him into answering "with clarity and precision," the minister determined to reply "in an evasive manner, at other times falsely, but always with a background of truth . . . to hide certain disagreeable details." Because he presumed that Canning would present a minute of this conference to the cabinet, he wished to make as good an impression as possible.

The General appeared at the conference, hopeful that his camouflage of truth would conceal necessary falsehoods. Canning scarcely looked at the answers which he had composed, but formulated a series of questions which somewhat duplicated those sent from the office. The rapidity of Canning's questions again gave Alvear the feeling that the British minister sought to throw him off guard, but he assured Rivadavia later that the strategem was unsuccessful: he carefully hid everything which would not reflect glory on the country.[27]

"So Señor Rivadavia is giving up the Ministry!" burst out Canning in a disgusted tone. Alvear had not heard officially the result of state elections held since he left, but newspaper accounts were quite as Canning had indicated.[28] Resignation of Rivadavia might indicate a continuation of national instability. Therefore, Alvear sought to distract the British minister by professing that he had not heard of it. But—here he skirted the truth—if such an event should prove true, it would be because Rivadavia had been so instrumental in reforming the state government that he would feel compelled to resign after elections had been scheduled in order to avoid charges of arranging a place for himself in the new administration.

Canning fired other searching questions related to national sovereignty and political organization. He wanted to know about the Assembly, whether two houses or one, the power of the executive, the resources of the country, population, the territory under control of the government. Alvear believed that his answers to these questions put the government in a stable light. When Canning asked if the United Provinces included Paraguay, Alvear equivocated: "Through its isolation the country is secure in its independence, but the territory is dominated by the private interests of a man who rules there with supreme power."

Canning shifted the discussion to Peru. Recent dispatches had brought news of Spanish victories, and he wanted to know if this indicated a decline of Spanish power. Alvear stoutly denied the contention. Spain had suffered great losses in former days when her strength had been much greater: now that the colonies had increased in strength and Spain had weakened, isolated victories could not affect the ultimate result.

While Canning surveyed the notes so hastily prepared an hour earlier, the envoy raised the question of the Banda Oriental, and orally supplemented his written declarations of the determination of the United Provinces to recapture the territory from Brazil. He declared that Brazilian occupation of that land and its refusal to arbitrate would certainly bring war. Canning appeared startled at this blunt statement and asked if such an eventuality might be avoided. Alvear thought not and justified the determination of his country by reciting its historical claims to the territory.[29] After employing all the peaceful and honorable means that became a nation, the United Provinces, he declared, had failed to change Brazilian policy from its course so obviously in violation of all law and justice. Since its independence this empire had exhibited unjust, aggressive aspirations that menaced its peace-loving neighbor. Some strong nation, he hinted, some nation full of the principles of justice could, by the wisdom of its councils, restrain the new and thoughtless cabinet in Brazil.

While emphasizing the importance of the Eastern Shore to the United Provinces, Alvear inadvertently introduced a painful subject. He confirmed Argentine determination to fight by declaring that the question of the Banda Oriental would be the first subject discussed at the next Assembly. Canning countered by saying that according to Woodbine Parish's report there had been no elections in the provinces, and with no elections there could be no Assembly. Without national feeling sufficient to elect an assembly, Canning would question the stability of the United Provinces. Again Alvear sought an evasion: although elections were long overdue, perhaps the British envoy had not heard of them: news traveled slowly in the back country. But Canning pressed him, and Alvear could not say definitely that elections had been held: from advance notices he supposed that they must have been completed. He revealed that he had no better information than Parish.

Canning continued the uncomfortable subject. He asked who had called the Congress. "Buenos Aires," responded the envoy. Canning dryly presumed that Buenos Aires had no authority over the other provinces. "None," Alvear confessed, "except by reason of its moral suasion and influence." "Then," pursued Canning, "do you go to North America as a representative of all the provinces or of Buenos Aires only?" "Of all," Alvear responded.

When Canning expressed understandable inability to find logic in such an answer, Alvear explained that a minister from the United States, Caesar A. Rodney, then living in Buenos Aires, had notified the provinces that he would serve as representative of the United States to them all. Since the other provinces had agreed to this arrangement, Alvear, as their joint minister, was sent to repay the international courtesy. It looked as if he represented the United Provinces by virtue of recognition of the United States rather than through provincial action.[30]

Canning then changed the subject. "What provinces have the United States recognized?" Magnificently Alvear answered, "The Viceroyalty of Buenos Aires." Still dissatisfied, Canning asked to see the letter of credentials to the United States. Believing this a trick to induce him to reveal official documents, Alvear avoided the issue by replying that he had already dispatched the originals to Liverpool, his port of departure.

Then he concluded the conference with a burst of oratory on the deep convictions of the United Provinces that England was the most progressive country in all Europe; how well the Argentine people realized that the English government was concerned for their best interests; how steadfastly they looked to it, the most illustrious and moral government in the world. Canning abruptly blocked this flow by saying, "Very well, Señor, very well; you understand our position."[31]

Why Canning behaved in a manner so blunt and unfriendly as to arouse the antagonism of his auditor is not clear. Earlier in the year he had assured the French minister that his government could not delay much longer the recognition of the Spanish-American nations.[32] Sentiment in England continued to favor the former colonies and English liberalism was blocking legitimist plans for counterrevolution throughout Europe.

England was more friendly toward the new republics than any other European nation, and there would appear to be no valid reason for concealing that good opinion behind a gruff exterior.[33]

Alvear had assumed that Canning would present the results of their conference to the cabinet. Perhaps he did. At a cabinet meeting the following day, July 23, it was agreed ultimately to recognize some of the former Spanish colonies, particularly Buenos Aires. Some decisive step should be taken to avert danger to the Old World "if such an extensive territory should be exclusively connected with one state [the United States] to which they are already indebted for recognition."[34] For many months Canning temporized. Publicly he insisted that he did not have adequate knowledge on which to determine the fitness of Buenos Aires to receive a formal recognition of independence. However, the decision of July 23 shows that lack of information was not his real reason for delay of recognition.

A month after the cabinet made its decision to recognize Buenos Aires, Canning wrote to Parish that he was postponing the step in the hope that Spain would act first. In order to realize this unlikely prospect, Canning suggested that the Buenos Aires government should buy its recognition from the mother country. Considering the impecunious state of the Spanish treasury, he thought the offer would tempt the restored monarchy.[35] Presumably he entertained no real expectation that the United Provinces would make a monetary sacrifice for Spanish recognition of independence. He admitted that Buenos Aires had irrevocably broken with Spain; that she had power to maintain independence; and that the government had a framework for providing internal stability.

Immediately after this conference with Canning, Alvear traveled to Liverpool and there dictated to Secretary Iriarte his report of the conference. His government found small comfort in it. Rivadavia's successor, General de las Heras, tried to console the minister with effusive congratulations, but at the same time confessed that England's vacillating policy was puzzling in the extreme. Only Canning's silence and English refusal to take positive steps against the new republics encouraged them to hope for recognition.[36]

In some respects the departing minister might have been pleased with his work. He had sent home reliable reports of the European attitude toward Spanish America. He had cultivated the acquaintance of the Spanish-American agents in London and had won their complete sympathy on the problem of the Eastern Shore. He had reliably reported English mercantile sympathy and the popular desire that the government should extend recognition. He had secured an interview with Canning himself, a meeting which the Buenos Aires administration had particularly desired. The conference may have prompted Canning's consultation of the cabinet and the decision presently to recognize the independence of some of Latin America after pressing Spain. If so, this was certainly important.

Yet Alvear found little satisfaction in the interview. It had come late. The request for information at an unexpected moment made him suspect trickery, and in defense he had told as little truth as possible. Canning had begun with a tone of disgust and had ended by questioning Alvear's credentials. At no time had the domineering British minister appeared friendly nor had he indicated in any way the future policy of his government. Instead of being encouraged by the prospects of immediate English recognition, the envoy from Buenos Aires felt that it would come at no early date.

As Alvear boarded his ship for the United States he must have felt a deep sense of unsympathetic treatment. What a contrast he was to encounter in the friendly United States, which two years earlier had recognized the independence of his country and was awaiting the arrival of its first minister!

2. President Monroe Interprets His Policy

During the wearisome forty-one-day passage from Liverpool to New York, General Alvear reflected upon the devious ways of English statemen and lack of contact with his own government. On his arrival in New York he found no letters, nor did he receive any during the next fortnight. Before leaving for Washington he complained of this oversight to his home office. He had not heard the results of elections held since his departure; if there had been a change of administration, as was widely reported in the press, he did not know the officials to whom he was writing. He felt embarrassed at such complete ignorance of home affairs.[1]

The new minister was detained for two weeks in New York and while there enjoyed the social life of the growing city. He immediately secured an introduction to a member of Congress—a leading member, he stated—and presently was being entertained "by the most respectable families."[2] His dispatches indicate complete satisfaction with his social reception.

The General had arrived in New York in time to witness the historic reception with which the city honored Lafayette, who was making his triumphal tour of the United States. Newspapers detailed to their readers the most minute plans for the entertainment of the nation's guest, Washington's comrade-in-arms during the American Revolution. Private conversation further extolled the virtues of the almost legendary hero of two republics.

With public adulation transforming Lafayette into an oracle, Alvear could not resist the temptation to present to him the cause of his own country. The great French leader advised him to avoid Brazilian negotiations as long as a monarchy existed in that country. He declared that Buenos Aires, in common with the other young states, could place no confidence in the nations of Europe. "The only nation," he said, "which can offer guarantee by a frank course and identity of principle is that of Washington."[3] A few weeks later the two men were in Philadelphia, where Alvear sought another interview. On this occasion he had no particular purpose except to call attention to himself by reflecting the glory of Lafayette, who sent the ambitious diplomat on his way "with the greatest proofs of consideration and politeness." Probably the introduction to Lafayette changed in no essential the result of Alvear's mission in the United States, but words of praise from the "Nation's Hero" may have served to enhance the General's estimate of the Republic of the North.

The dilatory manner in which David C. DeForest, unrecognized Argentine Consul-General in the United States from 1818 to 1823, had surrendered his files of official correspondence had caused Alvear initial delay in New York.[4] Rivadavia, on canceling DeForest's commission, had ordered him to return all his records of office. This order DeForest had not obeyed, for he was unwilling to trust to spying sea captains certain incriminating correspondence about privateers. Instead, he wrote Rivadavia that he would send his records when he should encounter a discreet traveler to Buenos Aires, but he would prefer to give the letters directly to an authorized Argentine agent. Since the former Consul-General had not then found a sufficiently confidential person, Rivadavia ordered Alvear to take over the files.[5]

As soon as DeForest heard of Alvear's arrival in New York City, he invited the diplomat to visit his Connecticut home and to enjoy the cooler and more healthful climate of "the little city where I reside and where all are warm friends of South America."[6] Alvear resisted the Connecticut Yankee's blandishments. He refused to visit the ideal little city of New Haven, but waited in New York until the cautious DeForest sent a trusted agent with his confidential packets. They included DeForest's correspondence with the United States government as well as all the documents remaining in his office or belonging to the government of Buenos Aires.[7] As soon as he received the closely guarded materials, Alvear, who had exhausted his small stock of patience, immediately left for Washington to present his credentials.[8]

The envoy reached Washington on October 2 and established himself at the capital's fashionable hostelry, Brown's Hotel. Prompt application at the Department of State revealed the fact that neither Secretary of State Adams nor President Monroe was in town, but that both were expected shortly. They soon arrived in order to prepare for the opening of Congress and to grace the reception of Lafayette.

Since Alvear's nomination in December, 1823, the Department of State had been receiving from its chargé in Buenos Aires news of the impending mission. There was plenty of information on Alvear's chequered revolutionary and political career. Monroe and Adams understood that Alvear had come to the United States by way of England for obscure reasons: possibly to conclude negotiations for a loan; to settle a shipping dispute; to bargain for independence; to see an elderly parent; or, perhaps, to act as secret agent for a monarchial clique.[9] They knew that the mission would visit the United States only for the purpose of initiating official relations. Then, presumably, it would go on to Mexico for a similar duty. These reports were fresh in the minds of Monroe and Adams when the first official representative from Buenos Aires arrived in Washington, in October, 1824. Although crowded by other official duties, Secretary Adams received Alvear on a preliminary call and presented him and his Secretary of Legation, Tomás de Iriarte, to the President on October 11.[10]

Alvear delivered on that occasion a prepared address stating the gratitude of Buenos Aires for the recognition which the United States had accorded that country's independence two years earlier. The speech, couched in the florid rhetoric of the times, overflowed with polite verbiage and generous overstatements:

> The government of the Republic of Buenos Aires . . . has charged me with presenting . . . the homage of respect, friendship and gratitude with which the Provinces are animated for the high consideration which the government of the United States has honored them in its solemn recognition of their independence. Such an act has inspired the purest joy. . . .

The minister added that his people were "following the example of the fatherland of the immortal Washington."[11]

These glowing words ill matched reports that Forbes had sent from Buenos Aires, but President Monroe, ignoring such realistic observations, answered Alvear in pleasing generalities. He spoke of the desire of the United States to maintain good relations with Buenos Aires; he hoped for the prosperity of the Provinces and expressed his satisfaction at the outcome of the struggle for independence. He concluded the brief interview by asking a few questions about domestic conditions in La Plata and the war in Peru, questions which Alvear took pleasure in answering.[12]

Although Monroe had completed what he would have termed a perfunctory presentation, Alvear was impressed by the President's words. The whole tone of the conference had been so different from the domineering manner of Canning that he immediately reversed the familiar Latin-American dictum that called England the greatest friend of the new republics. After one brief conference Alvear had succumbed, as had many Spanish Americans, to Monroe's sympathetic personality.

The day after his reception Alvear began a letter to Rivadavia in which he catalogued each day the main events of his mission so far. Following the date "18th" the letter changed to an ecstatic paean for James Monroe and the United States. The envoy explained that he had secured recently another interview with the President, this one longer and much more important than the first, in which Monroe had explained the relations of the United States with all the nations of Europe and had indicated their attitude toward each other. Much of this information Alvear considered entirely too important to entrust to the mail: in fact he did not intend to forward his report of the conference, but to carry it to Buenos Aires himself. To these accounts of official secrets Alvear added reports of private hospitality. He believed that the President had honored him "beyond example" by inviting him to visit his Virginia home if opportunity should permit. Alvear declared that he had passed some of the most agreeable moments of his life in Monroe's presence, causing him the "profoundest sighs" at separating himself from the nation where he had received so many demonstrations of friendship.[13]

In considering the probable nature of the conversations between Carlos de Alvear and James Monroe, it is necessary to recall what problems then faced the President. The officials of the United States believed that Spanish Americans generally ignored their country when they considered the international scene.[14] It would be natural for the President to try to impress favorably the minister from the United Provinces. He might be expected to explain policies of the United States toward the

South American revolution in such a way as to make Alvear believe that the United States, rather than England, had been of greater assistance to the revolted colonies. Monroe would normally seize every opportunity to advance the prestige of his country, an occasion such as the reception of the first minister from Buenos Aires afforded. Alvear's report of a second conference indicates that the President made the most of his opportunity.[15]

On this occasion President Monroe delivered himself of an extensive summary of world opinion relative to the Spanish-American revolution, and proudly indicated the importance of his famous message of December, 1823. A considered survey, given by the President while still in office, to an accredited minister of a Latin-American republic forms a document of some historical importance.[16] We must view with interest this commentary on the message, its principles, and purposes by its original sponsor, within less than a year after its pronouncement.

Monroe, says Alvear, opened the second interview by explaining the motives which had caused him to announce the declaration of the preceding December, the declaration which later came to be called the "Monroe Doctrine."

> Fearing that France, for many motives, after her fine success in Spain would try to send an expedition to South America, he President Monroe had made the solemn declaration by which he had promised in an unequivocal manner to protect the new states of America. . . .

Thus, according to Alvear, the President feared French intervention in the New World more than that of any other nation. Research on the background of the Doctrine has revealed a variety of fears and eventualities which thoughtful men of the period considered. We cannot safely say that one particular motive or situation dominated the thinking of all the statesmen actively concerned in the formation of the doctrine, but it is plain that Monroe and his advisers had been greatly concerned about the menacing attitude of France.

John Quincy Adams's *Memoirs* bear out the President's fears of French aggression which Monroe mentioned to Alvear. The Secretary of State had found his chief on November 3,

1823, "unsettled in his own mind" and "alarmed beyond anything I would have believed possible" about the likelihood of restoration of all Spanish America to the mother country. Ten days later he further elaborated, "The news that Cádiz has surrendered to the French has so affected the President that he appeared to despair of the cause of South America. . . . I never saw more indecision in him." Prompt collapse of Spain made the President feel that the Holy Alliance, with French support, would continue its conquests overseas, and up to the eve of the deliverance of his address these fears preyed upon his mind. Adams found him "singularly disturbed" at the prospect.[17]

The President's fears of French intervention did not abruptly subside like a three-day fever, as Adams had predicted in November, 1823, but continued in a fluctuating degree through the first half of the following year. During that time he heard varied rumors of French attempts to undermine the unstable republics by offers of co-operation to set up a monarchial form of government.[18] The President's apprehension of direct and forceable intervention had subsided by the time of Alvear's visit, but recollection of his former uneasiness was strong upon him. Monroe began by giving voice to his apprehension; later in the discussion he spoke at length of his existing fear of indirect French intervention through propaganda and native royalist sentiment. Monroe accurately described the real motive that he had personally entertained for pronouncing his declaration. He could not have hit upon an explanation which Alvear would have accepted with greater alacrity. Disturbing rumors of an impending French invasion had circulated throughout Buenos Aires at the time of Alvear's departure. In England he had gathered more reports of French sympathy with Spanish attempts at reconquest. Since such fears coincided with his own ideas on the European menace, Alvear accepted readily the President's reason for his declaration of the previous year.

Monroe assured Alvear that his declaration constituted an unequivocal promise to protect South America. On this point the President knew very well that neither he nor his associates had interpreted his message in such a positive manner.[19] In August, 1824, a few weeks preceding the conference with Alvear, Señor Salazar, the Colombian minister, had put a direct question to Secretary Adams:

> In what manner [does] the government of the United States intend to resist on its part any interference of the Holy Alliance for the purpose of subjugating the new Republics or interfering in their political form?

John Quincy Adams, after consulting with the President, gave a reply remarkable for its indirection and evasiveness,[20] quite contrary to Monroe's later resolute and categorical statement to Alvear. Presumably the President resorted to this disingenuous explanation in order to win the visitor's confidence and to impress the diplomat both with the power of the United States and with its determination to enforce its policy.

So foreign to Monroe are the robust sentiments that Alvear attributes to him that the first impulse may be to discount these reports as a serious misunderstanding. But in other respects, Alvear represents the President as voicing sentiments verifiable from the President's personal letters, from the writings of his most trusted advisers and friends, or from the official correspondence of the government. Since he reported accurately other sections of this long interview, it seems fair to conclude that he was not far wrong on this point.

After explaining the anxieties of the previous year, the President remarked that earlier he had asked the British government to declare what would be its conduct if any power other than Spain should wish to intervene in the subjugation of the former colonies. He had received no forthright reply, but Canning's speeches in Parliament satisfied him that British and American policies were identical. He said that he had next urged England to move from nonintervention to a more positive role, joint recognition of the independence of Buenos Aires. But Canning, without further explanation, had answered that the time had not come for such a step.

With accuracy Monroe was here summarizing the efforts of the United States to prevent intervention in South America and to persuade England to adopt a proper policy toward the new nations.[21] The most interesting omission was the date of these offers. He did not say that the proposals which he mentioned took place as far back as 1818 or 1819. Consequently they were not the immediate causes of his "unequivocal declaration." Perhaps he supposed that the major steps in the program were well known to the South American leaders.[22]

The President realized that the envoy would want to know what steps the United States had taken to enforce its declaration. He anticipated any such question by stating:

> The government of the United States on formulating the declaration had taken all possible means for making it effective—fortifying its coasts, increasing its naval armament and sending a part of it to distant seas, and that in making this show of force its object had been to demonstrate to the other nations that it was prepared to act if necessary.

By such a positive statement Monroe may have misled the receptive diplomat. Anyone properly informed about the public policy of the United States would have known that it had no armament capable of resisting determined intervention in South America. Nor had it taken steps recently to increase the military program beyond normal requirements of the country. There were a few patrol ships in the Mediterranean to safeguard national commerce in that area. One or two vessels patrolled the southern Pacific where whalers hunted. During the South American revolution United States ships regularly passed from one harbor to another or patrolled the Caribbean to watch for pirates. These were the only armament on distant seas to which the President could have referred accurately.[23] That there had been no especial program of fortification of the nation's shores is seen in Monroe's own famous message of 1823. Its sections on military affairs refer to the "usual" force. For the Army the President reported regular improvement, construction of three forts, coastal surveys for defense, and increased efficiency for the arms factory. Since he recommended an appropriation to provide cannon for the new forts, they could not have been very impressive fortifications when he promulgated the Doctrine.[24]

Whatever we may think of Monroe's disingenuousness to his auditor, this expressed determination of the United States to defend its position deeply impressed the envoy with the sincerity of the policy.[25]

If Alvear and Salazar received contrary information about a given situation, it is important to remember the differing circumstances under which the information was given. Salazar asked his question of Adams in order to learn if the presence of Spanish forces in his country, with France in control of Spain, violated the President's declaration. He hoped for an affirmative reply and, after that, a treaty of alliance, with direct military aid from the United States. And he wanted his answer in writing. Monroe, speaking to Alvear of a hypothetical condition, could afford to be expansive. By delivering his opinion orally the President could speak with less responsibility for his words, a condition which encourages brave replies.

We must note one further difference between the two occasions and between the two American statesmen. Salazar received his written answer from the Secretary of State who was not accustomed to exaggeration, a man who kept his enthusiasm well under control. Alvear talked with a President known for his public enthusiasm and indiscreet tongue. On his mission to France in 1794 Monroe's speech to the convention had exceeded customary diplomatic reserve. For years before recognition of the Spanish-American republics, his desire for precipitate action had been checked by the cabinet.[26] When the cabinet first discussed his message of 1823, his first impulse had been to include strong opinions on French occupation of Spain and on the Greek war for independence, but the cabinet persuaded him to moderate his statements. The Argentine representative, without knowledge of the foreign policy of the United States or of its public servants, accepted without qualification just what the President said.

From one source only could Alvear have acquired a basis for passing critical judgment on the President's statement. He might have compared notes with Salazar. Before coming to Washington he had talked at length with that diplomat and corresponded with him thereafter about Brazilian iniquities in the Banda Oriental and about their common relations with Europe. After consultation with Salazar about some of the President's "unparalleled confidences" on defense of the two Americas against European invasion, Alvear might have been less credulous.

We should remember that the minister, still a comparatively young man, appeared before an elder statesman whom the great Lafayette delighted to call a fellow-soldier in the war for Independence. Monroe had served as a diplomatic representative to France, Spain, and England; he had occupied many offices within the domestic administration of his country. This man in his most gracious manner had excused "excesses of revolution" which Alvear knew so well. He showed understanding of national travail after revolution and even called himself "a man of revolution," a term which exactly described Alvear also.

These circumstances worked to excite Alvear's sympathy and to dull his critical capacity. The American President furnished answers to European perplexities in such lucid terms that his auditor not only accepted the statement of the problem, but also approved of the resulting policies which the President declared that his country had adopted. Much of what Monroe detailed was common knowledge to men in foreign service, and Alvear's ebullition at some of the President's observations reveals the inadequacy of his own foreign office. A reading of official messages and published Congressional documents would have shown the essential facts of North American policy. Monroe was presenting to a man totally ignorant of statecraft a two-hour summary of the nation's ten-year policy toward the Spanish-American revolution. To Alvear the facts of the past years came with the freshness of morning news, and by reason of Monroe's sympathetic personality the impact was tremendous.

The President next turned to another phase of his program, benevolent neutrality, which he well knew the Spanish Americans had misunderstood. He began by stating that a certain party in the United States had favored a more active policy. The President explained that if the United States had interfered by force in Spanish America, the other countries would have felt free to do the same, and if this had come to pass, none could tell where the war would have stopped. Then South America might not have benefited from a less considered policy. Probably he was referring to the opposition which had crystallized under Henry Clay's leadership, but the Spanish-American countries themselves had clamored also for assistance beyond the limits of neutrality. While passing his judgment on such statesmanship, the President was also giving his estimate of the Spanish Americans who thought that the United States had done nothing to aid their struggle for independence. He sincerely believed that his country by its neutrality had served the interests of their revolution, and he regretted that its policy had won "very feeble if any support."[27]

By the time the conference had reached this stage, the President had won the confidence of his auditor, who began to ask him questions of extreme importance to Buenos Aires: What was the attitude of the various members of the Holy Alliance toward Spain's former colonies; and what reason did England give for not recognizing the independence of the American States?

Monroe gladly answered the inquiries, but first he reminded his listener that the United States had long urged the European countries to grant recognition to the rising republics. He placed himself well within the bounds of historical truth when he assured Alvear that

> he had never ceased to recommend to his ministers in the various courts of Europe that according to the distinct desires and inclinations which they should discover, they were to moderate the evil disposition which they should note toward the new republics, and that they should contribute to the good disposition in others, influencing them whenever possible to speed up the desired recognition.

This phase of Monroe's foreign policy is now well known. Diplomatic correspondence after 1818 shows that the United States vainly exerted its influence to induce European governments to recognize the struggling republics. As late as August, 1823, Rush had refused to consider a common policy with England unless that country would immediately recognize the former colonies as the United States had done, and Monroe had approved his minister's stand.

Proceeding further in his interview, the President gave his own estimate of European attitudes toward the former Spanish colonies. This information would be of particular value to a young republic which was still without a regular diplomatic corps. Beginning with Russia, he discussed in turn European policies toward the Spanish-American revolution. Alvear received the surprising news that relations of the United States with Russia were more friendly than with any other European nation. On the basis of this intimacy the President promised the envoy that Russia would not take part in any hostile move toward the colonies.[28] He developed this point at length, and, as Alvear's dignified phraseology expressed it:

> he was pleased to assure him who writes that there existed the closest friendship between the Emperor of Russia and the government of the United States. He had reason to believe that the Russian government would not enter into any plan that should have hostility against America as its object.

Assurance of Russian friendliness came as good news to Alvear. His government, denied direct communication with Russia, had supposed that the guardian genius of legitimacy had picked Buenos Aires for special treatment. He welcomed a program of neutrality toward the revolution.

Monroe began his explanation of English policy by declaring that more recently—for a second time[29]—he had invited England to recognize the independence of South America, but that he had received as before only evasions, with no discussion of principles. Here the President, of course, was alluding to the Rush-Canning conversation of August, 1823. Briefly the American President sketched his estimate of English indecision: conservative and aristocratic influences in the British government prevented Canning from taking a step which the majority of the people seemed to desire. These opposing forces had effectively paralyzed English action: neither could they decide to intervene on behalf of Spain nor could they agree to recognize the independence of her former colonies. This hiatus would lead the English to tolerate, then to recognize the new republics.[30] With a vivid recollection of enthusiastic merchants toasting him in Liverpool, Birmingham, and London, Alvear agreed that the English people were forcing recognition upon a hidebound ministry.

Finally the President presented his estimate of French diplomacy. He pointed out that France believed Spain incapable of securing her colonies alone, and therefore had hoped to aid her, "a thing that would have taken place if the message of which he had made mention and the declaration of the English had not stopped the Cabinet of St. Cloud."[31] Desires of French Ultra-Royalists to assist Spanish recovery of her colonies had become well known to the American government through the correspondence of its sage observer, Albert Gallatin. Publication in February, 1824, of the proceedings of the Polignac-Canning conference held in the fall of the previous year made it clear that English opposition to French intervention in behalf of Spain had settled the matter in European circles. The importance of this conference Monroe freely acknowledged to the Argentine envoy. Doubtless this modest restraint, which granted equal merit to English influence over France, served only to enhance the minister's estimate of the United States.

The President then turned his attention to a type of intervention which he believed that the French were actively sponsoring. French government circles, he said, still believed that republican institutions were not well established in the New World. Even, on the contrary, that the majority of the people preferred monarchy. Spread of this idea in Europe "was greatly prejudicial to the new republics, because with the rising hopes of establishing monarchies in America, recognition was postponed." Monroe promised that the United States would continue to urge recognition by European nations, but reminded his auditor that the best inducement to Europe would be the practical proof of stable republican governments in South America.

At this point the Argentine minister observed that the President hesitated and seemed slightly embarrassed. Well might he pause, for one of the last dispatches from Buenos Aires had named Alvear as a possible agent shopping in Europe for a king, even for a tarnished Bourbon king.[32] Taking advantage of the hestitation, Alvear boldly protested that within the whole range of his experience there had been no events on which the countries of Europe could have based hopes of establishing a monarchy. "On the contrary . . . everything conspired in the New American nations to implant the republican system, the only one that general opinion admitted and which the circumstances of the people made indispensable and necessary." With this protestation given, he urged the President to speak frankly, telling him what he believed that Buenos Aires should know.

Monroe responded by giving a long lecture on the evils of monarchy in the New World. The seriousness of his purpose is indicated by the fact that almost one-third of Alvear's report is devoted to this question. Without naming specific countries, the President explained that "some have fluctuated in the system of government they should adopt and others have proclaimed in certain periods for the establishment of monarchy, a thing which has fomented the hopes of the governments of Europe." He declared that he had lately won an admission from royalist Russia that republican forms were entirely suitable in the Western Hemisphere. Therefore, he urged that all countries unite in repressing that vociferous group which was always calling for a king. Alvear agreed that the conduct of some states had been "ambiguous," but he insisted that Royalists represented small groups who, on occasion, had been responsible for false interpretations.

Monroe explained that he placed no blame for these monarchial leanings on the people themselves. "All new governments," he observed sympathetically, "have not progressed in the course of the revolution equally in a firm and regular manner." He, for his part, was firmly convinced that the republican system was well established in the colonies to the exclusion of any other.[33] By this personal appeal for a stable government to one of the former leaders of Buenos Aires, Monroe did all that he could to advance the cause of republican government in this hemisphere. Whether or not his plea would be effective he could not judge. The young man answered him with easy affirmations, and disparaged the Royalists as a vocal minority.

If, as Alvear stated, he had never in his whole experience seen evidence of monarchial desires in Buenos Aires, he had moved within a circle of singularly narrow radius. Letters from the United States representatives there carried reports too specific to be denied, and Monroe with good reason believed that his warning was both timely and necessary.[34] That a strong movement for monarchy existed in Buenos Aires is, of course, an accepted historical fact.

Monroe then shifted to a problem which long had troubled him. He spoke of the difficulties which privateering had raised and of the piratical atrocities which, even recently, these raiders had committed. Some of the South American countries, he said, had objected to detention of any ship bearing their commissions. He explained the piracy laws of the United States and the methods of enforcement, because some of the South American countries, he said, had objected to detention of any ship bearing their commissions.

Alvear broke in to declare that his country had abandoned the practice of issuing patents. Recognizing the fact, Monroe explained that he introduced the matter solely to enlist support of La Plata in persuading Colombia to abandon the practice also. The President declared that privateering irregularities by any of the new states heaped public disapproval upon all the other Spanish-American countries. He expressed reluctance to use force to restrain the heartless raiders; drastic action on his part, he feared, might invite similar action from Europe. But unless he could find some way of allaying the anger of American citizens, public opinion would no longer support the South American cause.

Alvear's record of the President's attitude on this subject fits in with Monroe's tolerance of Spanish-American privateering excesses. Adams himself explained Monroe's restraint by kindly sentiments toward the rising republics: "The President rests much on general considerations—upon our interest and policy to sustain the South American nations."[35]

After the discussion of piratical evils, Alvear pressed a question which his government had instructed him to ask: What was the attitude of the United States toward Brazil and its conquest of the Banda Oriental? The President answered briefly: "It was the wish of the United States that Brazil would have chosen a republican system, but his administration would not say what form of government another should adopt." He declared that his own private wish—and that of his country—was that Brazil should establish a republic, and he confidently awaited the time when, sooner or later, it must follow the example of the other American nations. He spoke of the hostile and unjust desires for conquest which the Brazilian Emperor had revealed, but he did not indicate that the United States would take sides in the dispute.

Reports of cabinet discussions on Brazilian recognition show that Monroe gave a fair estimate of the official attitude toward that country.[36] The instructions which Adams had prepared for Caesar A. Rodney in 1823 on his assignment to Buenos Aires gave no expression of favor for either side. The Secretary of State regretted the war for its "distractions" and thought that with the Eastern Shore reunited under a free and republican government embracing the old viceroyalty of La Plata there would be less cause for Brazilian intrigue in Buenos Aires.[37]

The President concluded the interview by promising that the new states could purchase any goods which they might desire in order to continue the war against Spain—as Colombia had already done. He assured the envoy that the United States, ignoring the protests of Europe, had always found "honorable means" of evasion. A policy of open ports to the rebellious Spanish colonies had constituted one of the earliest points in the neutrality program of the United States, and Secretaries of State had answered many complaints on that score.[38] That the United States should help the former Spanish colonies by every means short of war had been the aim of Monroe's administration; the burden of the complaints of the Spanish ministers to the United States was that such help had been given. Alvear's recollection of two magnificent fifty-eight-gun frigates under construction in Philadelphia for Colombia confirmed the President's statements.[39]

We can best describe Alvear's reaction to this interview by his letter to Bernardino Rivadavia, who had, by this time, relinquished his post in Buenos Aires and accepted a diplomatic appointment to France and England. The minister had left Monroe's presence feeling that he had received information so important that he dared trust delivery of the report to no one. He believed that his report of the improbability of European intervention would be welcome to his government; perhaps it was. The United Provinces, maintaining no regular representatives abroad, had no reliable news service. Authoritative interpretation of the divergent policies of Russia, England, and France should prove valuable to the Minister of Foreign Relations. It was, of course, a great advantage to the United States that international news should be accepted with an interpretation which discounted transatlantic sincerity when European countries dabbled in the affairs of the New World.

Alvear had acquired a new estimate of the policy of the United States toward the southern republics. He now believed that this country had greatly aided the Spanish-American nations by its benevolent neutrality and by supporting their revolutionary cause in European courts. The restraint of privateers who boasted South American patents seemed to be based on highly unselfish motives. If the impending struggle with Brazil should materialize, he asserted that the Republic of the North would favor Buenos Aires on account of its natural sympathy for republics. He concluded that the United States, as the protector of South America, would not permit European invasion in the Hemisphere. If, through any eventuality, such intervention should occur, he was confident that the United States was preparing a formidable armada and would use it effectively in defense of the sister republics. The Argentine minister left the conference captivated by the personality of Monroe, "a man of knowledge, prudence, and of great experience in the management of public affairs." After this conference Alvear believed that by the side of Monroe he would render his greatest service to the United Provinces. The President could not have hoped for a more successful conclusion.

3. Views and Dispositions on the Banda Oriental

After the encouraging conference with President Monroe, Alvear pondered the uses of friendship. The President had expressed personal dislike of the New World monarchy and had believed that his countrymen shared these sentiments. He had spoken of "hostile and unjust desires of a Brazilian monarchy" in the Banda Oriental, and though the general tone of the conversation was neutral, these words suggested positive support for the United Provinces.

The problem of the Banda Oriental long had plagued the best councils of Buenos Aires and had made insecure all republican governments in the La Plata region. Alvear himself, as Supreme Director, had sought to mollify Artigas by surrendering to him the city of Montevideo, which had been won after so much toil and sacrifice. But the self-styled "Protector of Free People" had been unable to hold the territory long against Brazilian invaders.[1]

Buenos Aires accepted what it could not avoid, and lived from 1816 to 1820 in uneasy peace with Brazilians across the estuary. Then out of the climactic, political confusion of 1820 arose the republican administration of Rodríguez-Rivadavia, whose first concern had been to seek restoration of the lost province. Alvear's good friend, Valentín Gómez, carried to Río de Janeiro requests that the Empire surrender its ill-won territory, but the Emperor's cabinet informed him in February, 1824, that it considered the Eastern Shore an integral part of Brazil. He recognized the failure of his mission and returned home.[2]

Fearing this rebuff, Rivadavia had already ordered Alvear to discover what assistance his country could expect abroad. The Minister should make it understood, wrote Rivadavia, that the United Provinces were irrevocably determined to reoccupy the "Province of Montevideo" and to drive the Brazilians back to their original limits. The United Provinces considered it intolerable that an American nation should occupy by force any part of the territory settled by a neighboring state.[3] One of the purposes of Alvear's mission would be to discover the extent to which England or the United States would use its influence to keep Brazil within its former limits. And yet—the instructions warned—he must avoid in every way the appearance of a beggar: he should ask for nothing.

Alvear had explained the problem of the Banda Oriental frankly to Canning and had declared that if England did not exert some moderating influence on Brazil, war was inevitable. Mention of "war" had brought a flash of uneasiness to Canning, but the gesture afforded no clue to his probable action. Whatever action England chose to take, Alvear had concluded that it would result in no good for his country. If they should not find themselves in a position to fight for all their rights, the United Provinces might be forced to arbitrate the aggravating problem. Recent reverses to liberating forces near Lima and Callao might call for concentration of armed forces in Upper Peru and so postpone indefinitely an opportunity to vindicate the national honor and violated rights across the river.[4] If faced with such an eventuality, his country would need a safe mediator. Friendly reception in the United States and a new appraisal of its rising influence in the world councils suggested that a helping hand might be found in the New World.

Before Alvear began his travels, he would have preferred England as mediator, but the long conference with Monroe had shown how the United States disapproved of Brazilian monarchy. However, Monroe was coming to the end of his term. The United States was then in the midst of a many-sided Presidential campaign.[5] Alvear decided to sound out John Quincy Adams as the candidate most likely to succeed Monroe: What was the Secretary's attitude toward Brazilian occupation of the Eastern Shore?

Under the pretext of asking for a day to take leave of the President, he secured an interview with the Secretary of State. But to Buenos Aires he wrote that he sought the conference in order to learn the "interesting and useful views and dispositions of the United States" in relation to the Banda Oriental.[6]

The exact date of this conference, like that with Monroe, is uncertain, for neither Monroe nor Adams made adequate record of their contacts with Alvear; and the General himself is not entirely clear. Adams's day-book shows the following entries:

October 11, 1824—President Alvear to P[resident] U[nited] S[tates]. Speech in Spanish. Iriarta.
October 20, 1824—Alvear—long conversation with him. Presented him and Iriarta to P U S.
October 21, 1824—Note from Alvear.
October 22, 1824—Alvear and Iriarta took leave.[7]

The long conference of October 20 may have referred to the Monroe conversation which Alvear reported as taking place on October 14, but there is no record of Adams having been present at that time. In all probability he was not, for Alvear specifically says that Iriarte, his secretary, was present on that occasion, and it is unlikely that he would have overlooked the presence of the Secretary of State. Presumably this entry refers to a long conference which Adams himself held with the newly arrived diplomat. Alvear does not give a complete account of all his conferences with Adams, for he declares that he held "several" conferences with the Secretary of State, yet he reported but one to his government.[8]

The Argentine minister began this conference by tracing the recent history of the Banda Oriental: the brutal seizure by Brazil, the attempted settlement by a commission sent to Brazil, the refusal of that country to treat on any terms. In conciliatory manner he pointed out the prudent steps taken by his government and the successive rejection of all proposals by Brazil. He professed to fear that the only monarchy in the Hemisphere would engulf the struggling republics. Therefore, he declared that he had assumed the responsibility of asking if the United States would be willing to arbitrate this dispute between the two countries.

Alvear flourished the prospects of glory accruing to the United States. Adams quietly sat through the recital, evidencing great interest. The appeal concluded, the Secretary pleased the Argentine by assuring him that the government of Washington would be glad to present itself as mediator in this dispute and thus hope to bring a happy ending to the question.[9]

The Secretary of State needed no reminder from Alvear to make him realize the unstable political situation in La Plata. In 1817 he had feared that Spanish attempts to find a mediator in her quarrel with Portugal over reinvasion of the Banda Oriental would furnish means by which European powers could aid in repressing the New World revolution.[10] In the winter of 1817-1818 he had conferred with Manuel de Aguirre, agent of the United Provinces, who had come to the United States to secure ships for San Martín's invasion of Peru. They discussed particularly the Portuguese occupation of Montevideo and its consequent menace to the independence of the United Provinces.[11] He had kept himself informed in detail on affairs in the Plata region, both by the official dispatches of John M. Forbes and by a voluminous personal correspondence from that agent and minister of the United States in Buenos Aires. He had profited greatly from all this information. President Monroe believed that his Secretary had keyed the negotiations of 1818-1819 for the acquisition of Florida to counterbalance Portuguese advances in the Banda Oriental. This aggressive action in North America had divided the councils of Europe just as the monarchs had sought to aid the weakened Spanish monarchy.[12]

The Holy Alliance, Adams had written in 1820, as a League of Peace had functioned well except in the New World.

> The Portuguese aggression, too, the European alliance has undertaken to control and in connection with it they have formed projects, hitherto abortive, of interposing in the revolutionary struggle between Spain and her South American colonies.[13]

The Secretary of State was alert to new European schemes which might not prove abortive, and he cautioned Forbes to be especially careful to secure correct, unbiased information on the Banda Oriental problem.[14]

Dispatches from American agents in Buenos Aires had long retailed the monotonous story of Portuguese intrigues to win not only the Platean area but all the United Provinces as well. Scarcely a communication omits some reference to a novel royalist scheme or a Porteño official newly enticed by an old proposal. As a superlatively careful and conscientious Secretary of State, Adams had ample opportunity to learn how an aggressive monarchy on La Plata would menace republican institutions in the whole area. He was predisposed to any peaceful plan to delimit Portuguese-Brazilian influence, but not without recognizing Brazil, monarchy or no monarchy, as an independent state in the New World.

Alvear would have been alarmed if he had known that even then Rebello, the Brazilian chargé, was soliciting a defensive alliance with the United States. Adams rejected the offer in January, 1825, declaring that there was no need for an American alliance against impotent Portugal unless she received assistance from other powers.[15] Secretary Adams was doubtless well pleased to have the United States petitioned in quick succession as mediator in an inter-American dispute and as a partner in a New World alliance against a European power. He accepted the Argentine offer promptly, but rejected the Brazilian proposal with a finespun sophistry.

Several interesting possibilities developed from this conference. For one thing, it shows Adams's willingness to project the influence of the United States to the limit of the Hemisphere. By accepting the offer to co-operate in settling New World problems within the New World he was following the logic of the doctrine that he had helped to formulate a year earlier: a co-operation based upon the identity of republican interest within the Hemisphere. Also, Adams's willingness to mediate in behalf of the new states forms a significant prelude to his support of the Inter-American Congress at Panama in 1826.

Attached to his report of the conference with Secretary Adams, Alvear enclosed a dispatch which represented for him a complete diplomatic reversal. He disparaged England's importance in New World affairs. His observations in London, he wrote, had convinced him that England had notoriously supported unbearable Brazilian pretentions. New World republics should consider England as another European power related to all the others through its royal family, a member of the Holy Alliance, and a hearty supporter of the detested Brazilian monarchy. The United States he placed in another category: its political institutions were republican, and the sympathy of its government and people lay with the new countries of Spanish-America.[16]

He sought to take advantage of this favorable situation. Elated at the conferences with Monroe and Adams and most enthusiastic about the sympathetic hearing on the Banda Oriental, Alvear sought interviews on this subject with the Spanish-American representatives. He was quite undismayed by official warning from his government to make no proposals until the administration could adopt a policy. He was stimulated to greater activity when he learned that Silvestre Rebello had already called upon the same men he intended to see and had told them how greatly his country had been abused for pacifying a turbulent province.

Alvear sought to overcome such false impressions at once. With Salazar of Colombia he met the most hearty response. The Colombian told him that Rebello had inquired about the possibilities of opening relations between Colombia and Brazil. Salazar declared that he had disdained the offer, telling the chargé that such a move was impossible as long as the Empire held the Province of Montevideo. Rebello countered with protestations that Brazilian troops had occupied the territory because Montevideans did not want to live under the Buenos Aires government.

Salazar warned Alvear that while he placed no personal reliance in these Brazilian tales, his government might soon establish friendly relations with Brazil—already Vice-President Santander had suggested the possibility of such a step. This disagreeable prospect excited Alvear to the greatest activity. Buenos Aires had counted on help from Bolivar's army if Brazil persisted in its nefarious conduct. It would lose this resource if Colombia reached an accord with the Empire. For Salazar's benefit, the Argentine envoy drafted an extensive memorandum on Brazilian iniquities in the disputed area.[17] He explained the failure of Valentín Gómez's mission to Río de Janeiro. He stressed the dangers to the new republican states of a monarch who pushed his claims without a shadow of justice; of a ruler who, ignoring all law, recognized no restraints but his own convenience and ability to conquer. "Thus can one be sure that the Holy Alliance will find in Brazil a faithful executor of its designs in everything that pertains to the new states."

The United Provinces, he continued, had tried every peaceful means to induce Brazil to return to the paths of justice and moderation. With great sorrow they had seen their best hopes ridiculed. The nation would defend itself. Even then the United Provinces were holding three thousand men in readiness in Salta under General Arenales' capable command; and these, united to the Liberating Army and commanded by the immortal Liberator, would prove irresistible. To control such a grasping neighbor, Alvear advocated a republican alliance: the republics, united, could sweep all before them.[18] The General's love of military victory easily overcame the statesman's preference for mediation.

And so Monroe and Adams tried to convert the South American envoy to the policy of the United States: settlement of New World problems without European interposition, and mediation of disputes rather than resort to force. But there is no evidence of any effort to follow the lead which Alvear had provided: mediation by the United States. An archival note was made of the offer, but by the time Buenos Aires was ready to settle the dispute it felt strong enough to fight for its claims. If governmental instability in Buenos Aires had not overthrown administrations in rapid succession, some portion of Alvear's point of view might have impressed policy-forming officials. Rivadavia had been forced out of office even before Alvear had left London, and Forbes characterized his successors as "day laborers." As such they were not interested in forming a national policy on foreign affairs. Before Alvear reached home, García, the new Secretary of Foreign Affairs, had already decided to delay establishing the Legation in Washington,[19] and the General, on his return, promptly immersed himself in domestic politics and paid no further attention to foreign affairs. The seed cast by Monroe and Adams fell on stony ground, sprang up quickly, and wilted under the heat of political conflict in the United Provinces.

With great deliberation Rivadavia drew up Alvear's instructions for his itinerary to England, United States, and Mexico.

The minister had begun his travels early in March and expected to be gone for a year and a half at least. Yet he had not completed his eighty-four-day passage to Liverpool when the Mexican phase of the mission was canceled and he was ordered to return after the completion of his assignment to the United States.[20] Rivadavia gave no definite reason for calling him home. He vaguely referred to "interesting circumstances in the country" which would make an early return advisable. Alvear, anxious to protect his own political interests, accepted the order without objection. He fretted at the delay in New York while waiting for the DeForest archives. He wasted no time in presenting himself to the Department of State, and prompt reception by Monroe and Adams must have been pleasing to him. No sooner had he concluded his interviews than he sent notice of his intention to leave.[21] He allowed the rumor to circulate that his government wished to place him in command of an army that would march into Peru and there assist in the final episodes of the War for Independence.[22] Salazar sent cordial letters of farewell, and when David DeForest read in the newspapers of the recall he sent to Buenos Aires belated letters of congratulation and best wishes. Trailing intimations of military glory behind him, Alvear returned to New York and impatiently waited for passage home.[23] Then he received a rude awakening: it was an appointment to Colombia!

This was the end. The General had enough. He had never fancied posting about, exchanging credentials in remote capitals. For all the advantages to himself which his friends said this mission would provide, he had never wanted the diplomatic appointment. Always he had regarded the revolution of 1815 and the five years of exile as a monstrous piece of personal injustice. The nation, not he, must make good. He must have again a field command commensurate with his military rank. Nothing else would do; no palliative could satisfy.

Everyone said that Rivadavia had done him a favor by providing a graceful entry into national affairs. In his heart the ex-Director must have known that Valentín Gómez, his business manager and faithful friend was right: "Your previous conduct has made you detestable and the province looks upon you as a thing that does not belong to it." He continued with well-meant advice, which Alvear did not care to follow: "Write few letters to private persons, for when passed about they can be misunderstood. . . . Save your money in order to be independent in your own country."[24] Notwithstanding this good advice, General Alvear continued to feel bitter. Diplomacy meant time lost from his career and chosen profession. To his protests Gómez returned kind words:

> You adorn your profession: you go with it: you perfect it. You will be the only General of your grade and knowledge of war that unites gifts useful and honorable in a republic. You are young yet. The country is only beginning, and while it is necessary to think of war, one must not lose sight of peace.[25]

In his absence the city had begun to build amazingly, wrote Gómez. Peace had encouraged the construction long held in abeyance during the revolutionary years. Such marvelous progress seemed to a resident of the Port like the United States itself—street lights, pavements, new shops. In the United States a man could gain new ideas; and Alvear, living there, could acquire the very spirit of the country. "Stay in that republic," urged his friend, "and see how the nation operates. Learn. Endure the inconveniences of travel. Go to Colombia. Find out how a new nation grows and on your return here you will contribute your part in perfecting the work."[26]

For all these well meant admonitions Alvear cared little. He would not go to Colombia. It made no difference if the opportunity to see the United States, as Gómez warned, should never come again. Such consolation brought little ease to the General in his diplomatic wanderings. "Talents for peace as well as war" meant little to him. The question "Suppose war ceases, then what is your future?" left him undismayed. He would shape his own future. By fulfilling his instructions on the English and American phases of his mission he had paid both personal and political debts to his friends—men who had by that time left the government. Now he should be free to return home.

Alvear indignantly declined the mission to Colombia, which had already passed from one political corner to another.[27] He declared that since receiving notice of his recall he had hastened every phase of the mission to England and the United States and had labored long without sufficient rest. He wanted to get home. Constant travel for months, eating at public inns, and partaking of foreign foods for so long had upset his digestion: his health would sustain no more culinary punishment. Also, he had done enough to deserve a recall. He stressed his many interviews on La Plata affairs, his remarkable conference with President Monroe, and the public announcement in the American press of his departure for Buenos Aires—but he said nothing of his supposed return to command a military expedition. Alvear objected to the trip through piratical seas; he feared yellow fever at the Colombian coast; he shuddered at the hardships involved in reaching Bogotá. He ridiculed this traveling mission as "postillion diplomacy," which carried only dangerous hardships to the envoy and required unnecessary visits of etiquette. He assured Las Heras that when he had expressed a desire to travel to foreign countries and learn the arts of diplomacy, he had not meant to include the new states whose leaders knew no more than he of such matters. Besides, Ignácio Álvarez, representative of the United Provinces in Peru, could call at Bogotá more easily than a minister in the United States.[28] With these injudicious and suggestive remarks Alvear closed his letter.

This communication reveals some of the General's more unpleasant personal traits: his egotism, personal ambition, intense pride—even selfishness. After years first in exile and then in complete retirement from politics he was in no position to determine what assignments were necessary and which were "merely for etiquette." He seems to have regarded his original nomination as a means of advancing himself politically, and only incidentally to serve his country. When his government made a nomination which did not accord with his notion of personal benefit and convenience, he rejected it. Scenting victory both in Peru against the waning Spanish power and in the disputed Banda Oriental against the Brazilians, he intended to be present for the final blows. He had let his acquaintances in the United States understand that he had been called home in order to command a conquering army, and to have them learn that he had been transformed into an obscure minister was more than his pride could take.[29] Without caring whether his rejection would be accepted or not, he boarded the first ship for home.

This remarkably blunt refusal of his Colombian assignment aroused no discernible wrath. His report of April 9, 1825, announced his return from the United States—making no mention of England—and expressed the hope that the work had been found satisfactory. Promptly he received an effusive letter acknowledging the efficient dispatch of commissions entrusted to his care.[30]

Despite the unusual accomplishments of this mission and the importance of the information acquired, no observable results accrued. Two of Alvear's dispatches from the United States were presented to the Assembly of Buenos Aires on January 15, 1825. One representative moved that the reports should be read to the House at once, but another favored sending them to the Committee on Foreign Affairs before permitting a public reading. After a short discussion, the report was referred to this committee: it never received general attention again.[31] The original dispatches were filed in the archives of the Department of Foreign Affairs.[32] No further attention was paid to them.

And so the commission ended, but Don Carlos's concern for his fortune continued. No Argentine looked toward the future with more misgiving than he. He had a large and growing family. Except for the period of exile, he had always lived well; and he expected to continue to do so.

But how? In the economy of the new state opportunities for affluent living were limited. Only public employment in the highest brackets would meet the demands of his purse and satisfy the cravings of his ambition. Personal economies he found impossible to make. While he waited in New York had come prudent advice from Gomez, "Save, my friend, and on your return you will find sustenance for your family and independence for yourself." Sound advice, but Carlos de Alvear disregarded it. Choosing the magnificent gesture, he returned with a New England coach for an impressive passage through the narrow streets of the port and with two English servants for his home.[33] Contemptuously he had tossed back the arduous Colombian assignment to the Secretary of Foreign Affairs, who could dispatch to those unhealthy latitudes some hardier soul who minded neither dangers of travel nor treats of disease.

Such headstrong action in no way injured the General's standing with the administration, but it threatened his own solvency. The salary of a general on inactive status would never support his expensive family. The army could provide at best only a thin living, and already too many military men contested for the few positions of command available.

Rather than join in this undignified scramble, and—perhaps—lose the prize, General Alvear turned again to the foreign service as the most lucrative occupation in the public employ.[34] The following month, May, 1825, he accepted nomination on a joint mission to Bolivia (then called Upper Peru). There he would represent his country before Simón Bolívar, the Liberator.

III

MISSION TO BOLIVIA: 1825

At the outset of their struggle for independence the rebellious Spanish colonies agreed that each nascent state would accept its boundaries as defined by the mother country and refrain from preying upon its neighbors at some opportune occasion. By the terms of this agreement (called the *uti possedittis* of 1810) Upper Peru would continue to be administered by Buenos Aires, because it had formed a part of the Viceroyalty of La Plata. But a contrary fact challenged this convenient understanding: the people of Upper Peru preferred their centuries-old contact with Lima.[1]

Spanish forces had controlled Upper Peru during the whole of the War of Independence. Every attempt to invade the country from the South failed, and ultimately forces from La Plata abandoned all serious efforts to march against the Spanish from this direction. Suddenly, after Ayacucho, Royalist grip on Upper Peru loosened and forces under General Sucre, the Liberator's faithful lieutenant, swept across the land, dispersing local concentrations of Spanish fanatics. Then the populace, freed from Spanish control, acknowledged no authority. Some would have remained within the boundaries of the Viceroyalty of La Plata and recognized the jurisdiction of Buenos Aires. But an ever-increasing group claimed the prerogative of democracy: the people themselves could decide their political destiny. Most of those urging this cause favored independence. The presence of the Liberating Army from Peru and the impending visit of Simón Bolívar made it easy both to urge independence for Upper Peru and to choose the Liberator as their first leader.

Political administrators of the United Provinces, centering their attention on Buenos Aires, cared little about these affairs in the remote highlands. They ignored the whole matter and gave the popular and capable General Juan Antonio Alvares de Arenales, Governor of Salta and of the northern frontier, no instructions on how to meet it. The public unrest that accompanied the final defeat of the Spaniards disturbed Arenales, and he sought to win public confidence by calling a political convention that should decide the status of the four provinces of Upper Peru.[2]

When General Sucre completed the conquest of the area, he confirmed this call for an assembly on behalf of the Liberating Army and notified the governors of the United Provinces of his action.[3] To this proposed assembly the Congress of La Plata gave its official approval on May 9, 1825. At the same time that body authorized the dispatch of ministers plenipotentiary to Potosí, where they would treat with the new convention and meet the Liberator, Bolívar, President both of Colombia and of Peru.[4] And it was high time that the United Provinces sent some persons of experience and authority into that area. A political crisis had developed suddenly, and nobody in Buenos Aires knew what to do.

Acting with quite uncustomary promptitude, the Secretary of Foreign Affairs, Manuel José García, named two ministers for the task—Carlos de Alvear, a general to take the lead in discussions with Bolivar, and José Miguel Díaz Vélez, a parliamentarian who would negotiate with representatives of the new political body.[5] The government announced only that the joint mission would congratulate His Excellency, the Liberator, General Simón Bolívar, on the victories which had crowned his years devoted to the destruction of Spanish power in the New World. But the members of the mission soon learned that felicitation to Bolivar constituted but a minor portion of their duties. Their initial purpose was to wean away from Peruvian influence the four provinces of Upper Peru. The government of La Plata really hoped that the areas would remain a part of the United Provinces. Failing that, La Plata would accept their independence. Anything would be better than seeing them become part of a Greater Peru.

Hastily prepared instructions indicated in a most cursory manner the duties of the two members of the mission. Since General Alvear was the only military commander in La Plata (San Martín having been exiled) who could boast of military triumph, the Minister of Foreign Affairs instructed him to present to the Liberator the compliments of the Republic for his unparalled victories. Before the aura of triumph had vanished, Alvear should explain how the imperialistic conduct of Brazil in the Banda Oriental endangered all the republics. The United Provinces would count it a great victory if the Liberator would take up their quarrel. Through the influence of his prestige no less than his authority as President of two countries he could lead a victorious, common action against the only New World monarchy. To win Bolivar's support of the national cause was Alvear's special task.

Besides this invitation to Bolivar, the government of La Plata appealed directly to Upper Peru. Upon Díaz Vélez, Secretary of the Argentine Congress, García laid responsibility for inviting the new Assembly to remain within the state "to which they have always belonged"—a generous misstatement. Gracefully the instructions continued, "recognizing that the strength of a union is based upon the solidity of popular will, the Congress leaves the provinces at full liberty to decide their fate according to their own interests and happiness."[6]

As the mission prepared for its departure, the government received news of a Brazilian invasion into the remote, eastern Bolivian territory of Chiquitos and Mojos.[7] Brazilian troops from Matto Grosso had, without provocation, crossed the upper branches of the Paraguay and there had burned the small villages, stolen cattle, and abused the inhabitants. This news led to a quick addition to the instructions of Alvear and his colleague. They were directed to conclude courteous preliminaries as soon as possible and to secure at once a secret alliance for the total destruction of the Brazilian monarchy. The United Provinces offered to guarantee the expenses of allied armies for an invasion and to support allied navies to ravage the coasts of Brazil.[8]

This Brazilian incursion came at the moment when the United Provinces needed good grounds for soliciting allies in their impending war against Brazil. None of the war-racked new republics felt its interests involved in the Argentine fight for the Banda Oriental, but the Chiquitos affair would spread the bad name of Brazil. Upper Peru had become the current darling of Bolívar. He was going to visit there and, according to general expectations, would set up a new republic that presumably would carry his name. He might very well take up the quarrel of the foundling republic and with the United Provinces wage war against their common enemy. But most of the troops would, of course, come from the settled areas of La Plata—Upper Peru having as yet no military entity. And then nothing could so well counteract the separatist movement in Upper Peru as the sight of the Liberator leading troops of the United Provinces as they fought presumably to avenge the violations of Chiquitos as well as to contain Brazilian aggressions on the Eastern Shore. Certainly, too, with the help of Bolívar and of his armies victory would more likely rest with the United Provinces. The cause was good. Bolívar might accept: he loved the martial accolade of victory.

Since the Liberator had not yet arrived in the upper provinces, Alvear and his colleague proceeded in leisurely fashion. For three months they protracted their journey with long delays at Tucumán and Salta. Then when they learned that he had reached Potosí, they moved out promptly, arriving there on October 7, 1825. The following morning Colonel Daniel F. O'Leary, adjutant to the Liberator and leader of a guard of honor, presented the respects of his commander and received, in turn, a request for an interview.[9] Two preliminary conferences preceded the official reception and on these occasions Bolívar both discovered the purposes of the mission and explained his attitude on impending issues.

To the great surprise of the Legation, Bolívar declared that he had no powers to receive it officially. Although he carried titles as President and Supreme Commander of Colombia and

Peru, he laid claim to military powers only! For all questions related to foreign affairs the ministers should present themselves to the proper civil authorities in the several national capitals. On successive days Bolívar raised this question and, according to the account in Buenos Aires, only their sharp refusal to be humiliated made the Liberator agree to receive them properly.[10]

At the informal conferences Bolívar revealed an element of hostility toward the government of La Plata. He resented the bitter interpretation of his work which Argentine periodicals such as *El Argos* were spreading for public delectation. The envoys promptly answered that, in a country with a free press, unwise and sometimes unjust criticisms were bound to appear; these irritating remarks in no way represented the attitude of the administration or of the people. To no avail: "Gentlemen, speaking with the frankness which we have proposed to observe," Bolívar retorted, "I say that *El Argos* is paid by the government."

Díaz Vélez sensed the basis of the Liberator's hostility. The paper, he admitted, had once received some governmental support, and had paid an elderly churchman, Dean Gregorio Funes, a nominal sum as editor. But the administration had paid the money more out of respect for the Father's age and for his prestige acquired in the early days of the Revolution than for his ability as a journalist. Ultimately the paper had passed into private hands and its new owners published whatever they pleased. The Liberator regarded all their explanations of the hostile press as unsatisfactory; therefore both parties agreed to leave the thorny subject for a later discussion.

On the subject of an alliance against Brazil, Bolívar assumed what Alvear characterized as "a more frank character," although he proved as intransigeant as ever. He declared that by previous arrangement both Colombia and Peru had agreed to sign no treaties with any other nation, even with America, except at the congress of new states soon to meet in Panama. Even if the United Provinces should open negotiations for an alliance in Bogotá or Lima they would meet rebuff.

Again General Alvear found himself at odds with Bolívar. He insisted that such provisions were never listed in the circulars relative to the Isthmanian meeting. Since the United States had been invited to attend, one could not remotely imagine that country renouncing its treaty-making powers in order to delegate them to a general Congress. Bolívar sidestepped this latter objection by saying that he had not favored the invitation to the United States. Besides, Santander had written that the northern republic probably would not accept. When pressed to account for the Peruvian-Colombian agreement, so the ministers reported, he evaded the matter with assurance that the documents could be found and discussed later. The subject was never raised again.

The Argentine negotiators turned to matters more likely to produce agreement. Bolívar showed great interest in the specific complaints which Buenos Aires directed against Brazil. The account reflects a measure of Alvear's eloquence as he urged him to assume personal leadership of the campaign to repress, even to overthrow if necessary, an Empire bent on destroying the republics.

Unwilling to commit himself at once on a Brazilian campaign, the Liberator turned the discussion to the outrageous conduct of Dr. Francia, tyrannical dictator of Paraguay. This unaccountable individual had imprisoned Bompland, a European naturalist, who had strayed into his bailiwick. Bolívar seemed quite ready to overthrow the Paraguayan dictator. He had already made a survey of the Pilcomayo; and having collected all available information on the best route, he professed himself ready to strike. Since the route of march lay across the territory claimed by the United Provinces, he needed only the acquiescence of that country. Would the United Provinces receive from his hands that territory which once formed a part of the Viceroyalty of La Plata?

Bolívar's love of the bizarre had been forgotten! Instructions from Buenos Aires had made no reference whatever to recovery of Paraguay. Therefore, in the absence of any mandate, the Argentine ministers again rejected a proposal of the Liberator, this time basing their objections on "the liberal principles of La Plata." While he pretended not to urge the matter, Bolívar emphasized the strategic location his forces in Asunción would command if they should be needed for a Brazilian invasion. The Liberating Army at the back door of the Empire, he observed, might prove much more effective than an aide-de-camp politely knocking at the front door in Río de Janeiro. At the least pretext, and a pretext was never lacking, the republican allies would wage war victoriously.

Discussions shifted to the anomalous situation of Upper Peru. Bolívar hoped that La Plata would legalize the secession of the four provinces at once so that he could check in Lima the agitation for re-annexation of the area. In his zeal to secure prompt action, His Excellency rashly proposed, "Recognize the Bolivian republic, placing as a condition the collection of four or five thousand men for the war with Brazil, and I will accept the proposition." Gone now were his earlier notions that he had authority only to receive congratulations for past exploits. But this plan won no more approval than the projected invasion of Paraguay.

General Alvear reported that at the close of one of the conferences he raised the problem of Tarija, a territory belonging to the province of Salta. This district was then being occupied by the Bolivarian armies of the north, and the government of La Plata took umbrage at the presence of foreign troops in the national domain. For the presence of his armies there His Excellency offered devious explanations, but the Argentine plenipotentiaries declared that they refuted every point "completely and victoriously." The problem seemed to merit a special conference. With this agreement the preliminary meetings concluded after effusive protestations of friendship.

At least the reports sent to Buenos Aires give the account summarized above. Secretary García might well have concluded that the agents of his government spoke with zest and assurance while their opponents stood at a loss to answer arguments so logically based and so effectively phrased. According to the Argentine reports, General Bolívar appeared evasive and impotent when they pressed their discussion. Fortunately, we have other reports of these conferences.[11] The Liberator's Secretary-General, Estenós, records a conference which the ministers from La Plata failed to mention. When they called upon Estenós in his office before they had met His Excellency, the Secretary-General informed them that Bolívar lacked powers to receive an official mission. At this news Alvear and Díaz Vélez "were thrown into greatest confusion, not to say desperation, which the first one named showed particularly." In addition, Estenós inserted into his files memoranda of the conferences with Bolívar in which he portrayed the envoys as fearful, anxious not to offend, and hopeful for the Liberator's good grace. In complete contradiction to the Argentines, he declared that they suggested the dubious project of invading Paraguay; but Bolivar's adjutant, O'Leary, in his *Memorias*, attributed the suggestion to the Liberator.[12] This faithful attendant particularly remembered, too, the evasive and dishonest tactics of Alvear and Díaz Vélez: how they tried to reject the Paraguayan invasion without seeming to do so; how they sought to blind the Liberator with invitations to dazzling military triumphs even while their countrymen were seeking peace through English mediation.

Bolívar also sent his own extensive summaries of the conferences to officials in Peru and Colombia. He remembered, especially, the request for his personal intervention against Brazil. Alvear had asked him to take all America as a protectorate[13]—a wild suggestion that he had promptly rejected. The Liberator makes it clear that he knew his political limitations: as President of two republics he could make no commitments without the approval of national representatives acting through federal organization. But he said nothing about his offer to supply an army for the Brazilian adventure if La Plata would recognize the independence of Upper Peru. Argentine pleas for his intervention in order to save La Plata and his refusal to act bulked largest in the Liberator's summary of his earliest conferences with the southern plenipotentiaries.

General Alvear's private letters to his friend, Manuel José García, Minister of Foreign Affairs, shine unblemished by doubt, fear, or failure. They show much less restraint than his official communications. "I will say to you that in any event we shall have him safe, even though he comes as chief of this state." Again, "In my opinion it would be very convenient to make a big noise with Bolívar in order to restrain Brazil and give events time to mature. . . . He is very sensitive to all attack and you must know that he is very prejudiced against all of you."[14] Each man looked at the conferences through glasses colored best to reveal his own ego or to suppress the anxieties of his readers.

Though he denied power to act in international affairs, Bolívar consented to an official reception of the delegation, with the understanding that he possessed no jurisdiction in such matters. To this unsatisfactory arrangement the mission had to consent, nor did its ministry in Buenos Aires protest the acquiescence of its agents.[15] On October 19, at high noon, the mission, accompanied by forty guests and officials, pushed through cheering throngs to the government palace, where the Liberator, his marshals, and the civilian officials of the new nation about to be born waited to greet them. Alvear, speaking for the mission, delivered a flowery address on the ravages of Brazil and the hope of succor. Bolívar responded briefly with what his Secretary-General considered his usual "precision and elegance."[16]

At four o'clock the group reassembled around a banquet table laid for fifty guests. As flattering toasts met noble responses, the wine induced still more cordiality. Alvear, "never forgetting the country he represented," raised his cup to Colombia, "the light of America, the sword of Bolívar"; to "Bolívar, the hero whose constancy gave liberty to the New World"; to "the Republic of Bolívar, shielded by a good name." Then a whirl of toasts, salutes, *abrazos*. Domingo de Oro, the vivacious secretary of the Argentine Mission, offered a tribute to the victory of Ayacucho. Sucre remembered "the Argentine people, who have proved their love of liberty." The Liberator toasted the government of La Plata and paid resounding compliments to General Alvear and Díaz Vélez. Estanós remembered that "the greatest happiness reigned until long after darkness."[17]

The round of banquets had only begun. Alvear attended them all, toasted everybody, and talked of republican union to restrain imperialistic aggressors. Upon Bolívar and his generals he urged a victorious campaign against the New World monarchy which was prompted by their old enemies of Europe. The United Provinces could have chosen no more eloquent an emissary than the General, and he could have urged his cause nowhere so effectively as over the convivial cup drunk to past glories.[18] O'Leary, who attended these festivities, particularly remembered the General's persistence and his fervent overtures to persuade the Liberator to lead the war against Brazil, either in alliance with Peru and Colombia or as commander of Bolivian forces alone. These proposals never failed to accent the appeal to glory. Such, he says, "were the inducements presented each day, each day exhibiting a facet more flattering than before, and always he urged them with the characteristic zeal of the courtier anxious to achieve his object."[19]

Between these festivities the Argentine delegation scheduled with the Liberator conferences on special issues. Both parties had referred now and again to the problem of the Banda Oriental because solutions of almost every issue depended upon decisions reached in regard to this supremely vexing and acute controversy. In past years both Portugal and Spain had claimed the area. Its inhabitants often appeared indifferent to whose flag waved above the fort at Montevideo. Sometimes favorably inclined toward Portugal or Brazil, more often toward the other La Plata provinces, the Eastern Shore had never known political stability.[20] Through its back-country galloped *gaucho* leaders who varied appeals for allegiance to the United Provinces with demands for independence. Failure to solve the problem years ago had hastened Alvear's overthrow as Supreme Director, and ever since then the Banda Oriental had been a disruptive factor in politics on La Plata.

Brazil, after winning a gentle revolution against the mother country, sought more aggressively than ever to recover this lost province which she had always regarded as her own. Her imperial influence was limited to Montevideo and Colonia; the ordinary countrymen of the area, though often disappointed, had looked always to their La Plata neighbors for support against the Portugese-Brazilians. For each victory they praised themselves; for each defeat they blamed the muddled Porteños with increasing bitterness, sometimes fairly, but always vigorously.

Some Argentine advocates of direct action frequently crossed the estuary to the Eastern Shore. There they organized roving bands which made judicious attacks upon unwary Brazilian detachments. The government, not willing to court unpopularity, dared not curtail the raiders who sailed the estuary every dark night. Yet these increased attacks, which always brought popular acclaim from the coffee-cup strategists in Buenos Aires, would inevitably lead to war. The United Provinces were ill-prepared for such a venture. National forces had dwindled until the generals of the field had metamorphosed into the "idle swords" of the drawing room. The Navy, once so ably commanded by Admiral Brown, had vanished. The Provinces needed help.

Therefore instructions to the mission in Upper Peru had ordered the ministers to seek aid, both military and diplomatic. Alvear first asked the Liberator to lead the conquering Army of Peru and Colombia into Matto-Grosso and across the mountains to Río de Janeiro. Fleets from Colombia should ravage northern Brazilian shores while the Peruvian fleet could raise the inevitable blockade of Buenos Aires. In repeated conferences he pressed for immediate military alliance, but Bolívar, who had expected such an invitation, continued to explain that he could not commit the army to action.[21] Unimpressed by constitutional restrictions, Alvear set himself to secure Bolívar's personal intervention. The government of the United Provinces never knew how far its agent pushed his proposals. To his correspondents Bolívar wrote that General Alvear, flattering him to the limit, "has come to propose to me (as a secret proposition) the reunion of the Argentine Republic and of Bolivia, all of it bearing my name. He abandons the plan for nothing and even calls on me to establish the destiny of Rio de la Plata."[22]

Unabashed flattery, unrestrained proposals, "agreements in everything" won over the Liberator; and for a time he chafed that the Colombian government held him "as a boy that needs a tutor." Long after leaving the new republic Bolívar meditated the problem of the southern half of the continent and wondered if he could unify Peru and all the nations to the south —as Alvear had suggested.[23]

The private bid for the Liberator's support was followed by an official proposal that the republics should simultaneously demand of the Brazilian Emperor that such depredations as those in Chiquitos must cease and that the Banda Oriental must be freed from occupation or war would follow.[24] Bolívar had three objections to this plan: he had no power to sign definitive agreements for Peru or Colombia; he felt that all agreement would be abortive unless the attitude of England was known; and finally, from his correspondence with Dean Funes he was convinced that the United Provinces had no intention of fighting Brazil.[25]

This last point, so damaging to the integrity of La Plata, the Liberator had learned through his correspondence with Gregorio Funes. The Dean despised the current administrators of his country, partly because they refused to sanction open and immediate aid to the Banda Oriental, and he had persuaded Bolívar that he could not trust the southern government. Although the Dean later confessed himself mistaken in some of his more violent judgments, Bolívar never lost confidence in the correctness of opinions expressed by the churchman. Had all other factors been in its favor, the mission could scarcely have succeeded against the negative attitudes which Funes had inspired.[26]

Bolívar finally consented only to send an adjutant to Río de Janeiro with orders to demand from the Brazilian Emperor redress and apology for the military incursions from Matto-Grosso. This official, representing the Liberator in his capacity as Commander-in-Chief of the Allied armies, could join a representative of the United Provinces who would make parallel demands in reference to the Eastern Shore. The two envoys while in the Brazilian capital could learn also the attitude of England toward a war in southeastern America.[27] Beyond the boundaries of Upper Peru, Bolívar would agree to do nothing

—except to invade Paraguay, a project always repugnant to the United Provinces.[28] He appeared quite indifferent to Brazilian aggrandizement in the Banda Oriential.

While these accredited diplomats formally discussed what they might do about this Eastern Shore, less responsible individuals were forcing a prompt solution. A guerilla force had defeated there a Brazilian detachment of two thousand cavalry. Under the impetus of this victory, so wildly acclaimed in the streets of Buenos Aires, delegates from the Banda had been seated in the Congress of the United Provinces and the Brazilian representative to Buenos Aires had departed in a huff.[29] Although cventual war between the United Provinces and Brazil became obvious, the Liberator did not alter his previous decision to make no more than a diplomatic gesture: La Plata faced the Empire alone. For this situation there were no regrets on the estuary. The southern republic prepared to trust to force, even while voicing the pious hope that the other republics would "appreciate the community of interests which lie in the [Banda Oriental] cause."

The "community of interest" about which the administration of Buenos Aires now appeared so concerned had formed the basis of Bolívar's call for a congress at Panama. There the new states could consider common action for their mutual welfare. Secretary García's first instructions to the mission had not mentioned the coming congress, but when questioned later he told Alvear and Díaz Vélez that if the Liberator made attendance at the congress the price of his assistance in the Banda Oriental, they should appear to accept the proposal and then promise to consult with their government. The equivocation proved unnecessary. In September the administration resolved to send delegates, though it had small enthusiasm for the project.[30]

While the government was slowly reaching a decision to attend the Isthmanian meeting, Bolívar was following closely events in La Plata. He chose to make no special appeal to the ministers for his project, apparently because he believed that the logic of its situation would impel La Plata to assume membership. Eventually the delegation began to take seriously the Liberator's references to the "general interests of America," and "a body to give consistency to the new republics." Tentatively they suggested to García:

Perhaps it would be very convenient for the delegates to the Isthmus to carry instructions on [the invasion of the Banda Oriental] in order that it might be advanced in the Assembly, where possibly the fate of Brazil hangs in the balance.[31]

Bolívar could not understand why the United Provinces were hesitating to endorse the congress: they had the most to gain by federation. But whether they joined or not, he promised, the problem of the Banda Oriental would be the first subject discussed at the general assembly, and Dom Pedro would have reason to fear allied republican action.[32]

At the first military defeat of Brazil—when it appeared that the United Provinces might win singlehandedly—Secretary García dropped all notions of presenting the national cause to the assembled republics. He ordered the ministers to return. Their duty was done. They should declare that the government of the United Provinces, although keenly conscious of appearing united on some occasions, did not believe that the proper time had come for the organization of a federal body of American nations.[33] By this decision La Plata left Bolívar and his new republic to settle the Chiquitos episode as best they could and it renounced any intention of supporting the Congress of Panama.[34] However, the decision not to support the congress was not widely known. Even Dean Funes could not find out why García had named no delegates to the meeting. He attributed this indifference to the recent arrival from Europe of Rivadavia, around whom he believed centered opposition to the Liberator's plans.[35]

Bolívar never received García's rejection of the Isthmanian assembly. It arrived as Alvear was leaving Bolivia, and relations then seemed so cordial that he hesitated to inject this contrary note, lest, in disappointment or anger, Bolívar should refuse to send his adjutant to Río de Janeiro.[36]

The subterfuge availed little. Months later, when it became evident that La Plata was delaying overlong the nomination of its envoy to Panama, Bolívar wrote to Alvear personally.

This time he warned that the Congress of the Isthmus could take no action until the United Provinces had presented its cause. He repeated again that as commander of the Liberating Armies he could not take the field except by consent of the general Congress, and he warned that in any event a vigorous Brazilian campaign might ruin Argentine hopes of victory on the Eastern Shore. Even the mission to Brazil, the sole gesture of interrepublican action which Alvear had wangled, failed to materialize because Bolívar was unwilling to dispatch it until the meeting of the nations in Panama, "for I see no benefit that would arise from doing things half-way."[37]

And so the mission saw its major commissions come to nothing. It had failed to secure support for the war against the Brazilian Empire, and Bolívar would not descend from the Andean heights at the petition of La Plata. But it did seem as if the two ministers would secure credit for one solid diplomatic achievement which might mean much in the local politics of his nation—the re-annexation of the northern territory of Tarija. This area, north of Salta, lay at the borderland between Upper Peru and the Argentine territory where administration under General Arenales was officially recognized and unofficially disregarded.

After defeating the Royalist forces in this area, General Sucre, as military governor of Upper Peru, established in Tarija an interim administration at first under General Miller and later under Colonel Francisco B. O'Connor. Scarcely had the Colonel assumed his duties when General Arenales called upon him to evacuate Tarija. But O'Connor refused to leave, and he aroused a great deal of enmity by his pointed allusions to the impotence of the Argentine administration.

When the mission had set out from the capital, the government had not heard of General Arenales's difficulties with O'Connor. Not until July 28, long after their departure, did instructions to secure the return of Tarija overtake the mission.[38] At their first meeting with the Liberator they referred to this issue, and he seemed favorably impressed with their appeal.[39] However, he arranged a hearing on the matter and invited Sucre to attend. The Marshal of Ayacucho immediately launched into a justification of his occupation of Tarija. He contended that the people there wished to remain within the new republic just forming. Their territory had always been regarded as the granary of the mountainous uplands and as such it was vital to the new republic. Besides, from a military standpoint, Tarija was essential for the defense of the country. Its boundaries projected northward in such a way that invaders, collecting inside the lines, could suddenly burst out and sweep victoriously across the country.

To Sucre's sound reasons presented in a forthright manner, General Alvear was pressed to find better arguments. He lamented the mention of war between the republics. Such a thing was unthinkable, but prudence demanded that the territorial limits be settled at once. Uncertain boundaries had caused interminable European conflict and the New World must avoid the tragic errors of the Old. Yet the probable hazards of war should not form the basis of their action. Indeed, he belittled the military reasoning of General Sucre by arguing conversely: that Tarija, jutting upward, would, in the unhappy event of war, be entirely surrounded by Bolivian forces.[40] Nor was he greatly impressed by Sucre's appeal to the whims of the populace. As statesmen, they must recognize that the wishes of the people in a particular province should not be the decisive factor in drawing national boundaries. Only the fixed principle of the status quo at the beginning of the struggle for independence would suffice. All else would bring confusion. He made no defense of General Arenales's original agreement to the secession of Upper Peru: his motives were honorable and, however unwise the General may have been in his decrees and promises, he could not jeopardize the national rights. No political entity could secede without consent of the parent body. Furthermore, he reminded his auditors, the United Provinces had generously agreed to the secession of Bolivia if it so desired. By the possible loss of this great territory and its resources, the parent state obviously had weakened itself considerably. But the permission applied only to Upper Peru. Further withdrawals of additional territory—such as Tarija—rich and well populated as it was, would dangerously weaken the United Provinces, which, alone, stood between the rising republic and an aggressive monarchy whose evil hand it had so recently felt.[41]

The Liberator tried to remain neutral. He lamented the political incapacity of General Arenales, who by vague decrees had made each district believe that by popular referendum it could associate itself with any country it chose. From time to time during the meeting he would interrupt, sometimes favoring Alvear, yet often showing a decided interest in General Sucre's point of view. Finally, he took the part of the Argentine mission: "Marshal, it is necessary that [Upper] Peru should give up its pretensions to Tarija. For a hundred years these claims will serve as an excuse for war if the governments consider it convenient." Doubtless Bolívar would have preferred to support his vice-commander, for he had no confidence in the stability of the United Provinces, yet General Alvear based his persuasive plea on such sound legal and theoretical concepts that the Liberator ordered the return of the territory. In this question, above all others, General Bolívar proved unfounded the Argentine charges of prejudice against La Plata.[42]

Having reached a decision, Bolívar moved quickly. He gave his recommendation to the Bolivian Congress, and on November 11 that body "being satisfied that [the Liberator] would do nothing contrary to the interests of the State," agreed to the reassignment of Tarija. One week later Lieutenant Ciriaco Díaz Vélez, son of Alvear's colleague, received orders to assume control of the territory in the name of the United Provinces.[43]

During the Tarija discussions, Bolívar raised the question of independence of the republic which he was sponsoring. Always the ministers answered that their government would undoubtedly recognize Bolivia. In proof they referred to the action of the La Plata Congress on May 9, which gave the Upper Peruvians permission to choose their political destiny. Their own presence in Upper Peru with credentials as ministers plenipotentiary indicated that the United Provinces regarded the territory, in fact, as a sovereign body. Even the claim for restoration of Tarija, by implication, argued that the rest of the country owed no allegiance to the southern body.[44] They assured Bolívar that a representative to Buenos Aires could in due time complete formal arrangements for recognition. So earnestly did the Argentine legation present the apparent willingness of its government to recognize Bolivia that the Liberator happily regarded the question as settled "beyond all doubt."[45] But recognition was not as determined a policy of the United Provinces as the ministers had led the Liberator to believe. Their instructions included no such promise. Upon Díaz Vélez was laid the special duty of inviting the provinces to remain within the Confederation. "However," read the orders, "if they should elect to separate, the mission shall report." "Shall report" carried no promise of positive action.

The instructions also had ordered the mission to win the good will of the Bolivians, and to confirm in their minds the constancy of La Plata friendship. This friendship the United Provinces needed. Certainly Bolivia had a direct complaint against the Brazilian monarchy, and the Argentines set out to win allies for their cause. But their task was not easy. Popular prejudice had anticipated and discounted their friendly gestures. Always a rumor ran ahead of them: that in their luggage they were carrying one million gold pesos—money with which to thwart the public will by bribing the Assembly to vote for union with the United Provinces. They discovered that Bolívar himself had heard the story; but he did not consider it seriously.[46]

The shortest path to Bolivian favor would be to win the support of the Liberator. Therefore, Alvear renewed yet again his insistent pleas that Bolívar take command of La Plata troops against Brazil. Apparently weakening somewhat under these blandishments, Bolívar himself thought of another expedient: he could renounce his ties with Colombia and Peru and wage war as commander of Bolivian troops. But when the Argentines proposed that he guarantee Bolivian assistance in return for recognition of their independence, he hesitated.[47]

His obvious approval of the Argentine cause against Brazil won popular esteem for Alvear and Díaz Vélez. They proposed toasts repeatedly to the "República Bolívar" with what the Liberator characterized as "enthusiasm beyond all exaggeration." Both envoys treated local dignitaries with friendly consideration. At no time did they protest the steps toward independence which the hopeful republic had already taken. Their conduct coincided with the declaration of their Congress on May 9.

Softened by these public demonstrations of friendship, Upper Peruvians dropped their former suspicions. Presently Bolivian leaders began to change from opponents to active supporters of La Plata. The ministers gave this rising friendship a superlatively hopeful interpretation: the new state would undoubtedly ally itself with Argentina in the impending Brazilian war. They felt particularly encouraged to report that one of their recent converts, Dr. Mariano Serrano, had been named to represent the new republic at Buenos Aires. They understood that while there he would discuss the proportionate forces neeed in the war. Also, he might proceed to Río de Janeiro in company with the Argentine representative; and both men, along with Bolívar's aide-de-camp, could present the complaints of their respective nations.[48]

Yet a Bolivian alliance should not be accepted too readily. The "Republic of Bolívar" had reasons of its own for wishing to secure Argentine assistance. Recognition should come at a higher price than mutual convenience. Therefore, while Dr. Serrano still was on his way to Buenos Aires the two Argentines joined in a letter that advised a shoddy expedient. They suggested that the government delay its recognition of Bolivia. This grant of recognition, if skilfully handled, could serve as a prize for special consideration in some treaty—probably for favorable settlement of the Chichas claims which it had not been expedient to raise while affairs in Tarija were so uncertain.[49] While the conduct of the mission had been publicly frank, its members did not hesitate, secretly, to counsel others to evade their promises if, by trickery, the government could win an imaginary advantage.

Both García and his successor, Francisco de la Cruz, followed this advice completely. After teasing delays in the port, Dr. Serrano finally retired without presenting his credentials. At a time when La Plata needed allies and friends, the government adopted means best calculated to offend the new republic and to violate both the frank promises made to Bolívar and the implicit assurance given in its legislative act of May, 1825.[50] No conduct could have been better calculated to cancel all good effects of the mission. No policy could have assured so certainly Bolivian distrust at a time when both countries urgently needed to co-operate against a common foe.

These lugubrious results were by no means obvious in December, 1825. A joint diplomatic representation to Río de Janeiro with the blessing of Bolívar seemed assured. The Liberator had returned Tarija to the United Provinces. On other matters such as removal of the discrimnatory trade rates, establishment of mail service between Upper Peru and Buenos Aires, and prohibition of political discrimination against citizens of La Plata who continued to reside in the new republic he had promptly accepted every contention of the mission and had made all possible adjustments.

Alvear summarized for Secretary García the accomplishments of the mission: deeds which he described in excessive and egotistical terms.[51] Under his blandishments, wrote Alvear, the Liberator had become "another man," free from all the unfavorable impressions of Buenos Aires which he had once entertained. That this change was due to the good conduct and ability of the ministers themselves Bolivar had recognized when he contrasted their success with the failure of Argentine negotiations in Peru: "You fellows have got everything from me that you wished."[52]

Really, they had secured but one substantive point: return of Tarija to the Province of Salta. All else had failed of immediate fulfilment. With Bolívar's departure the glory would vanish, and General Alvear spurned negotiation with ordinary persons. It was time to go home. He had lived "in this damned dung heap long enough." Besides, men at home might pass him by. Already a revolutionary colleague (no more deserving than himself) had pulled a choice plum, the appointment to England. The General felt that he should have had that place after working in Upper Peru "like a dog for a year."[53] In a private communication García replied in an understanding manner. At the same time he reflected the unfortunate Porteño disdain of the back country:

> I would like for you to come back whenever you can leave those areas which cannot be really agreeable to one who is familiar with anything else. . . .
>
> Friend, if you had wanted to go to London with the mission of Sarratea, nothing would have made me happier than to please you, just as I, myself, would have desired a change in position.

And then, as if to explain that the successful appointee boasted resources beyond their puny strength, "Who can do anything against money!"[54]

Quite suddenly new positions had become available in the Army. Prospect of a war with Brazil meant that the armed forces would be expanded, and the likelihood of missing a command while absent in "this terrible penitentiary" galled the restless General. He enjoined García to consider his military qualifications, the credit his appointment would reflect on the government, his zeal and loyalty, and the great expenses necessary to support his large family.[55]

Either García effectively intervened on behalf of his friend or else the administration had no intention of overlooking its restless envoy. On February 15 the Minister of Foreign Affairs wrote that he had easily secured for his friend the post of Secretary of War and Navy in the new cabinet. He sent the flattering news that everyone was highly pleased with the results of the mission, and—to ease a worry that the General had mentioned earlier—the drafts given for current expenses had been honored.[56]

With the ambitious General promoting his personal interests, the mission withered away. When he judged the time ripe to re-enter the Buenos Aires administration, he left his post and thus divided the mission and ended its possible usefulness. But Díaz Vélez, quite satisfied to stay in Chuquisaca, remained there for a year working mightily on little matters.

Fancied slights and affronts to national officials absorbed his whole attention. Editors of a Bolivian newssheet, the *Condor*, had made false charges against the United Provinces, and Díaz Vélez demanded that punishment be meted out to the mendacious editors. Later he entered categorical denials that any official in La Plata had pried into the diplomatic correspondence addressed to Dr. Serrano in the port. And then there was the matter of Tarija again. Young Lieutenant Ciriaco Díaz Vélez had assumed administration of the district, but the populace would not abandon its preference for Bolivian control, and he could not win them over. The father sought to help his son by protesting the activities of Upper Peruvian adherents, and in so doing began to argue once more the question of Argentine rights to the district. This proved to be a most unfortunate gesture. Bolívar was gone now and with the La Plata administration bending every effort to defeat the Brazilians, the Argentine officials had no army to enforce the revived assertions of national right. The Cabildo of Tarija promptly took advantage of this opportunity to renounce its allegiance to the United Provinces and claimed Bolivian protection.[57]

Nor did this imbroglio mark the end of the minister's mismanagement. While vainly attempting to hold Tarija by dint of legal argument, Díaz Vélez let the appointment to the Panama congress go by default. Apparent acceptance of Bolívar's invitation had been one of Alvear's concessions to Bolívar. But when Díaz Vélez learned that he had been named to the post, he made no effort to undertake the assignment. In the meantime the government of Buenos Aires became so engrossed in the Brazilian war that it did not attempt to discipline the laggard or to nominate another delegate.

One thing La Plata did eventually make clear to Díaz Vélez: he was to return home. The reluctant envoy kept postponing his departure under many pretexts.[58] By the time he started home the administration had almost collapsed. Its enemies roamed the pampas, and Díaz Vélez felt himself a marked man as he furtively darted from one town to another on his way south. For months he bided his time. In the end he evaded the hostile *gauchos*, presented himself before the Minister of Foreign Affairs, and was officially and honorably discharged on June 7, 1827. By that time it was clear that the mission had failed and that the government of Buenos Aires itself was teetering on the edge of an anarchical abyss.

IV.

ARGENTINE MINISTER TO THE UNITED STATES: 1838-1852

1. Return to the United States

When General Alvear left the United States in 1824, he had been greatly impressed by the importance of keeping a representative of the United Provinces in Washington. He recommended that the post be filled at once; he could scarcely have imagined that thirteen years would elapse before a minister from La Plata would appear at the American capital. Still less could he have dreamed that he would be sent to the United States again. But so unexpected were developments in La Plata that both Monroe's confidences and Alvear's enthusiasm were lost in the devious turning of Platean politics.

The leaders of the United Provinces had not intended that the Washington post should be left vacant for so long. Repeated internal crises distracted them from international relationships, and the rapid shift of administrators prevented the consummation of long-range planning. Within less than a week after Alvear's arrival from Washington in 1825, the United States' chargé d'affaires, John M. Forbes, called on the Secretary of Foreign Affairs, Manuel José García, and inquired about the next representative to the United States. Forbes began his interview by discussing the high Argentine import duty on flour, and then presently observed that General Alvear had just returned from his mission. He asked if a public representative had been left in the United States. García replied in the negative. The Secretary assumed no responsibility for Alvear's return, saying that he had been out of office ill when Rivadavia originally had ordered the mission and that its itinerary had been arranged without his knowledge. Forbes asked if the government had any intention to make another appointment to Washington. García confessed that it had none. He protested that his country was too poor to pay for establishments abroad. It was true that Rivadavia had been accredited to the courts both of England and France as a chargé d'affaires. It might be interesting, García admitted, to have in Washington, now the focal point of New World politics, a general chargé to all the American nations; but the whole subject of the diplomatic system lay within the competence of the Congress, and that body would decide the question.[1] There the matter stood. Neither García nor his colleagues proposed to send immediately a representative to Washington.

Throughout the year 1825 Forbes's inquiries about the dispatch of a minister, or even of a chargé, received only evasive replies.[2] To emphasize the desirability of a representative in the United States, he raised again the question of a contested import tax on flour. He urged its abolition as a means of promoting trade with the United States. García countered that there should be a general trade treaty.[3] Suppose, queried Forbes, the President of the United States should ask for one to be negotiated in Washington? There would be no representative there to conduct negotiations. García had thought of that. He had often considered sending Manuel Moreno, a great friend of the United States, but such things could not be done in a week.[4]

Over two months later Forbes called again on the Secretary, and the men repeated their conversations. Once more García mentioned Moreno as a possible minister, and Forbes replied that many capable men were available. García held to his old line: ". . . but Dr. Moreno is a great friend of the United States!" To which Forbes wearily agreed. It seemed that a paralysis had struck the government since Rivadavia had left it, and the successors (such as García) he characterized as "day laborers." He left the conference with the conviction that the government would send neither Dr. Moreno nor anyone else to the United States.[5] He considered the insistence on naming Manuel Moreno a clumsy evasion to conceal absence of any plan to send a representative.

He had misjudged the Secretary. From the Argentine records it is evident that García and his colleagues in the Ministry sincerely strove to persuade Moreno to accept the position. Twice he agreed to accept the nomination and twice he refused—even after public announcement of the appointment. Publicly Moreno declared that his health would be ruined by the change of climate, for he could never endure the long voyage and the rigors of the frigid north. Privately, he asked, instead, for the position of Director of the Library.

De La Cruz, who succeeded García, could not force Moreno to accept the appointment, but at least he could preserve official evidence of the bibliophile's irresolute behavior. The Secretary, filing both the official and the private letter in the departmental archives, endorsed an angry "Resolution":

> The renunciation by Manuel Moreno of the charge entrusted to him having appeared—in violation of his consent given verbally before the Minister—. . . file this rejection with the preceding correspondence in order to have present the conduct of this individual.[6]

Besides the problem of personnel—always a very real one in a new nation—a multitude of mounting national problems further delayed an appointment to Washington. By the end of the year 1825 the country was on the verge of war with Brazil over the disputed Banda Oriental. A national administration had to be improvised, even though the interior provinces wanted neither war nor national unity under an administration that would inevitably lead to centralization. But these objections were ignored. A Constituent Congress created the office of executive for the nation and designated Rivadavia, recently returned from England, as President. For a second time he assumed the responsibility of government amidst intense opposition.[7]

And for a second time Alvear was identified with the party of Rivadavia. In the hastily assembled cabinet, General Alvear, as Secretary of War and Navy, capably organized an army and revived a moribund navy which again fought under Admiral Brown's command. As commanding general the aging Martín Rodríguez proved himself unwilling or unable to handle the dissident elements in his army. Therefore, Alvear promptly resigned his portfolio, replaced Rodríguez, and at long last achieved a field command: his first since 1815. He did not silence the criticism that ran rife under Rodríguez; but he surmounted it, and pushed the campaign energetically. The Army crossed the Brazilian frontier, and, at Ituzaingó, against a numerically superior force, Alvear won a decisive victory which his detractors attributed to the efforts of everyone but to the commander-in-chief.[8] None would have denied him the onus if the battle had been lost.

Military victory brought little relief to Rivadavia. Opposition to his conduct of war as well as to his domestic program prevented establishment of an effective foreign policy. He regretted the continued absence of a national representative in Washington, and while in the midst of hectic controversy he found time to discuss with John Forbes the hope of dispatching another minister. He expressed himself in such a friendly manner that the American chargé pronounced him "a great friend of the United States." In one interview Rivadavia declared that he had sent to the Assembly a proposal that it make appropriations for re-establishing the mission which had ended with Alvear's return. But just as the Executive was on the point of telling Forbes whom he might name to the post, other visitors intruded and serious discussion was abandoned.[9] This was the last time that Forbes talked with him on the subject.

Domestic insecurity increased. Dissatisfied soldiers returning from the fighting area threatened revolution. The peace mission sent to Río de Janeiro threw away the fruits of Alvear's victory. Rivadavia's opponents increased in number and bitterness; the whole political structure in La Plata disintegrated. Since there seemed to be no end to the struggle, Rivadavia resigned the following year rather than endure the calumny which his opponents heaped upon him. Following his resignation factional hatred knew no bounds, and for years the state trembled on the edge of anarchy.

The downfall of Rivadavia eclipsed the career of Carlos de Alvear. His fortunes were linked to that of his party which had assumed the name "Unitarians"; and when this party of unification lost its hold on the government his very existence became precarious. From time to time his name appears insignificantly in the scanty newspapers of the city. American representatives in Buenos Aires occasionally mentioned him in their dispatches, but he remained in the background of national life. His star became further obscured by the turbulent clouds of Argentine political strife and civil war that marked the anarchical struggle between the Unitarians and the Federalists for the domination of the capital.[10] The Federalists won out in 1829 when Juan Manuel de Rosas, *gaucho* leader of the pampas, assumed power as governor of Buenos Aires. From that time until 1852, if one excludes an interval of two years from 1833 to 1835, Rosas was Dictator of the Argentine. He ruled with a rod of iron. One of his first tasks was to rid himself of all political opponents.[11]

He issued decrees against Unitarian leaders and imprisoned, executed, or exiled many of Rivadavia's former party members. Many of Rosas' opponents fled to the north, to Uruguay, Paraguay, or Bolivia, where they found more or less secure refuge. "He bought off the leaders he could not readily subdue, and sent into exile those he could not readily buy." General Alvear, a traditional Unitarian, was apparently too important a man to handle violently; indeed, in Rosas' first period of dictatorship his violence was less marked than in later years. The General had not taken a leading role in the Unitarian government that briefly succeeded Rivadavia. His integrity was suspected. Men feared his support more than his opposition; and on one occasion when he offered to lead an attack against the Federalists, his own party men threatened to shoot him if he dared appear in the square. Fortunately for Alvear! Failure of the plot brought Rosas into power, and the discarded General assumed an air of innocence. The initial outbursts against the enemies of Federalism passed him by.[12] The Dictator let him alone, at least for the time being.

Rosas' suppression of his political enemies did not rid him completely of opposition. Many foes escaped his heavy hand by fleeing to Montevideo. There they continued their activities, seeking to overthrow him by promoting an intervention from that city. The Unitarians allied themselves with a Uruguayan leader who felt that he had been cheated out of the presidency of that new republic. He welcomed this support; his opponent naturally turned to Rosas for assistance. To stamp out these adversaries Rosas marched into Uruguay. Then the Unitarians in their desperation turned to France, which had already become involved in a quarrel with Rosas over the status of French trade and French subjects in Buenos Aires. The French accepted the invitation.[13]

They established their blockade of the city in March, 1838. Immediately Rosas felt the pinch. He released the few Frenchmen previously interned; but the French would not leave until he admitted the errors of his policy, and that Rosas refused to do. The overwrought populace, judging the Unitarians as traitors for inducing the French to intervene in the politics of the estuary, posted terrifying slogans everywhere. "Death to the savage Unitarians" was the shortest and simplest. Others were longer; they elaborated the theme of Unitarian corruption and eternal hatred for the party. This party feeling grew so intense that display of any sky-blue object—the party color of the Unitarians—was forbidden. Search-gangs invaded homes and destroyed dishes or any other blue objects. True patriots wore Rosas own color: red. These terroristic activities silenced Unitarians or others who resented highhanded Federalist action.

Besides this domestic turmoil, which required a considerable army, Rosas simultaneously became entangled in a brief war with Bolivia in 1837. But blockade of Buenos Aires by the French fleet forced him to abandon the contest with the Bolivian Dictator, Santa Cruz, who was also engaged in a war with Chile and Peru. With the blockade before the city pressing so heavily, Rosas was lucky to conclude the Bolivian hostilities before they seriously threatened his administration.

Domestic troubles, a foreign war, blockade of the main port by European powers: these did not encompass all of Rosas' troubles. He fell into a bitter controversy with the United States over fishing rights in the Falkland Islands. The Argentine governor of the Falklands had seized three American ships which he found fishing there in violation of his decree. In retaliation the captain of the U.S.S. *Lexington* had sacked the small settlement on December 31, 1831, and then departed. In January, 1833, the English occupied the islands.[14]

Negotiations with the United States proceeded too slowly for Argentine welfare. Not until December, 1832, did Rosas finally name a Minister Plenipotentiary to Washington, Carlos de Alvear. But nothing came of the nomination. When Rosas left the governorship of the Province of Buenos Aires shortly thereafter, the minister-designate to the United States was still in the country, his instructions still unframed.[15] Succeeding governors, unable even to control the province, never felt certain enough of their tenure to conduct negotiations with the United States on a matter involving national honor.

Alvear's appointment was kept on the record, but his departure was postponed month after month. Postponement did not help matters, for when the English seized the islands in January, 1833, the Argentine difficulties were compounded. As long as the Argentine government hoped to induce the English to restore the islands, it delayed dealing with the United States, for repossession of the territory would greatly enforce the plausibility of Platean demands for reparations. But Great Britain had no intention of returning the islands, and the representative from La Plata, Manuel Moreno, vainly pressed his petitions in London.[16]

When a new United States consul, Eben Dorr, arrived in Buenos Aires in December, 1834, he bore regrets from Washington that no Argentine minister had yet arrived. On assuming the executive authority once more in May, 1835, Rosas found the affair dragging along about as he had left it. But when presented with a sharp inquiry from the United States asking when the promised envoy would be sent, the Dictator made an explicit promise: within the next year.[17]

Apparently he meant business. For Rosas the choice of diplomatic officers was always narrow. Capable men whom he could trust he needed at home. And he hesitated to send abroad the inept or untrustworthy. His former nominee, Alvear, had been suffering from such a serious illness that the Dictator cancelled his appointment. Instead, he directed Moreno to leave London, where he was accomplishing nothing, and to present in Washington the complaints of his country.[18] Mention of the United States sent Moreno into another period of ill health from which he recovered only sufficiently to reject the appointment and to return directly home. His refusal caught Rosas by surprise, and the Dictator waited until the reluctant envoy had landed in Buenos Aires before coming at last to a decision to rename Alvear, who seemed to have recovered from a persistent infection.

This wavering procedure may have passed as statesmanship in Buenos Aires, but in Washington it indicated evasiveness if not downright dishonesty. It was well known that Argentina had kept Moreno in England for years but had given to the United States nothing but excuses.[19] President Andrew Jackson, who had dispatched Captain Duncan to secure respect for American rights in the Falklands, noted with satisfaction the Argentine reluctance to appear and demand settlement. In each annual message he commented trenchantly on the disinclination to negotiate any settlement of the "outrage" committed at the Falkland Islands.[20] Secretary Forsyth wrote more explicitly to the Argentine Minister of Foreign Affairs, Felipe Arana, of the President's disappointment at the "extraordinary and unexplained delay."[21]

It may be that these words caused a temporary activity. Arana began to draft instructions—a tedious process that involved months of equivocations. Dorr, the American consul, expected daily to send word of Alvear's departure, and even predicted his early arrival in Washington,[22] but he eventually ran out of explanations for delay and simply waited. After two years he thought he saw some signs of action, only to be disappointed once more.

Even as Dorr penned these explanations, hard necessity was forcing Rosas to dispatch the mission. The Argentine Confederation found itself without a potent friend abroad as France began to tighten the blockade of Buenos Aires. The United States was the most likely of all the larger powers to sympathize with it sufficiently to influence France to modify her demands or to withdraw. Suddenly the long-delayed instructions were signed. The Dictator obligingly named Alvear's son, Don Emilio Marcelo de Alvear, as Secretary of Legation; and father and son impatiently awaited the Dictator's permission to sail.[23] Strictness of the blockade caused further delay, but near the latter part of May, 1838, the mission sailed on the United States packet-ship *Nile*. The General left his wife and family behind him as he departed into diplomatic exile. He never saw them or his homeland again.[24]

This time he no longer regarded his position as a stepping stone to political heights. Instead, it was a refuge from the unchecked will of a resolute dictator. As a leader of revolutionary fame and as a victorious general in the war against Brazil, Alvear initially had enjoyed a fame which the younger Rosas could not readily destroy. But a widespread Unitarian plot had been discovered and all its leaders but himself apprehended. His unparalleled luck could not last forever. Rosas might soon suspect him: already his erstwhile Unitarian associates questioned his remarkable immunity from Federalist vengeance. It seemed best to escape all uncertainties by accepting a second assignment to the United States.

Rosas supplied the mission well: fifteen packets of official documents relating to the Falkland Islands; Rosas' message to the Buenos Aires legislature; his declarations against Santa Cruz, the Bolivian dictator; and Argentine-French correspondence concerning the blockade. The minister had ample opportunity to examine his packets as he sailed toward the United States. And it required a good deal of time to wade through the voluminous documents and to peruse his verbose instructions. First, Arana stressed the necessity of tact and caution in dealing with the United States. He curbed Alvear's impetuous manner by reminding him that he must abide by instructions and make no unauthorized declarations. To the end of his life Alvear never forgot these precautions. Frequently he reminded the Secretary of Foreign Affairs that he was observing the very letter of his instructions. He could do little else, for he had left his large family in Buenos Aires at the mercy of the Dictator, and as an envoy in a foreign land he enjoyed no income except by Rosas' good will.

In his first letter acknowledging receipt of all diplomatic materials, Alvear promised to pay particular attention to the Falkland Islands affair, and "to exercise prudent caution, always excusing previous acts or conferences which seem unworthy of the dignity or moderation of the delicate matters entrusted to me."[25] The pressure of events had caused Rosas to re-evaluate his administration. His minister could now see evidence of indiscretion and of undiplomatic acts for which he might find it necessary to apologize.

To be sure, no mention of prudence or caution marked the public announcement of Alvear's latest nomination. In bombastic manner Rosas declared to the Legislature that the minister would fulfil his "sacred duty" by protesting the affair of the U.S.S. *Lexington* and by seeking prompt redress for that scandalous event.[26] Concerning those "other subjects" such as the French blockade, to which Alvear made reference, Rosas said nothing publicly.

The main body of instructions was in two parts: the longer section dealt with the Falkland Islands episode, while the shorter postscript related to current disputes with Bolivia and France. Curiously, the postscript took precedence over the main directions, and only after an eight-point program of additional instructions had been observed could the minister take up the Falkland Islands dispute. He should protest "the scandalous event," but not until more immediate problems should be settled.[27]

According to Arana's prescribed order, Alvear should first express "with all possible vehemence" the zeal with which the Argentine Confederation[28] was pressing its war against the Bolivian dictator, Santa Cruz, a usurper, a tyrant who menaced the political equilibrium of the new states and by his insane ambition compromised their dignity and existence. After convincing the Secretary of State of the justice of the war, Alvear should try, said Arana, to circumvent possible agents of Santa Cruz if they sought supplies, munitions, or aid of any sort. If the United States with stiff-necked obstinacy should permit aid to reach Santa Cruz, then Alvear, after gathering all pertinent information, would suspend further relations until he could receive additional instructions.

All these vigorous declarations about Santa Cruz were wasted, for by the time Alvear had established himself in Washington, that little war in northern Argentina had dwindled away.[29] Additional points on the French blockade he found more pertinent to Argentine interests. Arana directed him to show that accusations of the French consul and the Vice-Admiral Leblanc constituted assaults on the independence and national dignity of the Confederation which the Argentine government would resist regardless of costs. Of the United States Rosas asked no more than good will. Arana directed the minister to secure the publication of all Argentine material on the causes of the blockade. At no time should he neglect the press: on every possible occasion he should insert favorable articles in popular periodicals. All replies to unfriendly comments should be stated in a dignified and prudent manner.

In addition, Alvear should cultivate the good will of other diplomatic agents and ministers residing in the United States. He should distribute all Argentine correspondence on the French blockade and carefully preserve a record of any communications which he might receive from them. Particularly Arana instructed him not to ignore the French minister, although he must avoid every act that might appear unbecoming. On every suitable occasion he should discuss with the Frenchman the detailed events which would demonstrate the justice of the Argentine government against unreasonable French demands. Perhaps Rosas did not trust the French officials conducting the blockade of Buenos Aires to present to Paris a complete account of events, and he hoped that the French representative to the United States would be more amenable to reason.

Finally, all domestic papers and communications should bear the heading: "Long live the Argentine Confederation!" and the aspiration: "Death to the Unitarians!" Never should the minister or any person in his service display the national color of earlier days, sky-blue; he should use only scarlet, symbol of Federal triumph under Rosas.[30]

Carlos de Alvear and his son, Emilio, arrived in New York on August 2, 1838, and there began their diplomatic duties. Congress was not then in session, and many officials of the government were absent on summer vacations. Alvear therefore delayed his journey to the capital.[31] For a few weeks he enjoyed the bustle of city life in New York. With characteristic energy he developed contacts with the local newspapers. They willingly published the official correspondence which he had brought with him. In his full-length dispatch to Arana on September 13, Alvear declared that already he could observe a distinct reaction in favor of the Argentine cause. North Americans were beginning to realize both the importance and injustice of simultaneous French blockades in Mexico and La Plata. This realization might offer additional opposition to French occupation.

Alvear further reported that while in New York he had cultivated the good will, not only of newspaper men, but also of diplomats whom he had met there. Among the representatives then in the city he moved promptly and easily. To the minister of New Granada (Colombia) he gave copies of official exchanges between Buenos Aires and France. To Venezuela he sent copies by a responsible citizen of that country. He dispatched another set of papers to Mexico and suggested an exchange of documents on their common resistance to French blockades. Alvear assured Arana that publication of Argentine correspondence in Mexico would strengthen even more the noble Mexican resistance. The chargés of Belgium and Holland also received a full set of documents.

As his instructions directed, Alvear sought the acquaintance of the French representative to the United States. The obliging envoy from new Granada invited the French and Argentine representatives to lunch with him, but at the last moment a sudden indisposition prevented the Frenchman from attending. Disappointed at his failure to meet on neutral ground, Alvear declared that he would yet manage an introduction. Come what may, he promised to do nothing unworthy of the government which he had the honor to represent.

Of Mexico he could send little news in this first dispatch. Alvear received no news directly from that country since the Mexican minister, Señor Martínez, was living in New Orleans. However, American newspapers indicated that the French blockade of Vera Cruz continued to encounter vigorous resistance. Because only English ships were allowed free access to this port, all news from Mexico, coming by way of England, suffered much delay. Therefore, Buenos Aires normally would receive word of Mexican developments from the minister in London before Alvear could send it, but if he secured Mexican accounts directly, he promised to forward them at once.

Alvear could report but one simple incident on the Bolivian War. He found no agent of Santa Cruz in the United States nor had anyone heard of purchase of war materials destined for that dictator. In the course of his New York visiting, the newly arrived minister met Dr. Gaul, representative of Ecuador, on his way to England. Alvear gave him a fervent essay on Argentine determination to force Santa Cruz from power, and supplied him with copies of the Argentine-French exchanges on the blockade. The Ecuadorian in reply limited his observations strictly to the Santa Cruz episode—a matter on which he was well informed. He predicted that an alliance of Chile and Peru would be sufficient to bring an overthrow of the Bolivian, and, with a seeming slight at Argentine prowess, Dr. Gaul stated that the Pacific countries expected Argentina to bear only a minor role in the war. This forecast, it turned out, was exactly correct.

Alvear did not conclude the dispatch without making his first of many observations on the press of the United States. The daily papers, he found, were so numerous and their special interests so diverse that one could not give entire credence to their columns. Nor could he determine from reading conflicting and often incomplete press reports the official position of the government on special issues. He could not state with certainty the position of the United States on La Plata problems until he had met members of the diplomatic corps and officials of the government.[32]

On September 28 the Argentine minister applied for recognition. Aaron Vail, as acting-Secretary of State, received him, and on October 11 presented him to President Van Buren.[33] This reception seemed to reflect some of the New World cordiality that Monroe had shown fourteen years earlier. Alvear developed at length the difficulties that his country had overcome in order to send a representative to Washington. The President replied that the Department of State had informed him of the great delay and, reported the minister, this additional explanation left him entirely satisfied.[34]

Some two weeks later Alvear requested an interview with the acting-Secretary in order to explain "pursuant to his instructions . . . the causes which have unfortunately interrupted the harmony of the relations between France and the Argentine Republic." He received a prompt appointment.[35] If there had been misunderstanding between the United States and Argentina, Alvear ignored it. He talked as to a friendly and sympathetic audience. Vail, pointedly ignoring all references to Argentine-French troubles, expressed a desire that the United States and Argentina should settle all disputes between themselves and wished for "an honorable and advantageous reciprocity." He hoped that Alvear would find his residence in the United States agreeable to himself and useful to his country.[36]

Not until he had presented the French trouble in its entirety did the Argentine minister revert several months later to the issues concerning the distant Falkland Islands. Before tracing Alvear's pursuit of his main purpose in the United States, it is now appropriate to turn to his other objective, the settlement of the Falkland Islands controversy.

2. The Falkland Islands Controversy

The previous chapter has explained the dispatch of an Argentine minister to the United States in 1838. It is recalled that as early as 1831 the first serious diplomatic breach between the Confederation and the United States had occurred in connection with interruptions of American fishing near the Falkland Islands. At that time representatives of the United States in Buenos Aires had failed to reach a settlement. For five years the North American republic waited for Argentina to send a representative to Washington to discuss the matter, but not until French intervention had threatened the existence of the administration itself had the government sought a friend abroad. Even then the proud dictator, Rosas, would not admit being hard pressed. He used the carefully preserved controversy over the Falklands, which he had no real intention of settling, as the excuse for dispatching his emissary, Carlos de Alvear, to the United States. While prolonging negotiations over the Falkland Islands his representative could offset the agents of France and thwart the machinations of Santa Cruz. For a second time Alvear appeared as the Argentine minister, and again his ostensible purpose but cloaked his real motives. How he vainly urged a settlement of the questions at issue between his country and the United States over Falkland Islands must, however, engage our attention. Unless the facts in dispute between the two countries are clear, the steps in Alvear's negotiations are meaningless. Let us begin by recapitulating.

A new phase in the history of these islands began with the outbreak of the Spanish-American wars for independence. Settlers returning from there to Montevideo in 1811 had left them deserted. Revolutionary wars and political upheavals prevented reoccupation: they continued uninhabited except for visits of passing whalers or sealers who needed fresh water or desired fresh meat from the wild cattle which roamed there. But in 1820 the government of the United Provinces declared its ownership of the islands and commissioned Captain Jewitt to establish its claim. And in good time, too, for he found as many as fifty foreign whalers anchored along the shores. He warned them off, giving notice that the United Provinces forbade unlicensed hunting and fishing and that offenders would be sent to Buenos Aires for trial.

The government followed this assertion of sovereignty by appointing a governor for the islands in 1823 and by granting concessions for settlement. After initial failures, some of the colonial promoters lost interest, but Louis Vernet, a naturalized citizen, kept working for the success of the colony. He secured in 1828 the appointment of Governor of the Shores of Patagonia as well as of the Falkland Islands and by this act became both an official of the government and an owner of the colony over which he presided.[1]

The governor immediately issued decrees against unauthorized fishing and seal-hunting, which were rapidly depleting the islands' principal source of income. He requested a man-of-war to enforce his order,[2] but the administration, then under the tenuous control of the Unitarian, Lavalle, could spare no warships for the distant colony. Instead, Lavalle, under the title of Delegate-Governor of the Province of Buenos Aires, issued in the name of the whole nation a decree on June 10, 1829, which proclaimed sovereignty over the islands and prohibited unlicensed fishing along designated shores. Supported only by this official document, Vernet continued to warn off whalers under penalty of seizure and of trial in Buenos Aires. One of the first ordered away was the America ship, *Harriet*, of Stonington, Connecticut, to whose captain Vernet gave a printed copy of Lavalle's recent decree.[3]

The United States had received no report of this decree, because its chargé, John M. Forbes, died before he could dispatch the notice to his government. His death left the consul, George W. Slacum, a young man of wilful disposition, as the only American official in Buenos Aires. Slacum assumed diplomatic responsibilities just as an unfortunate controversy arose, and the results proved singularly unhappy. On the other hand, England was better served. Her Consul-General, Woodbine Parish, protesting Lavalle's Argentine claims of sovereignty, declared that the islands belonged to Great Britain, and promised that his government would reoccupy the islands in due season. The Argentine Minister of Foreign Affairs, in acknowledging receipt of this unexpected document expressed the vague sentiment that his government "would take the matter into particular consideration."[4] Then all was quiet.

For two years Vernet guided his struggling colony while it gradually increased to about one hundred persons, largely men, of many nationalities. He secured a few German settlers by offering to loan them a few milch cows. To others he furnished agricultural equipment. Farmers tried to make a living from the stubborn soil, but early frosts killed their crops with discouraging frequency. A Dutchman set up a small merchant shop to serve the needs of the colony. Now and again stranded Portuguese or Italian fishermen remained there as farmers or plied their old craft. A few Indians from the mainland toiled as free laborers, while almost a score of Negro slaves tilled the governor's extensive holdings. The frontier group, at the usual price of privation and hardship, seemed about to establish itself.[5]

No heavy scruples embarrassed Vernet in his search for settlers. Perhaps the fate of the American schooner, *Bellville*, was not particularly unique. This vessel was wrecked while fishing off the Falkland shores, and at least seven of her crew and the first mate saved themselves. The men managed to secure, in some way, a portion of their ship's cargo in sealskins and whalebone. Her mate, Matthew Brisbane, a native Englishman, promptly entered Vernet's service, and became his military leader and director of later seizures. The members of the crew found themselves facing charges of what Vernet called "piracy" for unlawful fishing, but he appears to have used this harsh word only to frighten the men. He presently agreed not to press these charges since the sailors, as he later declared, "according to all appearances . . . are a hardy set of men and of an industrious disposition, capable of becoming useful members of this colony if set at liberty to follow their favorite pursuit of sealing." As a price for not pressing his piracy charge, "which, whether favorable or unfavorable, . . . would always become an evil to them," Vernet signed an agreement to buy their salvaged whalebone and sealskins, and, at the end of the season, the small boat they were already building. He further agreed to supply them with equipment in return for a share of the seals which they might kill around the rocky islands.[6]

Occasionally French, English, and American whalers stopped on their passages around the Horn, and to those who applied to him Vernet furnished needed supplies for a consideration. Sometimes fishermen killed seals in nearby waters without consulting him, but the governor took no positive action until he discovered the *Harriet*, warned away two years before, again sealing in his waters.

The circumstances of the seizure we gather only from the participants, and all of them lent color to the fact, if they did not alter the fact itself. Captain Davison of the *Harriet* dictated to George W. Slacum a connected account of the affair; and Slacum, in spirited tone, protested these events to Buenos Aires. Vernet never presented an orderly version of his seizure of the vessel, but contented himself with replying to Slacum's charges. From the indignant accounts of the one and the bitter defense of the other we must construct a factual survey of the governor's actions.[7]

Captain Davison declared that he had stopped at the Falklands on his way outward and met Governor Vernet. At that time Vernet had explained his authority as governor (Davison says that he *pretended* to act as governor), and warned the American captain not to catch seals within his jurisdiction. Returning to the United States after a sealing expedition into the Pacific Ocean, Captain Davison stopped again at the islands. He had to remain there windbound for over thirty days, and during that time he caught some thirty to forty seals around rocky points. This, he swore, he had done with the knowledge of Vernet, who assured him that it made no great difference. Then, one day an armed band, headed by Matthew Brisbane, arrested the American captain and placed him in solitary confinement; a boarding party took possession of his ship. Neither Davison nor his first mate was permitted to talk to each other or to the crew. With each passing day their suspicions mounted. Presently Vernet noticed that the American sailors had purchased all the long knives that they could find and were distributing them to disaffected settlers. The governor met this menace by shipping these colonists "by their own free will" to Río de Janeiro.

Before Vernet could reach any settlement with Davison, other American whalers appeared. Vernet's men, again led by Brisbane, captured the *Superior*, a ship belonging to the same owners as the *Harriet*, and jailed her commander, Captain Congar, with Davison. A few days later they swooped down upon still another unsuspecting whaler, the *Breakwater*. The crew of the latter ship organized resistance, overcame their guards, and slipped out to sea. This ship brought to the United States the first news of events on the Falkland Islands.

Vernet finally signed a contract with the imprisoned captains. They agreed that the *Superior* under Captain Congar should proceed with her fishing, while the *Harriet* should sail to Buenos Aires, where Captain Davison, representing both men, would stand trial for illegal fishing. In order to guarantee the return of the *Superior*, the governor held her sealskins as security. In the presence of the two captains Vernet took an inventory of the ship's stores and then sent her on her way.

As for the *Harriet*, Vernet and Captain Davison completed a second inventory of her supplies and then prepared her for a short voyage before seeking court review of his actions. The *Superior* previously had left several seal hunters on the Statenland, the very tip of South America. The governor promised Congar that he would pick up these men so that the *Superior* could sail without delay to newly discovered sealing grounds west of Chile—territory conspicuously beyond Vernet's jurisdiction.

Scarcely had the *Harriet* begun her voyage when she put about and sailed into the harbor once more. Davison said that after Vernet failed to capture an armed American whaler which he encountered, he ordered the ship back to port, thus leaving the marooned sailors in Statenland to starve. Vernet declared that the whaler which he met (he made no mention of attacking her) belonged also to the owners of the *Harriet* and the *Superior*. He intimated that he returned because he expected the third ship to rescue the sailors.

It was now high time to head for Buenos Aires to file before the courts his charges against the captured *Harriet*. Leaving a good portion of the ship's goods for sale in his island commissary, he loaded his personal effects on board, and set sail, with Captain Davison now serving as navigator. Upon arrival he paid Davison passage money and his wages as captain.[8] As proprietor he had stopped trespassers on his property; as governor he had enforced the decree of the nation.

On landing at Buenos Aires the governor made his way promptly to the courts, where he filed charges against the Americans. Davison directed his steps with equal promptness to the office of the American consul. Vernet, in his published defense some two months later, declared that he and Captain Davison had reached open and friendly agreements; but to Slacum, Captain Davison poured out a tale of violence and injustice.

Vernet angered the Americans on several counts. He had broken up a trade which their countrymen had been pursuing since the days of the Spanish monarchy, yet he dared not arrest British ships for sealing along the same shores, for fear of reprisals. At least, so the Americans interpreted his reticence when they pointed to an English ship sealing within sight of them all. He had threatened to charge stranded seamen with piracy unless they agreed to work for him. His failure to rescue the men on Statenland had outraged their sense of common humanity. They believed that on the voyage to Buenos Aires from the Falklands he had attempted to starve one American sailor into testifying against his comrades, although the governor said that he had imprisoned the sailor only as a precaution against mutiny. Vernet had made Captain Congar promise to communicate with no other ship except on a signal of distress, a promise which looked as if Vernet wished to conceal his seizures either for fear of their legality or in hope of catching other unwary fishermen.

For satisfaction of these affronts, the Americans looked to the agent of their government, not to Argentine courts. Consul Slacum, believing every word which Davison indignantly reported, addressed a short note to the Secretary of Foreign Affairs, asking if his government expected to approve Vernet's action. This inquiry the Buenos Aires government regarded as impertinent.[9]

Eventually the *Breakwater* reached the United States with an account of Vernet's activities. President Jackson, without waiting for an official report from Slacum, made vigorous allusion to the incident in his message of December 6, 1831:

Occurrences have lately taken place at the Falkland Islands in which the name of [Argentina] has been used to cover with a show of authority acts injurious to our commerce and to the property of our fellow-citizens. In the course of the present year one of our vessels, engaged in the pursuit of a trade which we have always enjoyed without molestation, has been captured by a band acting, as they pretend, under the authority of the government of Buenos Aires. I have therefore given orders for the dispatch of an armed vessel . . . to afford all lawful protection to our trade. . . . I shall . . . send a minister to inquire into the nature of the circumstances and also the claim, if any, that is set up by that government to those islands.[10]

Secretary Van Buren had anticipated trouble ever since reports had reached him of Vernet's claim to jurisdiction over the archipelago. He had long since ordered Forbes to investigate the matter and to remonstrate against any provisions which in the slightest degree would limit the enterprise of United States citizens in those regions, or impair their undoubted right to use the common fishing grounds. Lavalle's decree of June, 1829, the Secretary noted, had asserted claim to Tierra del Fuego and the Falkland Islands as a part of the Viceroyalty of La Plata by succession to Spanish sovereignty. Van Buren, in a blanket denial, declared that Buenos Aires had no right to those islands on the basis of past history, discovery, or possession by Spain. Those waters, he asserted, had always been considered open to all nations, the exclusive property of none.[11] Such an attitude implicitly denied English as well as Argentine ownership. If Edward Livingston, Secretary of State in 1832, had been aware of English claims to the territory, he did not mention them.

Slacum, acting as Forbes's successor in Buenos Aires, fulfilled these instructions bluntly. He protested the captures in an accusing manner. He acted as if he could expect no fair consideration of Captain Davison's plight, and so enraged the government by denying its sovereignty to the islands that the

Minister of Foreign Affairs requested that he abandon diplomatic questions and limit his correspondence to consular matters.[12]

The dispute had reached this bitter stage when Captain Duncan of the U.S.S. *Lexington* arrived in Buenos Aires under general orders, as President Jackson had reported to Congress, "to afford all lawful protection to our trade." Captain Duncan immediately applied to Slacum for details of any violation of American rights. Impressed by the consul's account of recent events at the Falkland Islands, Duncan decided to act. "I consider it my duty," he wrote home, "to proceed to the Falkland Islands with the force under my command for the protection of the citizens and commerce of the United States engaged in the fisheries in question."[13]

By protection Captain Duncan meant dismantling the colony and destroying its feeble military fortifications. But he did not depart without warning Buenos Aires of his intention. In addition, he demanded that Vernet be surrendered to him for trial in the United States courts as a robber and pirate, or else that he be punished under the criminal code of Buenos Aires. Slacum, on his part, also sent an ultimatum which demanded admission of no right to capture United States vessels and ordered a restoration of property already taken. Both American officials allowed the government two days in which to accept their demands or else Captain Duncan would sail.[14] The required time elapsed without a reply to either of these drastic notes: at high noon of the third day, Duncan, accompanied by Captain Davison, set out upon his mission of reprisal.

No sooner had the *Lexington* cleared the harbor than Slacum received an official reply which did not meet any of their demands. Ignoring the ultimatums which the two Americans had addressed to him, he added the solemn warning: "If any official or commander shall do anything which would tend to deny the right of Buenos Aires to the islands or to impede the seal fishery it may wish to exercise in them, prompt complaint will be made to the United States."[15] The minister refrained from discussing the possible justice of Vernet's action and stressed only his country's rights to the islands.

While diplomats haggled over rights or privileges, Captain Duncan settled the affair in his own way. Accounts which Duncan's prisoners presented to their government when they finally landed in Buenos Aires agree in general with American versions of what took place. Captain Duncan had waited, the island settlers testified, offshore for two or three days, windbound. No one had paid particular attention to the ship, thinking it a French whaler, since it appeared to be flying a French flag. Nor did he attract further notice again until he appeared in the harbor and a landing party of marines pulled for shore.[16] Vernet's deputy governor and Matthew Brisbane, his military commander, went down to the shore to see what the marines wanted. They were promptly captured. Others who ran to see what had happened suffered a like fate. The marines spiked a few small cannon which they found on the beach; they seized the commissary and supplies, burned the ammunition, and broke the small arms. Some residents fled to the interior, but an equal number stood their ground and asked the reason for such behavior.

The Captains Duncan and Davison answered all inquiries emphatically. They declared that the government of the United States, angry at Vernet for having stopped American shipping, had ordered them to destroy the settlement. The captains improved their story by adding that Vernet was already on trial in Buenos Aires for his highhanded behavior. Captain Davison pronounced the islands free of all government and offered to transport any who might wish to leave before other ships should come to complete the destruction of the colony. Many chose to accept the offer because, as one man frankly stated, the "New Yorkers" always did what they said they would.

Once the Americans had spread word of the impending fate of the colony, hitherto concealed discontent broke forth. One farmer posted over his door a placard announcing his poor opinion of the climate. The Germans, whom Vernet had induced to migrate by loaning them milch cows, killed the animals. After selling both skins and meat to the captains, they sailed away in search of more profitable fields. Others gathered their goods and waited to depart.

Curiously, the seven men from the *Bellville,* who had contracted to hunt seals on shares with Vernet, chose to remain and continue their work. Duncan gave them a pretentious document guaranteeing to them the right to fish and to enjoy in those latitudes the full freedom of the seas.[17] William Dickson, a Dutch merchant who wanted no trouble in court, received from the American captain a certificate that he had taken no part in the capture of American ships some months earlier. About fifty settlers who were willing to risk the early frosts chose to stay. They retired to the hills until the Americans had left. Captain Davison identified such property as had been taken from the *Harriet*—sealskins, small firearms, and sailing gear—and repossessed them.[18] Duncan carried away in all about twenty-five settlers, together with officers of the colony and Vernet's slaves. He had not hurt a single person nor could his enemies charge his men with private looting. But he left the island settlement completely useless as a military fortress.

Captain Duncan wisely forbore landing at Buenos Aires on his return, but chose Montevideo across the estuary. He had already touched along the shore and released the slaves and settlers. He retained in chains six of the men whom Davison recognized as members of the party which had seized his ship. He intended, he said, to hold these men until their government acknowledged that they had acted under its authority. If he did not secure this statement, he threatened to take them to the United States, where they would be tried as pirates. Reluctantly Buenos Aires confessed that Vernet was the recognized governor of the islands and that the men had acted under his authority—an obvious evasion of Duncan's question but direct enough to secure their release.[19]

The Argentine Foreign Minister, in his correspondence with Slacum, had kept his anger within bounds until he received word that Captain Duncan had destroyed the settlement and transported many of its inhabitants. Immediately he notified the consul that he would have no further dealings with him. Since popular indignation demanded that the government should make some positive gesture of disapproval, the minister first considered arresting Slacum, but ended by canceling his commission. Slacum professed great surprise and at first refused to acknowledge the act. He did, however, abandon his diplomatic correspondence and limited himself to commercial clearance papers and to indiscreet private conversations which drew upon him further ill-will.[20]

Slacum did not confine his complaints to Buenos Aires, nor his diplomatic representations to Secretary of State Livingston. He discussed his problems with the British minister to the United Provinces, Henry S. Fox, and the Consul-General, Woodbine Parish. Parish read to him the British protest over the Argentine claims of sovereignty made in June, 1829. He assured Slacum that England had no intention of taking the islands, but had filed the protest solely to keep the claim alive. So sympathetic did the Englishmen appear that Slacum thought that the two countries might unite on a joint policy of resistance to Argentine pretentions. He concluded his report on the conversations with the curious sentiment, "the most powerful reasons exist why England should not be permitted to colonize these islands." In his next sentence he pointed out reasons why England or some country able to exert effective control should take over the islands.

Francis Baylies, whom Livingston sent out in the autumn of 1832 as chargé and successor to Forbes, inherited Slacum's controversy. To his agent the Secretary of State gave a long letter of instructions which, besides maintaining views first expressed by Van Buren, developed additional points at great length. He cited historical evidence to show that since Argentina did not own the islands, she had no right to assert sovereignty over them. He questioned the authenticity of Vernet's appointment as governor. Furthermore, American sailors had customarily fished along the deserted shores for years, and any attempt to extend regulations into those areas should have been accompanied by adequate and official warning. He declared that Vernet's sudden violence, seizure of ships, enticement of seamen, and abandonment of marooned sailors did not comport with consideration due the citizens of a friendly nation engaged in a customary trade.

Although Livingston denied Argentine sovereignty to those islands, it appears that he did not intend to contest it seriously. He concluded his instructions by authorizing Baylies to draft a convention covering offshore fishing and sealing, instructions predicated on the assumption that the land hitherto had been unoccupied. This denial of Argentine sovereignty, like that of Van Buren, took no account of English claims to the islands. Both Slacum and Baylies mentioned English counterclaims, but the Secretaries of State ignored them.[21] In addition to the fishing convention, Livingston authorized the envoy to sign a treaty of amity and commerce. If the current dispute should interfere with the proposed fishing convention or the commercial treaty, then the Secretary of State authorized the chargé to postpone the Falkland matter for later discussion. The instructions closed with sympathetic expressions of good will toward the southern republic and a warning to Baylies that he should arouse no enmity while negotiating the question.

If these instructions carry a touch of unreality, we should remember that Livingston knew nothing of Duncan's extreme measures. He supposed that the Captain would recapture the vessels if he could. If not, then the chargé was to demand their release. Neither did the Secretary of State know of the enmity that Slacum had aroused. Nor did he take measure of Baylies' unsympathetic personality. The chargé did not appreciate the delays in dealing with the new Latin-American countries. Quibble over small points wrung the patience of this exacting Massachusetts lawyer, and within two months he was "embarrassed by the arrest of that prompt course of action which he had determined to pursue." The longer Baylies delayed in Buenos Aires, the more disgusted he became with the government and the people.[22] At no time does he seem to have applied himself to the latter portions of his instructions, but concerned himself rather with attempts to induce Argentine statesmen to admit that in the Falkland controversy their nation was completely in error. His conduct, therefore, marked not the easing of a strained situation, but its intensification.

Within a month after his first interviews Baylies despaired of getting a direct reply to his question: "Did Argentina claim authority to stop United States' fishing and whaling in Tierra del Fuego and Falkland Island waters?" After a teasing delay, Vicente de Maza, successor to Anchorena, finally answered that his government would not discuss this matter until the United States had settled for outrageous acts subsequently done by one of its men-of-war, and therewith enclosed Vernet's account of the affair.[23]

The United States envoy saw no reason for prolonging his mission if the Argentine government first demanded a settlement of claims which he was not authorized to discuss. After reading the Foreign Minister's letter, he instantly made up his mind to leave, but delayed sending official notice for a few days in order to appear not to have acted on impulse. When he did send a request for passports, he returned, unread, Vernet's account of Duncan's conduct.[24]

Before leaving his post, Baylies, like Slacum, talked the matter over with the British Minister, Henry S. Fox. The chargé declared that the United States laid no claim to the islands in dispute, but would defend its fishing rights in those waters against all comers—even the British themselves. Yet he further inquired if England, after asserting her sovereignty over the islands, would permit that area to become the resort of pirates. If so, the United States would have reason to complain at unfriendly treatment from England.[25] Fox reassured him by saying that he was preparing a strong remonstrance against Argentine reoccupation of the islands under another governor. When reporting this conference, Baylies rightly predicted that if England took possession of the islands she would not surrender them again, and that the services of Captain Duncan would not be needed to reduce the settlement a second time. The United States, he concluded, should be satisfied that it had compelled the Argentine Confederation to respect its rights.[26]

On the return of Baylies, Rosas named General Alvear as minister to the United States with authority to continue negotiations of the affair in Washington.[27] Rosas appears to have done this as a routine gesture, and he postponed departure of the envoy while he vainly sought to better his bargaining position by first securing return of the islands from England. By the time Alvear arrived in Washington in 1838 government officials no longer paid serious attention to the repeated excuses for his absence. Argentina gained nothing by the delay. England made no concession whatever on the return of the islands, and the United States during these intervening years lost confidence in the sincerity of Argentine promises.

Besides, when Dictator Rosas finally sent Alvear, he gave him no authority to conclude negotiations, nor did he allow any bargaining alternatives. Felipe Arana, his faithful Minister of Foreign Affairs, drafted instructions which required first of all an adequate reparation for Duncan's destruction of public and private property. In addition, the United States should acknowledge the Argentine right to regulate and control in any manner whatsoever all fishing and seal-hunting in *and around* the Falkland Islands. Finally, Alvear should secure from the United States its official acknowledgment of Argentine ownership of the islands. His instructions declared that such an admission should not be difficult, for the United States had no claim to that territory. In past years many American ships had submitted to Argentine authorities and had obeyed their orders. If the minister could not gain complete satisfaction on every point, Arana ordered him to retire from the capital, but made no mention of a return home.

If this major problem should be settled favorably, Arana ordered Alvear to defend the suspension of Slacum. He should contrast Slacum's disrespectful, offensive, and irregular communications with the more quiet and proper correspondence of the Buenos Aires government.[28] Arana included in the instructions information relative to certain claims of Thomas Lloyd Halsey, a former consul of the United States to Buenos Aires. Since the Argentine House of Representatives was still debating the problem, Alvear would not take up the matter himself. In reference to the debate itself, the minister should state that the House had been examining Halsey's bill when his lawyer suddenly removed all the papers. (They had been before the

House for seven years.) Obviously, the House could do nothing further until the necessary documents were returned.[29]

Buckled within his diplomatic strait jacket, Alvear prepared to negotiate a difficult problem. During a conference with Secretary of State Forsyth in January, 1839, the two men initiated a discussion of the general situation. Alvear began with complaints against the conduct of Captain Duncan. Forsyth, affecting surprise, asked if the General did not know that the United States had approved of Captain Duncan's actions. Alvear declared that he had never been informed of that fact. Still, reminded the Secretary, by that approval the United States meant no offense to Argentina. Alvear could not imagine approving that violent act without offending his country. Forsyth illustrated with a metaphor: Suppose a man discovers that his absent neighbor's house is on fire. He runs into his neighbor's yard and vigorously puts it out. Forsyth considered Captain Duncan's suppression of Vernet's piratical colony the equivalent of destroying the neighbor's door in order to smother the flames.

The Argentine minister thought the figure inexact. The neighbor was at home and saw no fire. If there had been a blaze, the neighbor would have been able to control it. Captain Duncan had admitted the presence and ability of the neighbor, Buenos Aires, when he delayed his departure two days while waiting for some word from the government. The man who smothers a conflagration in his neighbor's house acts within the law, or at least for the good of the community, while Captain Duncan had violated the laws of all civilized nations. The figure of a house afire scarcely applied to Vernet's acts, which he committed while under an Argentine commission and while subject to judgment by Argentine courts.

Forsyth countered with a question: "Who is this Vernet who dared to operate as if he were a pirate?" Alvear identified him as a man of wealth, culture, and of strict accountability whose conduct as governor conformed to his authority. Even if his conduct had been irregular, Captain Duncan had no right to resort to highhanded measures. Vernet was responsible to his government: only his government had authority to judge his criminality.

Secretary Forsyth did not further defend his figure of speech. Instead, he resorted to generalities by stating that his government had found the whole affair very painful and wished to end it soon with satisfaction to both parties. Then cordial relations could be re-established between the two countries. Alvear could agree heartily to the painfulness of the episode. All the Americas were united by a homogeneity of principle. This unity Duncan and Slacum had sought to destroy. Baylies had questioned Argentine sovereignty—an attitude which had encouraged England to seize the islands.[30] Argentina had lost these islands as a result of this encouragement given to England. Perhaps soon it would have to fight England—as it would do with all honor—for possession of Patagonia on the mainland. He continued with a broad hint, "Perhaps we shall have the misfortune of seeing those who ought to be our natural allies leaving us alone in the question. Already the Minister can see the extent to which France pushes her unjust claims to Río de la Plata and to Mexico."

The heart-warming spirit of Monroe had vanished: the Secretary of State offered cold comfort. "Your southern lands to Cape Horn are sterile and unsuited for agriculture." "To the contrary," Alvear insisted, "it is most excellent soil and very useful."

Forsyth drifted back to the original subject. Although the United States could not pass judgment on the proper ownership of the islands, he said, it certainly preferred that they remain in Argentine possession. The United States, he added, would never permit any European country to take an additional inch of territory in all America. The Argentine minister approved these sentiments as expressed in the abstract, but again lamented the actual fate of the seized islands.

"Then what does your country wish the United States to do?" inquired the Secretary of State. A fair question and promptly answered: "To make complete satisfaction for outrage to the nation's flag, to its subjects, and to its dignity." Notably, Alvear did not ask the United States to make good with force this latest declaration against European appropriation of additional American territory. The minister immediately offered his documents as basis for establishing the amount of damage Duncan had committed. His government, he insisted, had always wished to negotiate, but Slacum's violent language had removed the possibility of fair consideration. Forsyth countered vaguely by saying that he would speak to the President and notify the minister at their next conference. He reminded Alvear that the United States citizens also had claims against his country—such as the case of Thomas Lloyd Halsey. In reply Alvear assured the Secretary of State that he would find his country always ready to settle such matters. With bland promises to each other—Forsyth to consult the President about damage claims for Duncan's raid and Alvear to urge a settlement of Halsey's claim—the two men parted.[31]

Pleasant diplomatic amenities did not conceal from Alvear the determination of the United States to offer no satisfaction. He dutifully filed with the Secretary of State a formal complaint for Duncan's activities.[32] At the same time he sent a discouraging report to Buenos Aires. He protested to Rosas that his mission was at an end, completed with dignity but devoid of results. The United States had approved of Duncan's actions and surely would refuse to give satisfaction for his attacks unless Argentina admitted damages from Vernet's seizures. Despite Alvear's protests, Forsyth had kept insisting that this approval meant no offense to Buenos Aires: it had been impossible to overlook Vernet's actions. Alvear neatly reported his country's difficult position:

> This manner of expressing one's self cannot be accepted as satisfaction which in many circumstances similar to our own has been admitted by many nations. At least such nations have accepted the explanations only with the object of avoiding war or of not wishing to find themselves in the position of an offended party demanding what will not be granted.

Yet the United States professed a desire not to sever relations on account of this controversy, because it did not wish to take advantage of Argentina while she was facing European intervention. This apparent consideration should not be construed, he warned, as a sign of weakness or lack of determination. "This government is, above all—even Europe—the one that has shown itself the most demanding and tenacious in all subjects relating to claims and interests of its subjects." To prove the point, he cited the aggressive way in which President Jackson had obliged France to meet its claims.[33] He lamented the fate which had destroyed the good harmony between the countries at a crucial time and suggested a change in his unrelenting instructions. With all its nagging obstinacy, the United States could be considered the one interested party in Argentine affairs which need not be feared as an intervening power. "No matter what the enticement, it will not be drawn into the coalition. On the contrary, the American people and its government can be counted on to use its forces to destroy it."[34]

In his dispatch to the Secretary of State, Alvear ably summarized the claims against the United States. With greater skill and considerably less heat than de Maza had exhibited, he argued his country's legal right to the islands. The Minister contended that the Confederation acquired them from Spain as a result of transfer of sovereignty by revolution, as the United States had acquired coasts in North America on winning its independence from England. Spanish control of seal-fishing around the Falkland Islands, while often protested by European countries, was always recognized ultimately.[35]

After establishing Argentine ownership of the islands, Alvear reminded the Secretary of State that Slacum had not questioned this sovereignty until after negotiations were well advanced. As a domestic matter the case would have been settled, except for the untimely and unwarranted intervention of this consul. When urged to submit whatever facts he considered outrageous to the courts, as was becoming to his office, the consul had continued to frame excessive diplomatic protests. The dispute had reached this state when Captain Duncan by his assault on national property completely altered the whole problem. Alvear concluded by demanding of the American government "solemn and complete reparation."[36]

During ensuing weeks the Argentine minister found himself in a most uncomfortable position, both personally and politically. Rosas had sent him neither funds nor additional instructions. The envoy met his ordinary living expenses with great embarrassment. Because he did not like the United States—either its people or its climate—he began early his repeated requests for a transfer to any other country in the world. But the Dictator made no decision on either point: he evidenced not the least concern for the personal accommodation of his minister, and he did nothing on the problem of the Falklands. On this latter point he was waiting, presumably, until he had heard the results of the conference which Forsyth, in January, 1839, had promised to hold with President Van Buren.[37] Since the Secretary of State never reported this conference, if it was ever held, the Argentine minister saw month after month roll by with unrelieved anxiety.

In the meanwhile Secretary Forsyth requested a copy of Argentine fishing laws which American whalers were accused of violating. The minister reluctantly answered that no such compilation existed. His country generally observed the old Spanish code, because Argentina had not set up its own fishing regulations. The answer presented as good a front as possible to an embarrassing situation: it looked as if his country wished to try Davison for violating a law which even the envoy of the injured country could not cite. Livingston had told Baylies that Davison was accused of violating "unknown laws": Van Buren, while Secretary of State, had complained to Forbes that the fishing regulations were ill-defined. If the Argentine envoy himself could not identify these laws, then such measures must be considered as unknown to Americans.[38]

For the next several months both parties dallied. To Forsyth's presentation of claims for Halsey, Alvear answered that he had no instructions. He promised to dispatch the claim to his government and to return a decision as soon as he should receive notice. Forsyth, in turn, bluntly rejected Alvear's attempt to hurry the President's decision on settlement for Duncan's raid. On October 30, the General called to ascertain the results of the conference which the Secretary in January had promised to hold with the President. Forsyth answered that pressure of business had prevented a reply; and then, reported

Alvear, "with a smile he added, 'I hope that in Buenos Aires they will forgive the delay because we ourselves have waited a long time before having the pleasure of seeing you.' "[39]

This uncomfortable interview brought to an end Alvear's first full year in the United States. It was clear to him that the northern republic intended to make no settlement of the dispute until his country should offer some concession, and he knew that Rosas intended to make no offer.

Suddenly, from an unexpected quarter there appeared a hopeful mediator. In February, 1840, Alvear called at the home of Baron Bodisco of Russia to thank him for favorable remarks which he had openly expressed concerning Rosas' resistance to French intervention in La Plata. The Russian minister declared that he had forwarded to his capital the public notices which Alvear had ordered to be printed on various occasions, and these had made such a favorable impression that His Majesty stood ready to grant recognition to Argentina if that government should make application.

The Baron continued his kindly expressions by remarking that he had urged Secretary Forsyth to pronounce on the problem of French intervention in La Plata in a manner worthy of the leading American country. The United States, he had said, should not leave to England the strange role of mediator in New World disputes—a role which she could not play adequately because of her many interests everywhere and on account of her declining power, which was dropping daily at a prodigious rate. He had pointed out that the United States had exerted its influence somewhat to aid Mexico, but had done nothing whatever for Buenos Aires. Forsyth had remained silent in response to the appeal, as if there were matters on which he did not care to speak.

The Baron paused. Alvear volunteered no enlightening information. Bodisco abruptly asked him about the status of the Falkland Islands. Alvear explained the state of negotiations and the principles of justice which had guided his government. Bodisco thought it most unfortunate that this problem should influence the United States to such a degree that it would not oppose French pretensions on La Plata. In a confiding manner he asked why Argentina did not put an end to a question which now had no meaning since England had taken over the islands—no meaning except to destroy good relations which would be useful in resisting the French.

The conciliator soon found out what significance the Argentine government attached to the dispute. Alvear volubly explained that his country had wished to settle the matter, but as long as the United States refused to give satisfaction for Captain Duncan's attack, then good desires gained nothing. Not only did his country take exception to the provocative act itself, but to the implied assumption that an American captain could believe himself authorized to act in that manner. Bodisco reasoned that the United States really did not intend to support the principle that American ships could seize Argentine property, but Alvear argued that the United States should signify its rejection of such principles by making reparation. If such should be done, the whole problem would be solved quickly.

In the midst of his heated discussion, Alvear veered away from the subject. Unfortunately the new states had no exact delineation of their population or resources. Lack of accurate surveys, he said, had doubtless encouraged France to attack Buenos Aires. Certainly that government believed that at its first angry look Argentines would drop to their knees like slaves. But Europe and the world would see with surprise the brave resistance which his country would make against one of the strongest powers of Europe. Bodisco agreed with Alvear on the delicate subject of national bravery and on this comforting note the conference closed.[40] The Russian minister heard no suggestion of compromise nor willingness to face an altered situation. If he spoke to Alvear with Forsyth's knowledge, he could report only failure of his friendly suggestions.

Throughout the following year and the next, Alvear made no progress on the problem of the Falkland Islands. The national administration had changed and he met new officials. President Van Buren lost the election of 1840 to old "Tippecanoe and Tyler too"; Daniel Webster succeeded Forsyth as Secretary of State. Alvear allowed ample time for the new officers to orient themselves; still there came no response to the formal demand of the Argentine government for satisfaction. Nevertheless, the United States officials had not forgotten Alvear's claims upon their attention. Finally, on December 4, 1841, he received as unsatisfactory an answer to his demands as he could easily have imagined. Webster declared that his government wished to postpone a definitive settlement of the whole Falkland controversy, "even if it be assumed that Captain Duncan knew that Argentina maintained an official colony on those Islands." Since that episode, he reminded Alvear, the English government had taken possession of the islands on the basis of claims long antedating Duncan's visit. With Argentine jurisdiction under dispute, it seemed fair to await the settlement of the question before proceeding with existing claims of damage. By this proposition Webster abandoned the ten-year contention of the United States that Argentina had no right to interfere with American trade in that territory because as deserted islands they belonged to no country. Instead, he assumed that *either* Argentina or England owned the islands, and he proposed to let these two countries settle the matter between themselves.

The Secretary of State recommended that Argentina and the United States pass by this knotty problem and proceed with all other matters of mutual concern, a proposal Livingston had suggested to Baylies in 1832. If Argentina would accept this solution, then the President would appoint a representative to Buenos Aires and complete the diplomatic exchanges between the two countries.[41]

Alvear faced a hard decision. Not knowing what to do, he hesitated. His instructions did not anticipate this contingency. After several weeks, Webster asked for acknowledgment of his note. Alvear, not wishing to express any written opinion on the subject, evasively answered that the whole matter required a personal interview and that as soon as he had recovered from a painful illness he would come to Washington and talk with the Secretary.[42]

Rosas found himself as much embarrassed for a reply as his envoy. A satisfactory financial settlement of claims against the United States must depend on Argentine reoccupation of the islands—a very unlikely situation—or else he must forgo reception of a United States minister at a time when he needed evidence of American friendship. In hope of some solution which would not involve specific agreement to postpone the whole subject, he did nothing. This procrastination won him no greater advantage than his delay in sending an envoy years before. He avoided accepting Webster's proposition, but he received no representative from the United States.

Eventually the Dictator capitulated, but not by frank acceptance of Webster's proposal. A naval officer who was pressing the Halsey claim in Buenos Aires some years later reported that officials there desired to receive a representative from the United States. They promised that if he were sent, they would settle all claims and sign a commercial treaty—a proposition which had been hanging fire since the recognition of the southern republic. Although the officials did not mention the Falkland Islands controversy, Secretary of State Upshur interpreted the request as an acceptance of Webster's proposition. To his special agent, Henry Watterson, Upshur explained the history of the Falkland Islands question and instructed him to enter into no discussion of this issue.[43] The precaution proved unnecessary, because the Rosas government never mentioned the matter. To this day the Falkland Islands controversy with the United States stands exactly as Webster left it.

Webster deliberately avoided Argentine claims for damages and tacitly admitted the legitimacy of English claims to the islands because he did not find the problem important to the United States. As far as American fisherman were concerned, the dispute had ended. They had already found other fishing grounds where they could pursue their calling without molestation and, by heeding warnings from the British patrols off the Falklands, they avoided seizure of their property.[44] Probably Webster would have agreed with Forsyth in preferring that Argentina rather than England should have continued in control of the islands, but he did not want to menace a settlement of the issues set forth in the Webster-Ashburton Treaty of the following year by taking up a matter in which the United States had no immediate or vital interest.[45] The United States has pursued a strict policy of neutrality—even indifference—in the English-Argentine matter.

Alvear's attempt to settle the Falkland Islands controversy ended in complete failure, but through no fault of his own. Rosas followed what he believed to be the national interest in postponing a settlement with the North American republic. Rejection of claims for damages for Captain Duncan's acts, while slighting to Argentine pride, was not essential to national life. Even if Rosas had won every point he sought from the United States, he still would not have won the islands. Therefore he finally accepted Webster's formula because he saw a way to advertise the good will of the United States during Argentine resistance to the French. Presumably, he felt that by refraining from mentioning the terms on which a representative of the United States would be sent he was saving, in some measure, that fragile thing called "national honor." At any rate, he never raised the question of Duncan's conduct at the Falklands.[46]

Thus, by a sort of mutual consent, the controversy passed into a quiescence from which it has never been effectively aroused. John Calhoun, in his instructions to Brent in 1844, declared that the problem was suspended until the question of sovereignty had been decided. This suspension, he conceded, meant that the Department could not ask damages for Vernet's action without acknowledging him a legitimate official. "The obligation to make amends for an improper exercise of jurisdiction would seem inseparable from the right of jurisdiction itself."[47] Five years later, Secretary Clayton, ignorant of this decision, ordered William A. Harris, chargé in Buenos Aires, to secure reparation for all damages suffered by Vernet's actions. Shortly thereafter Webster succeeded again to the Secretaryship; Harris was recalled and a new chargé assigned. The aging claims were never presented. An unsuccessful Argentine attempt to revive the problem in 1886 resulted in a citation of Webster's proposal to Alvear.[48]

The United States never explicitly recognized English sovereignty of the islands. Once, in a routine convention with British colonies and possessions the Falkland Islands were listed as one of the areas to which the agreement would apply.[49] Perhaps this indirect reference to British sovereignty was made more through oversight than by intention. Although Argentine patriotism demands that their postage stamps representing the national domain shall include the lost islands, only a shift of international power will restore to her the islands which now provide England with an important base and repair station while her squadrons patrol the sea paths of empire.

3. The United States and Foreign Intervention in La Plata

The French blockade of Buenos Aires in 1838, although sudden in its advent, arose from questions of long standing. Some ten years earlier France, eager that her citizens should enjoy the same privileges as those possessed by the English, had tried to force this concession from sorely pressed Lavalle, the last Unitarian governor of Buenos Aires. Even the Federalists resented pressure on the governor; and the French, seeing that the Argentines stood as one against them, patched up their differences.

Yet the issues persisted. A few French merchants lost goods during civil disturbances; others were forced to serve in the army. In fact all foreigners were legally subject to military service save the British, whose treaty provisions exempted them from this obligation. Argentine governors generally allowed to American citizens the exemptions accorded the English and, in practice, few foreigners were forced to serve against their will. However, the French government, desiring to protect its nationals by a treaty equal to that which the English enjoyed, chose to put pressure on the Rosas administration.[1] Unfortunately the list of French grievances was short, and the charges of questionable merit. With a will for peace the French could have avoided hostilities easily.

The validity of these issues was never determined. Rosas would not discuss them with unaccredited agents, although Felipe Arana, Argentine Secretary of Foreign Affairs, promised investigation. This reply was not satisfactory, and so the French intervened rather than grant the credentials which Rosas demanded. The French had not intended either a full or a prolonged intervention: they had not planned to care for a large occupying force or to establish a base of supply. As months passed they needed a near-by port for sale of captured ships, for landing materials, and for shore leave. Upset conditions in Uruguay furnished occasion for French favoritism toward one faction, which, in return for support, opened the port of Montevideo to France. This faction was led by a former Uruguayan president, Rivera. The defeated party, under President Oribe, charging "foreign influence," fled to Buenos Aires and claimed the protection of Rosas, who adopted their cause as his own. French agents then encouraged the governor of Corrientes to rebel against Rosas, and this action caused the outbreak of hostilities up the Paraná.[2]

The *British Packet*, an English-language newspaper under control of Rosas, announced the blockade to its Buenos Aires readers as a minor incident worthy of a two-inch notice on the back page.[3] Before many months the incident had become a serious matter. Firewood for the city became scarce. Rosas' diplomatic correspondence frequently went astray, and in time government communications had to be concealed by forwarding them in private covers to business firms abroad. Sometimes the visiting man-of-war of a neutral power provided the only safe carrier for government dispatches.[4]

Against this background of international recrimination and intrigue we must picture Alvear's mission to the United States. Need of support for Argentina on the French issue superseded discussion of an attack on the Falkland Islands. Immediately after his arrival in Washington in October, 1838, the minister requested an interview with the acting-Secretary of State, Aaron Vail, in order to explain the resistance of his country to the blockade.[5]

While waiting for his reception in Washington, the new minister called upon members of the diplomatic corps in their proper order. At that time the duty was not too heavy, for foreign representation was not numerous: Mr. Fox of England; Baron Bodisco of Russia; Baron Mareschal of Austria; M. Pontois of France; Señor Martínez of Mexico, and several chargés. On each visit he explained the blockade as a violation of his country's rights, and justified recent hostilities against Santa Cruz, the Bolivian dictator. Alvear reported that he found sympathy and expressions of good will in all the chancelleries and secret joy that his country, by its resistance, had repelled the French.[6]

Interviews with these emissaries passed without comment, save the one with Baron Mareschal. The Austrian minister expressed indignation at French conduct in the New World as well as in Europe. Despite the French monarch's cleverness, the Baron explanied, he was not secure on his throne, and the radical doctrines he tolerated at home kept his neighbors on guard lest they be overthrown. Both Mexico and Argentina, he observed, did well to resist with force these French encroachments. France had not expected national resistance either in Mexico or in Buenos Aires, nor had she anticipated English opposition once that nation's flow of commerce had been interrupted. The Baron felt that if France had not met active resistance in the New World her demands would have known no limits. Then, as if to even the score against France, he declared that the Austrian Emperor had failed to recognize Argentina only through lack of opportunity to do so. He was prepared to take this step in the near future.[7]

According to instructions, Alvear did not except the French minister from his diplomatic courtesies. Naturally the meeting involved real problems of tact. As the Argentine minister entered the French residence, M. Pontois rushed forward calling out the name of his visitor and showering apologies for not being properly dressed. In flattering vein the host declared that he knew his visitor by reputation for his victories in Brazil; and to these gallantries Alvear responded in kind.

When the two men reached the subject most important to them, M. Pontois was all conciliation. He professed ignorance of the latest news, but expressed regret for early trouble. He insisted that instead of being hostile to the new republics France should protect them, and declared that on his impending trip home he would say as much to the King.[8] Alvear, in turn, protested Argentine friendship for France, but the blockade of Buenos Aires made it difficult for Rosas to stop the rise of popular resentment against her. Rosas was ready to negotiate, he repeated; but it must be done through legitimate, diplomatic agents. Under the circumstances the Dictator could have done nothing but defend the honor of his country. To match these noble sentiments Pontois replied that Leblanc had proceeded according to instructions, but that he must have mistaken the intention of the Argentine government.[9] Diplomatic courtesies thus exchanged, Alvear withdrew.

During the course of his visits with the diplomatic corps, Alvear kept an appointment with the Secretary of State. To him he presented at length the cause of his country and, as befitted a case of special pleading, assumed an air of injured innocence. He stressed the insignificance of the incidents over which France had made issue: demands for a most-favored-nation treaty; demands for exemption of French citizens from military service when Argentina had none in her armed forces; demands for a treaty stating French right to indemity for losses to her nationals when every nation has the right to seek redress of grievances. Surely France must have some bigger reason for maintaining the blockade! He declared that his government was completely ignorant of real French motives, but as a sovereign nation it could never negotiate while the blockade continued. He assured Vail that Rosas would continue to resist by every means within his reach—a declaration which the acting-Secretary of State understood to mean a revival of privateering.[10] During this interview Alvear asked for no assistance from the United States; he was presenting to a neutral and friendly power the plight of his country.

In addition to his duties as diplomatic representative Alvear also served as press agent. Arana sent him reports of successive French attacks: the alliance in Uruguay with Rivera; French capture of the Argentine island of Martín García, which controlled the entrance to Río de la Plata and the waterfront of Buenos Aires. Arana forwarded many newspapers in English and French, which reproduced the official correspondence between France and the Rosas administration, and ordered Alvear to secure its publication "in the newspapers of that Court." Rosas believed that the record would win the sympathy of the

United States.[11] Any sympathy which the United States may have had for Argentina was curiously difficult to find.

An early violation of American shipping rights by the French appeared likely to arouse the desired sympathy. Therefore, Alvear carried his report to Secretary of State Forsyth. Two ships, the *America* and the *Elizabeth Davidson*, had sailed with full cargoes to the Argentine port of Lobería Chica, to the south of Buenos Aires along the Patagonian coast. This port lay beyond the areas which the French had declared in blockade. No French vessels patrolled the entrance to the harbor. The ships discharged their cargoes and were reloading again when a French corvette seized them and took them to Montevideo, where they were held as prizes. An American commodore protested this infringement of neutral rights, saying that such action was without precedent and would not be tolerated by the United States.[12]

The General found Forsyth well acquainted with affairs in La Plata. The Secretary bitterly termed the acts of the French consuls there as unworthy of a civilized nation. The French had destroyed the rights and privileges of neutral nations, not only by blockading Buenos Aires itself, but the whole coast as well. Alvear readily agreed with these strong opinions and reminded his auditor that Rosas had protested the French violation of international law. Once the Secretary said: "The French wish to make a paper blockade, and we are only waiting to see what they will do with our seized ships." Alvear interpreted this statement to mean that the Secretary rather hoped that the French admiral would sequester the property. This act would arouse public opinion in the United States to such an extent that its officials could then take vigorous steps which as individuals they strongly approved.[13] Alvear, if not Forsyth, was destined to be disappointed. The United States never seriously challenged the French government in the pursuit of its blockade, and American merchants abandoned their trade in that area.

The business interests did not wait in idleness. An American newspaper, reporting the Lobería Chica seizure, carefully understated: "The issue of this affair is awaited by the commercial community with much interest." In the newspapers of the Atlantic seaboard the businessmen exporting to Buenos Aires aired their pro-Argentine sympathies and protested the blockade which was destroying their business.[14] Congress, generally responsive to economic distress of American citizens, was seldom treated to a discussion of the problem. Only Caleb Cushing of Massachusetts seemed really concerned about French intervention in the New World. He submitted to the House in December, 1838, a resolution which quoted Monroe's declaration of 1823, and in the light of this statement asked what justification there could be for French intervention is Mexico.[15] On February 11 of the following year the House approved the resolution which by this time included a query on La Plata intervention also. Cushing's speech in support of his measure has been called a "slashing attack on the Administration," yet its comments seem mild enough. Cushing commended the protests against French action by William Brent, the American chargé in Buenos Aires. However, the Senator did not condemn the administration for indifference or for failure to act more positively. Rather he used the French action to warn his countrymen that they must assert their rights in Oregon, or a parallel situation would develop in North America.

This tinge of sympathy could give Alvear small grounds for expecting effective action or even a positive declaration of principle against the French in La Plata. Shortly before the passage of the Cushing resolution he accurately summarized the situation in his dispatch to Arana:

> The opinion of the businessmen of this country is every day more pronounced against the hostilities of France in Buenos Aires and Mexico; but however great the influence of this opinion, it will never be consistently strong enough to alter the neutrality constantly observed by this country. One cannot hope, as a consequence, to expect any act in favor of the cause which the sister republics sustain except that of an official friendship. . . . Although the United States sentiment is favorable to Argentina in the question with France, this country is circumspect.[16]

To this circumspection Alvear attributed a selfish motive. The United States, he believed, would not show a decided interest in a country with which it was not certain of adjusting existing questions. As proof of his contention he cited the agreement made between the United States and Mexico—an agreement which gave all benefits to the United States and recognized no Mexican claims. This overweighted bargain Alvear declared to be the price Mexico paid for the favor of the United States. He knew very well that Rosas would never abandon the Falkland Islands claim against the United States in return for dubious support against the French.[17]

Rosas needed assistance, but he made no gesture of conciliation to win it. Secretary Arana responded to his minister's evaluation of United States policy with a more specific appeal than the instructions to Alvear the year before had indicated. The blockade was becoming tighter; the populace was feeling the pinch; and Rosas was hoping for relief.

> Rosas hopes that the illustrious Government at Washington, recognizing the good rights which sustain so much those states as well as this state against the unjust pretentions of France, will decide to demonstrate its sympathies which are demanded by justice no less than by convenience of neutral interests compromised by the unjustifiable French blockade.[18]

Intimations of possible aid were not entirely lacking. In April, 1839, the American Commodore Nicholson, while stationed at Buenos Aires, offered to negotiate with the French for abandonment of the blockade.[19] Soon thereafter news of the Congressional comments on the Cushing resolution became known in the beleaguered city. Rumor, reflecting accurately the wishes of the sorely pressed people, if not the facts, announced that the blockade would soon be given up because the North Americans were mediating the French question.[20]

Because the Mexican affair was of greater importance to the United States than a distant blockade in La Plata, the government in Washington had protested French conduct in Mexico. For Buenos Aires it did nothing. The unsettled Falklands controversy had cost Argentina sympathy in official quarters. Neither the American people nor their leaders knew a great deal about La Plata affairs. None could feel that events so far away genuinely threatened national interests—especially when overthrow of a political faction rather than seizure of territory was the real issue. Also, French and English deadlock in remote La Plata enabled the United States to press its own policies more firmly in reference to Texas and to Mexico.

No action, therefore, followed the passage of Cushing's resolution in 1839. In a second protest of July, 1840, Cushing declared that the blockade in La Plata was illegal and that neutral powers should never have been silent about it. But with all his declarations of its illegality he made no claim that it violated basic policies of the United States.

While the French were pressing their blockade, Alvear received favorable notice from Russian and Austrian representatives. Probably their motive was not so much to aid Argentina as to irritate the French. At a diplomatic ball given at the Austrian embassy the Russian minister, Baron Bodisco, approached Alvear and, gesturing to the bystanders, observed:

> General, I am going to say to the Secretary of State and to these gentlemen [referring to several Senators nearby] that it is grievous and singular the conduct which they observe toward your country—letting it be oppressed and abused by France, a big maritime power. I have told them that we look to them to stop this sort of thing.

Thus challenged, the Senators began to talk energetically. The Baron continued:

> It is said that England could not use the language of force, because . . . she fears in the present circumstances to give offense to France. But the position of this country places it outside all fear. I have said to them that I am impartial. My country has not recognized your country, but my Emperor and all the Russias are friends of this republic and we see with pain the position it must take.[21]

Bodisco was not satisfied with these thrusts. Later in the evening Alvear again encountered him playing cards with Secretary of State Forsyth, Mr. Fox of England, and the Swedish representative. As Alvear approached the table the Russian observed in a loud voice, "General, do you know how Mr. Fox treats me? He has me oppressed and blockaded with the same injustice which the French use upon you. But I resist!"

The Baron's conspicuous behavior and his positive speech made Alvear believe that he had received communications upon the subject of the blockade from the Russian Court, especially since Russian envoys had the reputation of never speaking on political matters without instructions. Alvear said that at a dinner a few days later he would try to engage Bodisco again on the same subject, and determine more exactly what the Baron had in mind. At the same time he gave assurance to his government that he had not failed to present to Bodisco the Argentine reasons for resistance, and that he would certainly "encourage this man in his persistent and laudable desire of demanding that these Señores [Americans] shake off the sad apathy in which they find themselves in respect to such an important and transcendental subject."[22]

The dinner offered no opportunity for a private conversation, but it did provide an occasion for another public declaration by the Russian minister. During the first course he proposed a toast to General Rosas, and Alvear returned a fitting response. The gesture excited considerable attention since it was not then the general custom to toast individuals or governments. Indeed, Alvear observed, in the United States the custom of private toasts had almost died. After the banquet many people congratulated him on the very close relations between his country and Russia. Thinking that this erroneous reputation would help Argentina in her resistance to France, Alvear answered all comments vaguely. "Unfortunately," he observed to Arana, "the minister of France was not present at this affair."[23]

The minister of France would not be outdone. A few days later the Secretary of State entertained the diplomatic corps with a dinner and a splendid dance afterward. Among the guests Alvear encountered M. Pageot, the French minister. In a voice that many could hear, M. Pageot asked if Alvear had received the latest news from La Plata. "No news in particular," he acknowledged, "for the blockade delays many dispatches. What news of especial import has M. Pageot received?" "News," he replied, "that perhaps the blockade is raised by now, for France has offered such good terms that only delay by Rosas could prevent the establishment once again of good relations." Because he had no information on the subject, Alvear felt that he should not continue the discussion before so many people. He resorted to platitudes: his government had long been animated by the best feeling toward the French and constantly sought to end the demonstration; however, Rosas was equally determined to sustain his nation's rights to the end rather than injure the dignity of the country.[24]

Report of public favors by Bodisco aroused keen interest in Buenos Aires and won for Alvear a more prompt reply than usual. Arana instructed him to thank the Russian for his sympathy at such a critical time. Further, he was to say that the government would be pleased if Russia would recognize the independence of the Confederation.[25]

Rosas realized that it would be to his advantage if he could establish relations with Russia while France was blockading Buenos Aires. Therefore, Secretary Arana notified Manuel Sarratea, the representative stationed at Río de Janeiro, of Bodisco's action, and requested that he make friendly advances to the Russian envoy there. Sarratea did so, returning a most discouraging report. Regardless of what Bodisco had done, the Russian chargé, Lomonoroff, conducted himself in a diametrically opposite manner. He conspicuously ignored Sarratea and trailed the French minister as if he were a member of his delegation. In order to give no offense, Sarratea had avoided him. At last, while attending an official function, he recounted the conduct of Baron Bodisco. Lomonoroff exclaimed, "My faith, I have not received instructions on the matter." Thus the Russian diplomats canceled each other at Río de Janeiro and at Washington.[26]

A full year elapsed after this diplomatic pantomime before news arrived that France would withdraw, leaving Rosas still master of La Plata. Immediately Alvear released the terms for publication. On that same evening he attended a banquet where the English, Dutch, and Austrian representatives, and Secretary Forsyth all joined in praising the victory. Everyone rejoiced that Argentina had dared oppose France and hoped that this experience would teach Europe that the young republics were not to be abused. Finally Baron Mareschal led the beaming Alvear to the French minister "to make peace" and there each smilingly exchanged congratulations.[27]

A month after the French had withdrawn from La Plata, Arana addressed to the United States an official notice of the peace. He appraised the treaty as a "classic proof of the high politics and honor of the King of France . . . but also of the justice, moderation, and dignity of the Argentine Confederation. . . . An interesting document for all those who are called to a like destiny with the Argentine government."[28] Certainly the United States had shown small interest in protecting that destiny.

Retirement of the French left Rosas confident of his control of La Plata. He continued to meddle in the affairs of Uruguay, where there were large French interests and many French residents. His interference became more and more serious until, in 1845, both France and England determined to smother his activities by another blockade. During this uneasy interim Alvear sent back to his government such intelligence as came his way. One such item was President Tyler's annual message of December, 1842.

In his message to Congress, President Tyler referred to European interference with the new republics in the Western Hemisphere. The message does not mention the French nor does any part of it suggest that he was conscious of affairs in La Plata. At the conclusion of his remarks on the terms of the Webster-Ashburton Treaty, at that time before the Senate for approval, Tyler added:

> With the rest of Europe we are at peace. Carefully abstaining from interference in all questions exclusively referring themselves to the political interests of Europe, we may be permitted to hope an equal exemption from the European governments in what relates to the states of the American continents.[29]

Quite probably the inciting cause of President Tyler's remarks was English and French activity in Texas aimed at encouraging that country to remain independent, but the principles of his address would apply equally well to La Plata affairs.

For this reason Alvear called attention to the President's declaration. Rosas was so impressed that he had the message translated and distributed to the French colonists in Uruguay.[30] Rosas saw, and he hoped the French would see in Tyler's words, a warning against European intervention and a promise of aid from the United States if trouble should arise.

This mild reaffirmation of a principle declared by President Monroe almost twenty years earlier found Alvear considerably less enthusiastic than he had been after Monroe's enchanting exposition in 1824. By 1842 he had begun to envisage the United States, not Europe, as the great menace to Latin America. His comments reflected both his memory of Monroe's explanation and his present fears that a newer generation had twisted the words of the author so that they would serve another purpose.

> This principle, declared for the first time by President Monroe when France was preparing to help Spain in the fight against her former colonies and adopted by Mr. Canning, freed us from this powerful enemy [So far Monroe had taught him.]. But today this republic is so strong with respect to us and her power and strength grow so rapidly that adoption of this principle cannot be accepted by the other American republics except in special cases that may be convenient.
>
> On the other hand, one cannot believe that Europe subscribes to it because this would be to grant in America a very decided superiority to the United States. Politics is no more than a science of national interests. . . . England, for example, is at once a European and an American power and she has as much interest in defending the rights of Mexico from North American invasion as the United States has in defending her from English invasion.[31]

Undeterred even for a moment by Alvear's cautious observation, Rosas accepted Tyler's words as a challenge to France. So did Guizot, the French prime minister, who felt that the American President was challenging French policy either in regard to La Plata or Texas. Privately he expressed his unwillingness to recognize such a policy.[32]

This lack of recognition became evident a few years later when both England and France again intervened in La Plata affairs. Willingness to attempt a second blockade after an inglorious retreat in 1840 indicates that English and French ministers were as short of wisdom as of memory. But because the Argentine Dictator had proved such a cantankerous opponent, they let bad tempers overcome better judgment, and by 1845 the two countries found themselves ranged against Rosas, whom they considered a vile troublemaker. In September of that year they began the second blockade without definite agreement on their joint conduct or responsibility except to destroy their enemy and to establish peaceful trade in that area. Unembarrassed by the absence of any real issues at stake, the two powers began another long and costly demonstration. They hoped to use victory in that part of the New World to counterbalance diplomatic defeats in North America. There the triumphant election of Polk had committed the United States to an expansionist movement which foreshadowed defeat for European machinations in Texas and perhaps in Oregon as well.

Both for domestic and foreign consumption Rosas took high ground in his protests against the new blockade. The Dictator declared that he was defending the American System: that America [the Western Hemisphere], like Europe, had its own special interests whose protection could not concern Europe at all. It would be as irregular for Argentina to interfere with those concerns of Europe as for Europe to interfere with Argentina. "No intervention of whatever European power in the internal affairs of America is a doctrine consecrated by the very act of its emancipation from Europe, emancipation bought at the cost of so much blood and the greatest sacrifices."[33]

The second intervention greatly increased Alvear's duties. In an effort to be useful to his country, he interviewed the English and French ministers themselves, and sent to Rosas excessively optimistic predictions that the information he gave to these officials would lead to an alteration of European policy.[34] He picked up gossip at the waterfront on the movement of French and English troops. He relayed from Moreno in London the prediction that England would not dispatch troops to support the blockade, for in addition to her other world-wide commitments she would need troops in the Oregon and California area. Even at the cost of war she would deny to the

United States access to the Pacific.[35] Rosas' public utterances do not indicate that he thought that North American expansion would divide his enemies or weaken their attacks.

His minister sought the Secretary of State, James Buchanan. To this official he asserted the illegality of the English and French intervention. Alvear, like Rosas, based the major emphasis of his protests on the principle of nonintervention by European countries in the affairs of the New World. This principle, he reminded Buchanan, had been proclaimed on various occasions by the presidents of the United States—though he did not mention Monroe by name. In Alvear's opinion violations of these proclamations would justify resistance to European powers. Resistance by the United States "with all the moral influence in its power" would furnish a suitable and useful opportunity for showing "that the governments of the New World, and most especially the one which by its power and elevation is at the head of them all, does not remain indifferent to the principles and declarations made by it."[36] The United States stirred not from its indifference.

While Alvear was engaged in his round of duties, events both in Europe and in the United States were shaping themselves for a general declaration of policy by President Polk himself: a declaration which should have advised Alvear exactly on the attitude of the United States toward his country's problem. During debates in the French Chamber of Deputies in June, 1845, opponents of Guizot had taunted him for passively awaiting the annexation of Texas. In reply Guizot revealed that his administration had definitely opposed the union and had sought to prevent it. He justified this active, though secret, participation in New World affairs in his famous "balance-of-power" speech: that France had an everlasting interest in the maintenance of independent states and balance of forces in the New World between England, United States, and countries of Spanish origin, a balance which would prevent any one of them from becoming too powerful. However, the minister added, France ought to act only by influence and expression of opinion (as she had acted in the Texas question), and with a constant recognition that protection of French interests should be the determining criterion. Not the Texas question alone, he said, but all future political decisions in the New World would be guided by this maxim.[37]

That France had or intended to have an influence in determining the political growth of one or more of the new republics was a challenge to the United States which the newly elected President, James K. Polk, could not overlook. In his annual message the President specifically repudiated the concept that a balance-of-power arrangement such as that in Europe could apply to the North American continent, and especially to the United States. "We must ever maintain the principle that the people of this continent alone have the right to decide their own destiny." He continued:

> We may claim on this continent . . . an exemption from European interference. The nations of America are equally sovereign and independent with those of Europe. They possess the same rights, independent of all foreign interposition, to make war, conclude peace, and to regulate their internal affairs. The American people cannot therefore view with indifference attempts of European powers to interfere with the independent action of the nations on this continent.

And then, after quoting a passage from President Monroe's declaration of 1823, he added:

> This principle will apply with greatly increased force should any European power attempt to establish a new colony in North America. . . . The reassertion of this principle, especially in reference to North America, is at this day but the promulgation of a policy which no European power should cherish the disposition to resist. . . . It should be distinctly announced to the world as our settled policy that no future European colony or dominion shall with our consent be planted or established on any part of the North American continent.[38]

The most conspicuous difference between Monroe's declaration and that of Polk is the insistence of the latter on its special applicability of North America. He plainly omitted South America from the areas in which his policy would apply "with greatly increased force" by particularly distinguishing between "these continents," and by declaring that "under existing circumstances" the United States was prepared to enforce the doctrine only on the North American continent.

To all these events Alvear was an interested and concerned spectator. He reported in August the great indignation expressed in the press against Guizot's address: "It has produced in this country . . . an alarm or indignation in all parties and in all sorts of people." The French minister, M. Pageot, had confided to him in a private conversation that France would fight before permitting the United States to secure California. France had protected the United States when it was small, but as it expanded and increased in strength Europe could no longer watch its growth with indifference. M. Pageot explained French assent to the recent reannexation of Texas, by saying that the French and English governments had agreed to let the United States annex that republic as a concession to future good will, but further expansion must cease. Neither country would permit, without war, the peaceable annexation of California.[39]

What really demanded explanation was the President's declaration that while he accepted Monroe's original principle of nonintervention by European powers in the affairs of the Western Hemisphere, he would limit enforcement of it to North America, thus explicitly rejecting any notion of interference in the southern blockade. Alvear's report to Arana indicates that he either misunderstood the import of the President's message or else he was trying to buoy up the Argentine government with false and unfounded hopes. Perhaps his intense desire for assistance deluded him into thinking that the United States would take up the cause of Argentina. At the same time he admitted that the United States had what he called "delicate relations" with England over Oregon and California which required that its attention should not be distracted with other subjects.[40]

Alvear's conjectures were true—in part. President Polk's papers show that he had in mind the future expansion of the United States into Oregon and California, and they carry no mention of La Plata affairs.[41] But his advisers had been calling for much more than that. John McKeon of New York, leader of Tammany and a Presidential adviser, suggested immediate purchase of Canada and annexation. Besides, he proposed a Presidential declaration against foreign interference "on this continent" and the appointment to South American countries as full ministers men of great ability who would teach the southern leaders the value of union in their resistance to European interference.[42]

This advice, excepting acquisition of Mexico and Canada, Polk followed in its general outlines. He made the same distinction between North and South America as areas of primary interest to the United States, while restricting activities in South America to that of counsel and expression of opinion. Like Monroe, he felt that a declaration of policy would deter the European monarchies in an attempt to build up in South America a conservative force to counteract the liberal principles that had been signally successful in the United States. A restatement of the policy of the United States, in the opinion of Polk's advisers, meant "doing something" for South American victims of European interference. In line with this policy Secretary Buchanan issued instructions to William Harris, the new chargé to Buenos Aires:

> Whilst existing circumstances render it impossible for the United States to take part in the present war, yet the President desires that the whole moral influence of the Republic should be cast into the scale of the injured party. We cordially wish the Argentine republic success in its struggle against foreign interference.[43]

In Polk's voluminous correspondence, which he so scrupulously preserved, no letter sent to him in reference to his speech mentions the problem of La Plata. Some correspondents congratulated him for having effectively answered Guizot; others were glad that he had thwarted England or France in Mexico, in California, or in Oregon. Apparently all understood what the President meant by "this continent," and none suggested that the blockade in La Plata was in any way related to the "high destiny" of the United States.[44]

After the President's message of 1845, Senator Allen of the Foreign Relations Committee sought Congressional declaration to cover both Americas. The resolution failed. It would seem that the President correctly interpreted the wishes of the people by refusing to commit the nation to a South American policy.[45]

From our perspective of today we can see that Alvear was too optimistic in feeling that Polk would soon make a direct statement about the La Plata situation. The President had no intention of including any portion of South America in the area the United States would insist should be free from European interference. Polk did not restrain himself on account of fear of public opinion: neither he nor any considerable portion of the United States saw the necessity of using force to protect South America. Every attempt to test public opinion in Congress shattered against an impenetrable indifference to affairs geographically beyond the vital interests of the United States. Privately, Secretary Buchanan, going further than Alvear ever knew, assured the British minister that the United States would not interfere in La Plata, and disavowed Brent's attempt to arbitrate.[46]

In Buenos Aires the chargé from the United States, William Brent, did not understand this drift in his country's policies. He deeply sympathized with Rosas' resistance to European intervention. He felt that as a key man in a crucial position he must arouse his government and his people to the significance of development on La Plata. To that end he published letters in Washington's administration paper, the *Daily Union*.[47] He sent to Secretary Buchanan many pieces of Rosas propaganda and copies of British and French exchanges. In order to refresh the memory of the Secretary of State on the traditional attitude of the United States toward European intervention in the New World, he interlarded his dispatches with pertinent quotations from Presidents Jefferson, Monroe, and Tyler.

Without instructions he volunteered his services to the blockading powers as mediator, but they refused his offer. The English and French officials, regarding him as a senile tool of Rosas, disregarded his repeated warnings of reclamations from the United States for all acts "committed under the shadow of a pretended blockade." Rosas, of course, appreciated these bumptious efforts to provide an early end to the blockade, and regretted the recall of the chargé in 1846. Alvear, completely without justification, led his government to believe that Brent's strenuous efforts in behalf of Argentina represented the real attitude of the United States. He sent repeated assurances that at all times the United States had supported its chargé and represented his recall as a political shakeup at home, not as a change in policy. "The President and cabinet of this country are desirous of giving Your Excellency all possible proofs of appreciation and esteem."[48]

Brent's efforts were unheeded. English and French officials ignored him. His letters in the public press in the United States aroused no comment, and Secretary Buchanan, far from making an issue of the intervention, instructed Brent's successor, William A. Harris, not to renew the offer of mediation.

Just as Baron Bodisco for personal reasons had publicly indicated special favor to Alvear, so Secretary Buchanan in April, 1847, chose to stimulate diplomatic comment by a similar action. The affair occurred at a formal dinner given by the chargé of Austria. Secretary Buchanan met Alvear's son, Don Emilio, at the door of the reception room and asked, after audible greeting, if the Argentine Embassy had received the recent news from La Plata. Since Don Emilio replied in the negative, the Secretary volunteered the report that England and France had agreed to meet Argentine terms. Then, turning to the attentive circle Buchanan exclaimed, "General Rosas is a great man whom I admire very much." The auditors chorused their agreement, the representatives of Chile and Peru speaking with especial vehemence: "with demonstrations truly American," says Alvear, of "a man who sustains our continent with such glory." The father reported that his son's Argentine heart swelled with pride at the tribute to the illustrious chief who was guiding so justly the nation's destiny.[49]

Sympathy for Argentina such as that found in Buchanan's instructions to Harris or as that encountered by Alvear at diplomatic balls amounted to little. Before Alvear could capitalize on public sentiment in favor of his country, he had to arouse it: a task at which he strove mightily during the years 1845-1846. He succeeded in the publication of occasional news notices in the Democratic newspapers of New York City, where Irish Tammany men opposed England more heartily than they espoused Argentina. He urged the businessmen of the country to protest the blockade which cut them off from Argentine trade. In Congress these representations were quietly disregarded by an administration which was pressing England for an agreement on the Oregon territory.

Alvear's dispatches made this clear to Rosas,[50] but the limitations of truth did not greatly restrain the Dictator when facing increased urgency on the home front. An editorial in his *Gaceta Mercantil* of February 25, 1846, declared that as a result of pressure in Washington the French and English would have to agree that the United States should mediate the dispute. Then, as if speaking to the United States rather than to his own people, the Dictator continued:

> The government and people of the United States ought to realize clearly that their influence in America and their prestige, and their own security would be greatly threatened if . . . they should permit England and France to decide arbitrarily and tyranically American questions and so they would place the United States in a secondary position which would be dangerous in emergencies.[51]

The Argentine people may have been consoled by these prospects so incorrectly presented to them, but the northern republic paid no attention to these trial balloons. The United States was standing firmly by the interpretation of 1826: that the Monroe Doctrine was not a pledge which other nations could call upon it to redeem.[52] When Harris arrived in Buenos Aires in 1846, he found that the people fully expected the United States to come to their aid. This idea persisted so stubbornly that as late as 1850 he was still trying to disabuse Rosas of the fond but vain hope that the United States was obligated to help him in the maintenance of an "American Doctrine."[53]

While Rosas stressed openly the ideal of American solidarity and of close agreement with the United States, he never persuaded the northern republic to declare publicly its opposition to the blockade. Buchanan wrote confidentially of the distinctive spirit in the New World which animated the Argentine people in opposing two of the greatest powers of Europe. He instructed Harris to remind Rosas of Polk's recent annual message in which the President had developed American doctrines for opposition to European intervention in New World affairs. He wished Argentina success in its struggle against English and French violations of these principles, yet declared that the United States, "due to existing circumstances," would take no part in the dispute.[54] Rosas surely took small comfort from such assurances.

Officials of the United States who were stationed in Buenos Aires finally came to oppose the investment of the city as heartily as Brent had done. The consul, Joseph H. Graham, emphasized the unfairness of the investment, its arbitrary seizures, and its illegal captures. But the blockade was effective. Since American shippers and merchants wanted to avoid lawsuits in the courts of the blockading powers, they obeyed the whim of the French or English officials.[55] Harris, the chargé, finally wearied of the bickering between all the powers. He gave a public scolding to England and France and sent urgent appeals to Washington for at least one ship to bolster the vanishing prestige of the United States on La Plata.[56] With Texas and Oregon questions so recently closed and the Mexican War in progress, the United States continued to ignore the whole issue.

The United States had no reason to interfere on its own behalf, because Alvear had promised that any privilege or concession which the blockading powers might wring from his country would be promptly granted to that country also. Since the administration won assurances from England and France that neither of them would make territorial claims, it was undisturbed by existing unpleasantness below the equator.[57]

The actions of the United States which appear so half-hearted and ineffective were the best that Rosas could win from the only country he could claim, with any appearance of truth, as a strong friend abroad. Therefore, he made the most of this tenuous friendship by expressing approval of an attitude much less effective or decisive than he had wished. In his annual message to the twenty-sixth legislature, a relic of democratic procedure which he seems to have kept for sentimental purposes, Rosas expressed the strongest regard for

> . . . the ardent sympathies of the United States for the cause of La Plata. Its decided repulse of the European intervention against them is notorious . . . and the North American press, faithful echo of the sentiments of that enlightened people, has diffused throughout the world execration of the United States against the armed interference of Europe in the affairs of the Republics of America. . . . That government . . . offers to the civilization of the world a grateful and consoling example.[58]

Sheer hyperbole published to comfort an harassed people.

As Argentine minister to the United States, Alvear was unable to assume an active role in defense of his country. During the two interventions he reported possible recognition of the Argentine Confederation by Russia and Austria, but nothing came of these offers. He correctly informed his government that the United States was so deeply involved in its own conflicts with England that little aid could be expected from the northern republic. In fact, it seemed indifferent to Argentina's plight.

At the onset of the first blockade his government held great hopes that destruction of American trade would bring such strong repercussions in Congress that the United States would use its influence to break up the intervention on La Plata. But the Argentine minister frankly stated that these interests would exert no influence upon the councils of the government. This estimate was exact. Yet during the whole of the second blockade he sent dispatches which frequently expressed high hopes for immediate intervention by the United States—hopes that were quite ill-founded. Why he let himself by misled so badly is not clear. It may be that his later activity promoting sentiment in favor of intervention made him overestimate the effectiveness of his own work. At least his own government felt that his public relations program was successful out of all proportion to its real achievement. Yet Alvear's mistaken appreciation of American sentiment extended also to the Presidential addresses. President Tyler's watered-down declaration of 1842 he understood to be a restatement much less vigorous than Monroe's original declaration. But three years later he missed the import of Polk's statement which particularly excluded South America from the area of special interest to the United

States. Certainly Alvear's analyses did not grow increasingly acute with his lengthening years of residence in the United States; rather the reverse is true.

On the authorization of Rosas at the beginning of the second blockade, General Alvear conducted a propaganda campaign in the United States in an effort to win for his country the attention of the American people. The Argentine Dictator hoped that an aroused public sentiment would force the government to intervene immediately in behalf of his troubled country. And so a century ago the Argentine minister in Washington secretely used the newspapers in a vain attempt to induce the United States to resist a European blockade laid against a republic of the Western Hemisphere.

4. Difficulties of a Propaganda Agent

When Rosas dispatched General Alvear to the United States in 1838, he expected that his envoy would serve as propaganda agent as well as diplomatic representative. The Dictator laid great store by an appeal to "American solidarity." He hoped to take advantage of the sympathy for beleaguered Argentina which was to be expected from the North American republic.[1] He pictured Federalist resistance to European interveners in the Río de la Plata as common American victories. With the eloquence of James Monroe both Rosas in Argentina and Carlos de Alvear, his representative in Washington, proclaimed freedom of the New World from European interference.

More immediate diplomatic issues kept the newly arrived minister from devoting his full energies at once to the program of propaganda. For a few years he sponsored in the public press information favorable to his country but in a desultory and perfunctory manner. During the period of the first blockade, he offered translations of official documents for publication, and editors used such portions as struck their fancy. While living in Washington, where the only newspaper of influential circulation was the administration's (Democratic) *Daily Union,* he had small facilities; nor could he have accomplished a great deal anywhere with inadequate funds to subsidize newspaper articles. He was content to see the official reports from his country spread in the public press. His government asked for nothing more.

But Rosas' troubles had not ended. Although he survived the first intervention in a creditable manner, he did not come through the fire unscathed. Exiled Unitarians had begun from Montevideo, Chile, Brazil, or Europe their literary campaign of hostility and abuse. As native and educated Argentines, writing in convincing fashion, they shaped public opinion abroad. Rosas could not stop their agile pens. He needed capable defenders and ardent sympathizers outside Argentina: he had none except his own diplomatic service. Therefore, the Secretary for Foreign Affairs instructed Alvear, as well as the ministers in London and Paris, to give special attention to the preparation of favorable press reports which might refute the vigorous Unitarian charges. Each representative received small sums in order to guarantee notices favorable to the home government.[2]

These orders came in a convenient hour. Alvear's diplomatic activities had become both routine and sterile: presentation of ordinary claims absorbed little time or attention. He accepted the task of propaganda with alacrity, and acknowledged his assignment by commenting upon the evils which Arana wished to eradicate: horrible lies about the administration were pouring from Montevideo and, spread by strangers, were being believed. Against these acts of private malice he would defend the country with truth by writing articles based upon official documents, Argentine gazettes, ministerial correspondence, and well-known facts of Argentine history. Then in a glowing, adulatory paragraph he enrolled himself as a defender of Rosas:

> I shall employ myself with greatest zeal in fulfilling the order, not only as an individual in the employ of the government but also by the sympathy of recognition and gratitude that, as an Argentine citizen, I profess to an administration whose worthy chief has known how to elevate the credit and splendor of our country to a height hitherto unknown.[3]

No one can dispute the record of his zeal, and his sympathy with the Rosas regime appears both real and personal.[4] For three years Alvear's major interest centered in the distribution of propaganda material—a task which he pushed to a climax in the fall and winter of 1845-1846. Thereafter his literary output waned, and by 1847 had almost ceased.

He did most of the work alone. Recognizing that a foreigner could not write within the mental pattern of the people, he suggested that Rosas appoint American citizens in various cities as consuls and vice-consuls. Even though their commercial activity might be negligible, they would feel called upon to defend the Rosas government on every occasion, and the Confederation would gain more defenders at no cost.[5] Rosas eventually named Schuyler Livingston of New York, Nalbro Frazier of Philadelphia, Fitz-Henry Homer of Boston, and, in 1851, Carl Morton Stewart of Baltimore as consuls, but beyond sending to Alvear material on La Plata problems which appeared in local newspapers, or publishing an occasional translation of a Rosas decree, they took little part in defense of the Confederation. Rosas appointed too few consuls to be effective, and he made no real effort to use the men whom he did appoint. They seldom corresponded with Alvear or Rosas and apparently limited themselves to their commercial duties.[6] Alvear recognized the needs of a propaganda campaign, but slow and inadequate support at home crippled his almost unaided efforts.

As his first project in 1843 he published five hundred copies of a small volume, *Sketches from the Public Life of Rosas*, which contained an account of the honors conferred upon him by the Argentine House of Representatives.[7] The task of translation and printing continued longer and—as such things usually do—it cost more than was anticipated. The minister's annual publicity allowance amounted to $500 per year, and the small edition which he prepared came to $1,555, a sum which he reported with reluctance and apology. The printers had reproduced a steel cut of Rosas so excellently that the Dictator's Secretary, after commenting upon it, paid the bill, although he cautioned Alvear never to spend so much money without special authorization.[8]

With the printing completed, Alvear distributed copies to men he considered the most important in developing public opinion. He sent copies to the President and his cabinet, to the governors of the New England and Middle Atlantic states, to the members of the diplomatic corps, excepting the English and French representatives, to the Congressional Library, five copies to his half-brother in the Spanish government, and nine copies to Rosas. He hoped that a laudatory account of the Federalist leader would counteract to some extent the Unitarian scurrility emanating from sources outside the Confederation.

On completion of this project, Alvear moved his residence from Washington to New York City, although for a time his son, Don Emilio, stayed behind to care for accumulating legation correspondence. As the minister explained to Rosas, Washington was a small country town. Prices were higher than in a city, because everything he needed must be brought from New York. In New York he would be in touch with more important newspapers and could communicate with the other sections of the Union more successfully.[9] After 1844 he appeared in Washington only periodically for official functions, and, disregarding repeated protests from the Secretaries of State, he never resided in the capital city again.

His newspaper activities demanded Alvear's constant attention. Soon after the editor of a Spanish-language newspaper, *Noticias de Ambos Mundos,* agreed to open his columns only to the defense of Rosas, the envoy read a hostile account in the sheet. When he complained at this betrayal of trust, the editor replied that he did not have time to read every item in his paper, and offered to write a favorable article in reply. Alvear thought that he should do it himself, and his homily upholding Rosas he signed "An Argentine."[10]

While editors of the popular newspapers such as the *Morning Courier* and the *Enquirer* never pledged themselves to Rosas, they permitted Alvear to reply to charges which defamed Rosas' good name. These replies he framed as a letter from one "Stephen Clark" of Río de Janeiro. The New York *Herald* of November 14 carried a similar letter. It seemed best to head his fictitious communications from Río de Janeiro or Montevideo, important centers of Unitarian propaganda, in order to make it appear that some of the educated elements in those cities had not fallen under the beguiling influence of Unitarians. During the first half of 1845 Alvear concerned himself with this type of newspaper work, offsetting a hostile article in one paper by a favorable one of his own in another.[11] Well supplied with news accounts from Arana and with communications from Guido in Río de Janeiro, he did his best to ridicule Unitarian charges of misconduct and robbery by Rosas' adherents.[12]

Just as the campaign had got under way, Alvear encountered Joshua A. Dodge of Salem, Massachusetts, who considered himself an authority on international affairs because he had held three consular posts in Europe. Dodge felt that his authoritative words would arouse the American people to the dangers of European intervention in the New World: soon he was composing flattering essays on the virtues of the Dictator. He secured the publication of a laudatory article in the Salem (Massachusetts) *Register* and persuaded the editor of the New York *Sun* to run another as an editorial in the issue of August 13, 1845. A discourse so couched, Alvear thought, would win American support by appearing to represent popular opinion; it would remind the readers that Argentina counted upon the sympathy of the United States.[13]

Even with the aid of Dodge and occasional assistance of friends in clipping relevant articles from out-of-town papers, Alvear's activities did not satisfy the Buenos Aires administration. Apparently Arana expected his minister to send complete clippings from the nation's press, but Alvear protested. "On account of the great number of papers published in this immense country, it would be necessary to spend a lifetime of many men in order to acquire and read them all besides the great expense of a prodigious subscription list."[14] Subscriptions cost more than Arana realized; extra copies of a desired issue could not be found later; and it was practically impossible for him to secure back numbers of out-of-town publications.

Alvear not only was pressed to collect published opinions on La Plata troubles, but he also had great difficulty turning out material of necessary volume and variety. His oral English probably was good, but his attempts to compose articles in English resulted in lamentable failures. His penmanship was atrocious; his spelling of Spanish was always slatternly; and his efforts to master English spelling by use of logic and phonetics left many words practically unintelligible.[15] But he recognized his limitations. When Dodge was not available, he dictated his account to an editor who would set the material into proper style. An article in the New York *Herald* for December 8, 1845, was prepared in this way. Often after Alvear had left the newspaper office, the editor would add other material that the minister felt was quite erroneous. Then, in another article, and signing his name as Argentine minister, he would deny the offending section. And so he got nowhere. This proclamation of egregious error in one part cast doubt upon the reliability of the whole account. Frequently editors were reluctant to take this extra trouble of composing his articles even if they wanted his material. At such times he paid them whenever he could out of his small funds.[16]

If we add these articles to the normal reporting of the blockade by returned shippers, we find that the New York papers were copiously supplied with information on affairs in La Plata. In time Alvear noted with satisfaction the increasing amount of news devoted to Argentina. Inland newspapers had copied the news (and his opinions) from New York publications. Other editors spontaneously announced opinions favorable to Rosas. As a propagandist, the minister claimed credit for the increased publicity. Alvear secured publication of one article in February and another in May; still a third appeared in August. In late November there appeared two more. December saw eight reviews from his pen, or that of Dodge. In order to make resentment of the blockade appear to be a national sentiment, not a party issue, he sought to scatter his contributions, so that Whig, Democratic and nonpartisan publications would carry his protests at the unwarranted intervention. For this reason he secured insertion of rather lengthy accounts in the New York papers: the *Sun*, *Herald*, *Journal of Commerce*, *Morning News*, *Commercial Advertiser*, and the *Evening Post;* as well as the Washington *Daily Union.*[17] Dodge devoted special attention in 1846 to the *Daily Union*, the Democratic administration paper, which accepted many articles—at a fee.

These sponsored effusions appeared anonymously in a variety of forms. Some pretended to be personal letters written from South American cities; others presumed to be news accounts gathered by "our correspondent" or taken from "latest advices"; and sometimes the publishers ran them as editorials.[18] Certain New York newspapers were unvaryingly hostile to the Argentine Confederation and hoped that the English and French would carry things their own way. At times even friendly editors published reports uncomplimentary to the Argentine cause. On such occasions Alvear did not try to insert an argumentative rejoinder in the following issue. Instead, a few days later, he would induce another editor to carry a favorable account which would cast doubt on the full truth of "recent reports" without actually refuting them point by point.[19]

The greatest propaganda activity coincided with the meeting of Congress in December, 1845; and continued during the course of the following two or three months. The Argentine minister cited a violent anti-English resolution passed by big Tammany meetings in the fall of 1845 as a great triumph which would surely influence the President and Congress. ("In a country like this the public must move before the government can act.") Parallel sentiments expressed in milder language by the Secretary of State and favorable opinions in the Washington *Daily Union* he attributed to his earlier publicity.[20] He supplied Congressmen regularly with copies of his articles in order to furnish factual material for their speeches which he hoped would ring out in defense of "American" rights. Simultaneously he was seeking from businessmen in Salem, Boston, Baltimore, and Philadelphia petitions against the blockade. He "planted" an article in the *Journal of Commerce* of December 3, 1845, which detailed great losses of American business and called upon the government to provide relief. The influence of the United States, he said, would be crucial in bringing the intervention to an end.[21]

The articles published during this period constitute a defense of the Rosas regime in every particular. They recalled the petty pretexts of the first intervention; they emphasized lack of popular support both in Uruguay and Argentina for the French and English in both blockades, despite outpouring of European gold. They stressed the illegality of the blockades, destruction of neutral trade, the renewed hostilities occasioned by European intervention. Occasionally his articles appealed to the cause of American solidarity in the name of President Monroe, and sometimes he cited later declarations by other American presidents or statesmen.

This Argentine propaganda defended Rosas personally from the charges made by his enemies. Alvear first denied the existence of the "Mazorca," Rosas' red-shirted, extralegal band to enforce acquiesence or death. Later, he presented this group as a voluntary patriot society whose violent actions were but natural outbreaks against hated French and Unitarians. Rosas' best efforts failed to stop these escapades of the Mazorca, he explained, for they represented spontaneous, popular anger. In short, Rosas had ordered no assassinations, was guilty of no cruelty. Instead, he protected religion and punished crimes, because he possessed an elemental austerity coupled with firmness and justice. His services were wholly patriotic: he accepted no salary from the State. The Dictator's administration strove for peace in La Plata. He did not desire to annex the territory of Uruguay, but fought there in order to aid Oribe's resistance to European aggression brought on by rebellious Uruguayans and exiled Argentines. As panegyrist of the Dictator, Alvear appealed to the vanity and self-interest of the United States by presenting Rosas as an admirer of the North American Republic: Rosas in power meant a friend in the South.

> General Rosas and the people he governs are strongly attached to this country and its institutions and eventually the Argentine Confederation will be modified on the same plan. . . . He is a truly great man and in his hands this country is the second Republic of America.[22]

During the height of this agitation, Alvear could never have completed his work without the assistance of Dodge, whom he first engaged as his copyist at the Voorhees courtmartial.[23] Since Alvear spent on newspapers alone more than the sum Rosas regularly allotted to him for propaganda, Dodge contributed his services. Perhaps he did this on the promise of remuneration in the future: at this period the General was urging Rosas to permit employment of a press agent. He submitted long and persuasive arguments in favor of this step, but Dodge, for all his "decided and passionate admiration," received from the Dictator only a message of thanks.[24]

The reports which Dodge made to Alvear reveal both the methods of a propagandist of a century ago and the difficulties which he faced in arousing the United States to favorable action. He wrote from Philadelphia on December 17, 1845, telling of his recent arrival and of his conferences with Nalbro Frazier, Argentine consul in that city. This official had composed an article on the blockade which he hoped a local newspaper would publish. In addition, he was preparing a strong protest against the intervention which the Philadelphia merchants would endorse and send to Washington. The realistic Dodge expected small results from the protests: unfortunately, the merchants trading with Buenos Aires were mostly Whigs.[25]

Then he resolved on a more effective scheme: he would organize the Democrats of the city to protest the blockade. With mass meetings and strong resolutions from party adherents, he hoped to impress the Democratic President and the Secretary of State. He laid his arguments before Richard Vaux, City Registrar, and Democratic leader. He argued that the blockade was but a test case by England and France to discover the reaction of the United States toward European intervention in American affairs. If this attempt should succeed without objection, the monarchs of Europe would unite to overthrow liberty, first in South America, and then in North America. After two long interviews which retraced the history of English and French interventions in La Plata, Vaux agreed to sponsor the rally. Dodge asked Alvear to send to their new convert all documents available on the subject. On second thought he decided that it would be best to send him only those materials which he himself had written: "we can be sure of them."

In Washington, Dodge found a still broader field of action. He conferred with Vice-President Dallas, whom he had known for fifteen years. This gentleman expressed such a strong opposition to intervention that Dodge requested Alvear to send him all relevant documents, omitting to state which ones he considered "safe." He was optimistic enough to believe that he had enough influential friends to pass a resolution in both Houses against the intervention.[26]

As events proved, Dodge had enough friends to secure introduction of a resolution but not its passage. He worked steadily from December, 1845, to March, 1846, secured conferences with many Congressmen, and distributed to them his articles and other published material. They all opposed what he called "the shameful intervention in American affairs," and "the impious league of monarchs." Dodge claimed credit for persuading Senator Allen, chairman of the Foreign Relations Committee, to present a resolution which not only approved President Polk's references to the Monroe Doctrine, but also pledged the use of force to maintain freedom from European intervention.[27] Dodge attributed failure of this resolution, and in all probability correctly, to the approaching crisis over Oregon and to Congressional unwillingness to complicate still further the issues with England. Senator Allen, although he optimistically predicted reintroduction and passage of the measure, did not again take up cudgels in behalf of his resolution.[28]

During Dodge's residence in Washington, the *Daily Union* published a series of articles which with growing bitterness condemned European intervention in La Plata. The one which appeared on February 18 was so extreme that the Whig *National Intelligencer*[29] prepared to take up the issue. The *Daily Union* abruptly discontinued the provocative accounts: the editor would not create a party issue without the consent of the President.[30] Dodge soberly concluded that after editorial tempers had subsided he would try again; but he would have to write in a more general vein. He continued to translate Rosas' bulletins and decrees, and these at least were published without protest in the *Daily Union.* He said that his articles had been copied in papers throughout the nation. Alvear knew this statement to be true, and he assiduously courted the *Union* for favors. He would hold an article for days in order to see it in this paper rather than secure immediate publication in some less strategic journal.[31]

As the minister surveyed his work at the beginning of 1846 he felt proud of his accomplishments. He had prompted in the nation's capital an energetic defense of the Argentine cause. He had seen that his articles were spread far beyond his subsidized circle of editors, and he proudly dispatched copies of his own work to Manuel Moreno in London, and to Tomás Guido in Río de Janeiro.[32]

A sudden burst of anti-Rosas propaganda roused Alvear from his complacency. The *Commercial Advertiser* on February 3, 1846, praised the victory for the blockading forces at the Battery of Obligado.[33] He immediately prepared a reply which appeared in the same paper the following day, and in the *Sun* two days later.[34] He also sought its publication in the *Daily Union* in order to give faithful Democratic editors throughout the country an opportunity to copy it. The point of view of the article may be judged from Alvear's own words: "It has been written to augment the moral strength which the United States gives to us and with that circumspection which is necessary in order to give a good effect."[35]

The next anti-Rosas discourse occurred in the monthly magazine, the *American Whig Review*. The issue of February, 1846, carried an article purporting to be written by a Mrs. S. P. Jenkins who had lived in Buenos Aires and then moved to Montevideo. From there she wrote a scathing attack on the Argentine Dictator. The article may well have been propaganda from Unitarian sources, although Alvear never seems to have questioned its authenticity.[36] Shortly thereafter the New York *Evening Mirror* published several editorials and news notices based on Mrs. Jenkins' revelations. Alvear declared that he had long since answered such threadbare tales "victoriously" but that for the benefit of New York and London, he would restate his defense. His reply, in a series of seven articles, duly appeared in the *Daily Union*.[37] The basis of these articles is the correspondence of a purported Englishman, Alfred Mallalieu, whose defense of Rosas was published in English newspapers as letters to Lord Aberdeen. Rosas was reprinting these letters in his own press, and Alvear incorporated this material in his replies "in order to make it plain that an Englishman in England has already blasted those calumnies which are now being repeated by a woman."[38]

As a part of his policy not to reply to a hostile article directly in the same publication that carried the original charges, he did not contest the diatribes in the *Whig Review*. Instead he gave his data to W. A. Hogg, who composed a long and effusive article for the *Democratic Review* of the following May.[39]

Against more extensive literary efforts he had no defense. There came to his notice a novel entitled *Dolores, A Novel of South America*, which recounted, said Alvear, the adventures of one Paula Monso, a woman married to a Portuguese professor of violin. Some persons supposed that the authoress was a German, others declared her Swiss, but regardless of nationality, Alvear complained, her book teemed with lies.[40] Beyond these protests to his ministry, he could do nothing. Certainly in retaliation he could not write a novel. And then in the summer of 1846 he encountered a sketch of La Plata life by one Anthony King, who carried, said Alvear, the courteous title of "Colonel." This "Colonel" had lived in the Plata area for twenty-four years, and on return to New York had increased his fortune to the respectable sum of $50,000. Against Colonel King, Alvear turned streams of abuse. He considered his book the most absurd, deceiving, ill-considered, foolish, lying account that imagination could encompass. He described the author as obscure and supremely ignorant; a member of the Native American Party, who, favored by his great fortune, continually stirred up agitation on subjects which met his fancy.[41]

A later generation finds in Colonel King's account a naïve portrayal of Argentine life from 1817 to 1837. The author was not a colonel by courtesy, as Alvear suggested, but won his rank through service in the Argentine militia after serving for more than ten years in the armed forces. He began his service in 1817 when he engaged in the campaign which finally eliminated Artigas from Platean affairs. Then King campaigned in the Argentine northwest until the collapse of Spanish resistance.

He withdrew from the service rather than engage in the Argentine civil war which broke out in 1829. For several years thereafter he lived in Córdoba, then under the rule of the Unitarians whom he supported. Alvear correctly interpreted the Colonel's hostility to the political principles of Federalism and his dislike of the Dictator. And as the servant of Rosas, the minister heaped his abuse on Colonel King. But this condemation should have hurt the pride of the glory-loving General whom King identified as "the brave General Albia [*sic*] who led Argentine forces against the Brazilians."

The summaries which Alvear made of the two books are so incomplete and so erroneous that one wonders if he bothered to read the texts, or, if he did, whether he deliberately falsified his report. King had campaigned for many years in the Argentine and repeatedly says that in La Plata his name was corrupted to "Quino," but Alvear identified him for Arana as "Mr. Bing." The novel, *Dolores,* a verbose imitation of Walter Scott's *Talisman,* certainly deprecated the Rosas regime, but Alvear's characterization of the text is ludicrous. The author, a Dane, Paul Harro-Harring, privately and anonymously printed his novel. Alvear was far beside the mark in attributing it to a woman of Swiss or German nationality. Now he was paying for the sketchy education of his youth.

In literary criticism he was beyond his depth: he could scarcely compose material for the daily newspapers. The New York *Evening Mirror* gave him the most trouble. Its continued barrage of the "most atrocious calumnies against our country and government" made it appear that this paper was receiving material from Unitarian and European sources. Since he felt unable to reply personally to all those charges, he renewed his plea for a propaganda assistant. Eloquently he outlined the difficulties which he faced: the activity of enemy agents; the need of checking the press; the necessity of frequent trips between Washington and New York; the strange administration of a country whose government operates under the direction of influential men from the masses; the need of seeing these leaders; the necessity of sustaining a consistent discussion where everyone wishes to state his opinion. He was constantly hampered by having to find first one man and then another to write his English articles. A paid assistant drawing upon Alvear's knowledge of the Argentine and upon the official documents of the Rosas regime could compose and present his material for publication at once. A prompt answer would prove more effective than one a week later. Besides, newspaper editors refused to accept a lengthy and detailed defense, but with a full-time employee Alvear could publish long articles in booklet form. He could secure such a person for $1,200 per year. "The flaming effort of our enemies . . . with the object of defaming our government testifies to the importance they attach to this country,"[42] wrote Alvear, pleading that his government could not afford to be less concerned. It is difficult to see how his work could have yielded appreciable results without the organization of a real propaganda bureau. If Rosas expected an effective newspaper campaign that would influence the United States to interfere in his behalf, he needed to support it much more liberally than he chose to do.

Dodge abandoned the project of enlisting aid for Argentina when he realized that he would never receive any fee for his work. Alvear continued the work alone, but thereafter very few articles came from his office or pen. By the spring of 1846 he had to content himself with short newspaper columns, and before the end of the year even this outlet was generally denied him. He seems to have abandoned all propaganda efforts except for the *Daily Union*. The Oregon question received increasingly greater publicity, and he knew that the editor was sincere when he said that he had little space available for La Plata problems. He found it impossible to promote further the various propositions on which he had been instructed.[43] His dispatches continued to stress the great benefit to his country if the United States would favor the national cause. For this reason he vainly renewed his importunities for increased subsidy, but Rosas never replied to these appeals. In time Alvear's propaganda encountered Mexican War sentiment which completely smothered all possibility of intervention in the Río de la Plata, or even of diplomatic protest about affairs in the distant south.[44]

With the foreign-language press Alvear had very little association. Two Spanish-language papers were published in New York, the *Revisor* and the *Crónica.* Two exiled residents of Havana who agitated for Cuban independence managed the former; the latter was financed by the Cuban Captain-General to defend the Spanish administration. None of these editors cared what happened in La Plata, and since neither had influence among American readers, he did not ask them often for favorable publicity.[45] He was much more concerned with the French newspaper, the *Courrier des États Unis,* which was subsidized by the French government. This paper carried articles hostile to Rosas and disparaged his feats of arms while praising the intervention of France and England. Alvear had several explosive interviews with the editor, and occasionally used the charges appearing in this sheet as a target for pro-Rosas broadsides. On one occasion he composed an unsigned article in French and engaged an agent to present it to the office of the *Courrier,* but the editor developed unexpected scruples: he flatly refused to publish at any price a discourse with whose sentiments he did not agree. Not to be outdone, Alvear sent the article to New Orleans, and there it appeared in a French paper as well as in translation in the Spanish publication, *La Patria.*[46] He found that the foreign-language papers, subsidized to advance special causes, were either indifferent or hostile to La Plata affairs. Only a Mexican editor of a shortlived paper, which was discontinued on advent of the Mexican War, exhibited real interest in the Argentine cause. When Alvear offered to pay for articles printed in his paper, the editor would accept nothing, declaring that he had done it as a favor "to the man [Rosas] who knows how to defend the dignity of his country."[47]

Rumors of Rosas' financial resources greatly exaggerated the amount he spent on propaganda. The French attaché of Count Walenski charged in 1850 that Rosas subsidized periodicals in France, England, Portugal, Brazil, and the United States, besides directing three journals in Buenos Aires.[48] The fact is that Rosas sent small annual grants to each diplomatic post, and so far as the United States was concerned, this propaganda fund of five hundred dollars had to be spread so widely that it could scarcely have merited the term of "subsidizing periodicals." This allowance Alvear exceeded three times over in the publication of one small book. His subscription list for newspapers cost one hundred dollars per year, and additional sums for postage, duplicate copies of all accounts for or against Rosas, and one hundred copies of the articles which he wrote consumed much of the remainder.[49] In some years the regular sums did not suffice and Alvear requested special outlays which, though granted, were accompanied with a flat order not to exceed the appropriations again. Rosas, ever fearful of graft, ordered that all expenditures should be accompanied by signed receipts.[50]

Apparently neither Alvear nor the editors thought it unusual that they should accept payment for articles appearing in their columns. But he did object to their tactics: they charged foreigners more than they required native citizens to pay for material of equal length. The editors as a group were quite unreliable: they would promise to run a series in their papers, and then would insert them at such wide intervals or cut them so severely that the major effect would be lost. They had a thousand ways, he complained, to make a person pay in a most arbitrary fashion, and after he had secured their promises of faithful performance, it was necessary to talk to them daily.[51] He found the editor of the New York *Sun* the most reliable in keeping his promise to run whole articles, and the most willing to serve as ghost-writer. During a two year period he paid him three hundred dollars. To the editors of the *Herald*, *Morning Courier*, *Enquirer*, *Evening Post*, and *Express* he paid during 1844 the total sum of six hundred and fifty dollars. The editor of the *Daily Union* had received one hundred and seventy by August, 1845, but since the *Union* published many more of his articles in 1846 than in any other year, his expenditures with this paper must have increased considerably.[52] By 1849-1850 the propaganda campaign had tapered off, and in an interim accounting Alvear submitted a bill for three hundred and thirty-three dollars. Of this sum he laid two hundred and forty dollars to what he called "investments." Arana's warnings had secured the desired effect: the remainder of his five hundred dollar grant Alvear reported "on hand." He incurred no further deficits.

Because the editors of the partisan press sympathized with Argentine opposition to European intervention in the affairs of the New World, they saw no objection to accepting both the article and the cash. But when the administration indicated that the Oregon issue was of particular importance, the *Union* dropped the La Plata episode, and Alvear's extant dispatches do not reveal payments or promises to publish further material.

The significance of Alvear's newspaper work is purely negative: a true estimate of public opinion in the United States on the La Plata imbroglio cannot be gauged by perusing the important newspapers of New York and Washington. It is obvious that frequently the articles were composed from reports by the Rosas government and were therefore biased. And no sentiment favorable to Argentina as it appeared in the American press can be accepted as the actual sentiments of the editor or of the presumed "correspondent," for these sentiments may have originated in the facile brain of the Argentine minister to the United States. However, the spontaneous copying of his articles by inland papers shows that he correctly interpreted the private opinions of the people. After publication of Rosas-slanted articles in the *Daily Union* ceased in 1846, few contributions sponsored by Alvear appeared in the American press. From time to time notices of the blockade reminded the public that the intervention continued, but these accounts did not originate with Alvear. He had to content himself with running a clipping service for the benefit of the Argentine press.[53] His later dispatches were filled with reports of the American scene. He found few pleasant prospects. He believed that the nation which had been deaf to the appeals of his country and had ignored the promises of Monroe would turn to conquest at the expense of its weaker neighbors. Soon it would become the menace of all Latin America.

To this bitter prospect Alvear devoted the last correspondence of his diplomatic career. By citations from history, by quotations from statistical tabulations of immigration, by appeals to racial feeling he identified the existence of a spirit of conquest in the people of the United States. He grieved that he had lived to see the Spanish-speaking nations despised by their northern neighbor, a nation bent on expansion. Vigorously he sought to arouse his heedless countrymen to their imminent danger. Like the prophet of old he cried out that all men had bowed down to other gods, but no comforting vision appeared to Alvear: he faced Manifest Destiny alone.

5. Facing Manifest Destiny

As an involuntary resident of the United States for fourteen years, General Alvear had ample opportunity to observe the people among whom he lived. Through his diplomatic office he met many national leaders and statesmen: Presidents Monroe, John Q. Adams, Van Buren, Tyler, Polk, Buchanan. He knew Henry Clay, Daniel Webster, John C. Calhoun, Joel R. Poinsett, and George Bancroft. He read the American press widely. While a member of the diplomatic corps he became acquainted with many foreign representatives such as Lord Ashburton of England, Señor Calderón de la Barca of Spain, and Washington's companion-in-arms, Lafayette. In short, few foreigners have been so favorably placed to observe, intimately and critically, American public policy over such a long period in the first half of the nineteenth century.

The core of this policy, as the General interpreted it, was westward expansion, a program that aroused his intense fear and distrust.[1] He considered the expansionist sentiment the more fearful because it was rooted not in the heart of a single individual, but in the hearts of a whole people. One "conquest" led to another; each success set a goal for the following generation and thus established an endless chain of disasters for Latin America.[2]

Occasionally he would grant an exception to this doleful prospect. The "expansionist" difficulties in Maine he considered harmless: the issues that culminated in the Webster-Ashburton Treaty he shrugged off as routine agreements.[3] In spite of the popular war fervor, he observed no military preparations, and everywhere he found both a sincere desire for peace and a genuine respect for England. Much of the agitation, he believed, was aroused to mollify the Southern states for the destruction of the slave ship *Criolle*.[4] When the final treaty was announced, Alvear commended the Secretary of State on a peaceful and honorable settlement, creditable to the government of the Republic,[5] but in his heart he believed that the United States had signed the treaty "in order to find herself free on the subject if she should become entangled in continental difficulties."[6]

The precise nature of these anticipated difficulties the Argentine minister did not state. But clearly he did not expect that westward expansion to Oregon and the Pacific would end without English intervention. He notified his government in 1843 of a recent bill to promote settlement in Oregon.[7] This measure, he declared, was the first ever passed by the government to sponsor emigration. Up to that time private citizens had accomplished the spread of American culture and civilization through voluntary movement. The Federal government had never promoted westward settlements under official auspices. By this latest proposal Congress hoped to encourage citizens to establish residence in Oregon in order to counteract English influence in the Pacific, which had increased tremendously after the notorious Chinese Opium War of 1842. The likelihood of war between the two nations seemed greater because England claimed the territory which the United States intended to take for itself.

He ventured no further analysis of the Oregon question. Nor did he feel that he had reversed his estimate when, at the height of the crisis, he seems not to have expected a war between the two countries.[8] Controversy over the Northwest had diverted Congressional notice from La Plata when it seemed that the United Staes might have taken a stand against the southern blockade. Rosas urged Alvear to promote discussion of La Plata affairs again when the Oregon debate had closed. But the expansion fever did not subside until after European intervention in La Plata had ceased.

The rising fever, though checked, lingered; the flush revealed traces of a recurrent malady temporarily quiescent. The

Oregon "compromise" to the contrary, Alvear did not believe that the United States had abandoned in the least its desire to possess the whole of Canada. Years later he observed that possession of this territory remained a dominant idea in the United States, but that respect for English power made national leaders discreet in public utterance.

> I must tell you that the ambitious fury which has taken hold of this country passes all boundaries of imagination and its inhabitants generally have the conviction that they are destined to possess and be masters of all America to Cape Horn, and look upon this as an inevitable event and as a question of fact which time will solve.[9]

If the Western Hemisphere were to avoid this destiny, then the apparent victims should bestir themselves. Let them reverse the adage and summon the Old World to redress the impending balance of the New. All need not be lost; help could be had. France, Alvear reported, regretted to see England come to terms with the United States over Oregon while she was still enmeshed in the La Plata blockade. The French minister had declared to him that rivalry between the two English-speaking nations was more apparent than real. In any crucial issue the two nations would league together because preponderant opinion in the United States was one of respect and admiration for England. The Latin-American nations, he warned, should consider France the most friendly of the great powers because of its cultural affinity. Concurrent French investment of Vera Cruz and Buenos Aires did testify to the contrary. But he explained French occupation in Mexico and Argentina as a terrible example of French carelessness in selecting special agents, and not as an evidence of imperial aggression. In spite of these lamentable difficulties he promised that the New World would see France withdraw without making any claims for territory whatsover. Neither England nor the United States, he boasted, could truthfully make such a claim.[10]

Reference to the claims of the United States against Mexico struck fire. Here was the issue—Texas; there the enemy—the United States. It had not always been so in Alvear's thinking. Toward the Texas Republic at first he assumed no hostile attitude. Having arrived in the United States shortly after the Texans had won their independence from Mexico, his early dispatches made no reference to the situation there. He believed that Mexican leaders had been lacking in foresight when they had invited into their territory an aggressive and hardworking race, and he did not at first accuse the United States of sponsoring Texas settlement or of aiding the revolt for independence. He paid no real attention to the problem until the possibility of annexation aroused his bitter objection. Then the "Texas Question" ballooned into "the most important problem between the peoples of Spanish and 'Saxon' descent."[11] All the new republics should note the outcome well, for Mexico served as a barrier to further expansion of the United States. He marveled that after the fighting for Texas ceased, the Mexicans could delay recovery of their lost territory by engaging in bitter domestic quarrels.[12]

Yet even as Mexicans ranged themselves against each other in domestic affairs, their government was seeking the assistance of Latin-American republics in restraining the United States. Alvear, as early as 1839, reported that Mexico had named to the governments of South America a representative who would attempt to revive the unfortunate Congress of Panama,[13] but he considered the Mexicans unwise in their insistence that the Congress should be held in Mexico City. If they were appealing in the name of the Spanish-American "race," they ought to be willing to accept such a place as a majority might select. In this way they would avoid the appearance of using the Congress as a tool of Mexican policy. Since Mexican leaders wanted a congress for this purpose and the other Spanish-American countries did not, this attempt to revive the dream of Bolívar failed.[14]

Failure dogged the Mexicans. Alvear judged the armistice with Texas another futile gesture. Mexico thus gave tacit recognition to the formation of a new "Saxon" state in her territory, and by so doing she postponed the struggle until too late to fight with success. She, in due course, he predicted, would be absorbed by the more powerful Texas race.[15]

Warm sympathies for Mexico and opposition to the national aims of the United States made Alvear complain henceforth of every official mention of Texas. When annexation became imminent, his indignation mounted. He hailed abolitionist opposition to the measure, and called the attention of his government to the speeches of the elderly John Q. Adams, who accused the United States of fomenting the Texas revolution and of aiding its successful completion.[16] Nor did he depend on partisan accusation alone to prove his contention. Publication of the correspondence involved in President Tyler's negotiations showed to Alvear's satisfaction that the United States was tempting Texans shamefully with offers of protection while posing as a friend of Mexico. This amazing, two-faced correspondence, he declared, characterized the nation at large. It entertained no respect or consideration for the rights of Mexico. "It has pretended to consider them only as a formula."[17]

The spirit of annexation was mounting. Alvear predicted that the next president, either Clay or Polk, would submit new schemes for incorporating Texas, and with party support they would pass. Soon after the election of 1844 the envoy had the melancholy pleasure of pointing out the accuracy of his prediction. He recognized the popularity of annexation and deplored the time Mexico had lost in recapturing her province. He hoped that the Mexicans would fight against the annexation of Texas; otherwise additional territory would be devoured piecemeal and their nation soon disappear. Consent to annexation would not permanently solve the problem for Mexico. Soon a question of boundaries would arise, for neither the old Spanish monarchy nor the Mexican government had laid out definite limits. Again Mexico would find herself on the defensive. He knew that in certain grandiose moments Texans had laid claims even to the Pacific coast. Since the American government had manifested a very live interest in acquiring California, he did not doubt that it would support these wild pretensions.

The disillusioned minister predicted that the program of expansion would not stop even at the Pacific. Annexation of Texas, he declared, would make much easier the ultimate acquisition of Cuba, the island so ardently desired by the United States. Probable success of the expansionists aroused a fatalistic admiration: "North American politics in its ambitious plans displays the hypocritical and perfidious manner, yet always approaches its object with planned and tenacious perseverance."[18]

On reporting the final annexation of Texas, Alvear sounded a warning for all Latin America. This *first* step in acquisition of new territory[19] he felt "ought to call for close consideration by all other American republics"—a generalization which may have indicated his approval of Mexican attempts to revive the inter-American congresses. His dispatches were long and emphatic:

> Until now this country has affected a kind of protection toward the other governments and peoples of the New World. It has shown some sympathy for them. This noble conduct has made the European countries believe that any ambitious plan on their part would find a strong resistance in the United States. The American cause, the same form of republican government—everything in fact—seemed to contribute to the belief that these fine policies would not change. . . .
>
> This country is no longer the former fatherland of Washington, composed of simple and modest citizens, pure and content with their state, without ambition, respecting the rights of others as equal to their own and making them admire the foreigner for the practice of all the social virtues. Then this republic had only a little more than 2,000,000 inhabitants scattered through thirteen states. Little more than a half a century has been sufficient to gain 20,000,000 and to create a union of twenty-nine states and territories. Likewise their sympathy and protection toward the rest of America has changed to hostility and ambition. Twelve years ago this ambitious program came to birth and with the rapidity with which everything grows in this country, it has been sufficient to take hold of the masses. . . .
>
> The voice of justice and right has lost all its force in this country and if a remnant of shame for the public morals of the world does not restrain the inhabitants once the first step is taken with the incorporation of Texas, this people will launch out and continue in this race of usurpations without it being possible to contain them by other means except employing force to resist them.[20]

In high alarm Alvear visited other members of the diplomatic corps and heard them condemn the annexation of Texas.

Señor Calderón de la Barca, the Spanish representative only recently transferred from Mexico, showed to him the Spanish response to an earlier French suggestion that the two nations forestall annexation by jointly recognizing the independence of Texas. The Spanish government had replied that it would not consider recognition because this territory had belonged to Mexico and that country, far from surrendering its rights, was preparing an invasion. Both men found in the document different meanings. Calderón de la Barca saw proof of Spanish friendship toward Mexico; Alvear interpreted these sentiments as evidence of Spanish forgiveness for the wars of independence. In reality, Spain was applying consistently the rule that she had proclaimed when her own colonies had rebelled a generation earlier. The era of revolution had passed for the aging Alvear—by 1845 he was acclaiming the rule which as a young revolutionary in 1812 he would have considered unjustifiable.[21]

Considering Alvear's deep resentment at the annexation of Texas, his existing dispatches on the Mexican War seem comparatively brief. From the year of his arrival he had observed the rising difficulties between the United States and Mexico, and he unfailingly sympathized with Mexico. Blandly ignoring awards made to the United States after adjudication of claims by impartial referees, he labeled all such problems as "claims." Mexican procrastination in payment, he wrote, gave the United States additional opportunity to take advantage of her southern neighbor. Successive "negotiation of claims" secured from Mexico terms which required that country both to surrender its just demands and to pay all claims presented by the "subjects of North America." Such was the price which the northern republic exacted for its friendship.[22]

Toward Mexico, Alvear had the natural sympathy of a kinsman. But he felt that by bad statesmanship and poor government that country had invited opposition from a ready troublemaker. So great, indeed, was his disgust with Santa Anna's short-sighted statesmanship that he seemed almost to forgive the United States for advancing in the face of such obvious weakness. Gauging national stability in terms of white populations, he lamented Mexico's high proportion of Indians.

He explained her declining fortunes on the basis of racial degeneration; otherwise he could not account for what he called great cowardice, imbecility, and lack of constancy. He saw no ultimate fate for Mexicans except national extinction unless—by a miracle—God should give them another type of man.

His despairing prescription required promotion of European immigration so that—perhaps—along the northern border a chain of white settlements with organized armies might stop an Anglo-Saxon advance.[23] Vain hope! Already Mexico had found the cure of that bitter medicine worse than the national illness. Early settlers under Stephen F. Austin and other *empresarios* were supposed to furnish just that sort of immunity to the western fever. Instead, they had raised the temperature of the countrymen they had left behind.

As one might have expected, Alvear's sympathies were violently aroused as he followed the negotiations which culminated in the Treaty of Guadelupe-Hidalgo. He followed with interest the acrimonious Congressional debates in Washington thereafter. He bemoaned both the lack of justice and the public morals which the United States was showing. He cited the charges by Van Buren, Gallatin, Henry Clay, and John Q. Adams to prove that the United States had covered atrocious aggression by lies that Mexico first had crossed the disputed frontier.[24]

If Mexicans were deluded by the prospects of peace, Alvear was not. Because habits of conquest would grow stronger with each success, he feared this latest victory, and he scornfully contemplated the prospects:

> As for the peace which they think they have obtained, it cannot be more than a truce, for far from satisfying or calming their enemies by their submission, they have only aroused them by the ease of overcoming them to take the rest of the national territory of Mexico.[25]

Yet for all his disdain of the Mexicans he felt that none of the sister republics could have accomplished more than she did, and that any territory belonging to the Spanish races would be taken by a conscienceless American people when they considered it convenient to do so.[26]

As Alvear followed Congressional debates, it became clear to him that the "Washingtones" (Whigs) who had blamed the war on the Democrats for the sake of political ambition would have done the same thing, had they been in power.

> It is true that the ambition of conquest, without considering the justice of its means, is unfortunately a fact which dominates a large majority of the people of North America, and thus threatens the future state of the people of the New World by offering them a bloody war, usurpations and impositions.[27]

On this despairing note Alvear's comments on the Mexican War came to a close.

Yet the continued boastfulness of Manifest Destiny set the Argentine envoy's teeth on edge. He found it painful to hear the effrontery with which various men were named for the Presidency—this one because he favors capture of Cuba, another because he favors taking more land from Mexico. Success in Texas and California made the Democratic party advance its plans to include both Cuba and the Isthmus of Panama. No place, it seemed, was really safe from the flaunting northern republic. Already men said that the United States needed bases for their ships rounding the Horn. Some spoke of purchasing the island of Catalina from Brazil: others said that they needed to buy or seize the islands of Chiloé from Chile. Rumor charged a pretender to the Inca throne with having appealed to the President for assistance against the existing government of Peru. On one occasion Alvear declared that the incident was of no importance; on another day he would warn that he was perfectly convinced that the United States hoped someday to annex Peru.

> There is not now the least risk that Peru should be invaded by North America. Many other countries lie between it and that nation, but this document on the Inca pretender shows the active spirit and vastness which animates the partisans of conquest . . . as well as the anticipation with which they begin to scatter the germs which facilitate the future realization of their aims.[28]

Dangerous germs, decidedly, which the Americans scattered so recklessly: the professed advantages which they claimed would be the certain reward of any Latin-American republic willing to annex itself to the United States. Did not 80 per cent of the American travelers in South America preach this idea? he asked. Even worse, returning travelers assured the party of conquest that the people of the Latin race were tired of wars and revolutions: they knew they were badly governed for the benefit of a top clique in each country. The masses of the people yearned for annexation. "Here it is curious to see how they think that this event would be for the good of those republics."

Rosas received these alarming reports in silence. No extant letter from Arana expresses any opinion whatsoever on the expansionist policy of the United States. Presumably what Alvear labeled "distance, rivalries, and other political circumstances" accounted for Rosas' reticence. Rather, the Argentine House of Representatives heard both praise of the United States for boldly resisting England in her attempt to persuade Texas to continue its independence and thanks to the northern republic for doing its best to prevent English conquest in La Plata.[29] Rosas, fearing that he might need the assistance of the United States against England or France, dared not adopt the attitude either of alarm or of opposition which his minister so obviously desired.

Alvear's alarm sprang from something much deeper than the partisan accusations of Whigs and Democrats: the United States drew its sources of strength from the manpower of all Europe. Territorial growth of the United States he found distressing enough, but unparalleled growth in population gave assurance that the historical processes would never be reversed. Land once taken by this new nation would not remain long unoccupied, left forgotten, and then—perchance—recovered by some clever Latin dictator. The whole of Latin America together could not match this westward swarming. He declared that the annual immigration into the United States had now reached the impressive total of 400,000; 173,000 had settled in the state of New York alone. The money which the immigrants brought with them, although small for any particular individual, greatly increased the national wealth. When he considered the investment of such capital, the profit from immigrant labor, and the natural increase in population, he understood the mounting real estate values and the pressure to expand into unpopulated territories. Alvear correctly predicted that immigration would increase and that eventually the United States, already one of the strongest powers in the world, would become the greatest of them all.[30]

This increase, of itself, need not have been too disturbing. His objection lay in the spirit accompanying national prosperity. A desire now gripped the masses themselves to secure even more territory. In a monarchy, he reflected, aggression usually ceased with the death of an ambitious sovereign; in a democracy it would die only with a decline of the whole people. Already Central America, Venezuela, and New Granada (Colombia) as well as Mexico ought to consider the future seriously. Ecuador and Peru should note (and with alarm) the rapid increase of population in California and Oregon. One day these people would control the Pacific.

To stop this westward tide appeared impossible. In developing new territory these North Americans were proving themselves active, hard-working, and enterprising. Soon they gained a superiority of numbers; they exploited natural resources in the occupied lands; they monopolized agriculture, commerce, navigation, and industry. Such vigorous competition paralyzed the Spanish races who could not survive it. In defeat, therefore, the smaller group either died in misery or emigrated to uninvaded shores. "Such is the power and such the country against whose ambition the South American republics see themselves opposed."

Against this rising aggression the Latin-American republics, so Alvear believed, could summon no effective aid from abroad. Russia, Austria, and Prussia, as land powers, limited their influence to continental Europe. Only France or England might possibly oppose the United States, and even then the result would be in doubt. A large and growing population gave it a reserve of manpower. Its fleet might be small, but its privateers, using well-constructed ships and a superior class of sailors, "would fight with bitterness and success."[31] He found no balm in Gilead.

Latin-American nations, for their part, must sustain at all costs a "balance of power" in the New World. This political principle Alvear defined: no part of the independent nations of America may separate of its own will from the home country in order to incorporate itself into another state; no nation may interest itself in such matters without the consent and approval of its neighbors. He declared that in defense of this principle the Argentine Confederation had resisted the union of Peru and Bolivia under Santa Cruz. True, the Confederation had lost Bolivia and the Banda Oriental, but with the consent of the mother country. Excepting these two instances, the Spanish-American nations had kept their old Spanish boundaries inviolate until Texas seceded from Mexico and joined the North American Union.[32]

The longer Alvear lived in that great Union and meditated the course of international diplomacy, the more he wrote, not altogether as an Argentine, but as a representative-at-large and prophetic citizen of all Latin America. To him, he felt, had been revealed the course of things to come. He never doubted the victories which the United States would gain at the expense of the Latin-American nations. And because he imagined that he saw the road ahead so clearly, he became embittered at the fate reserved for his people. His feelings were hurt by slights to all the Hispanic nations. England and France, no less than the United States, offended, so that his dispatches were weighted with leaden prophecies. All the great powers, ignoring the new republics, would do as they wished: Latin America had no influence in their councils.

During his residence in the United States he saw the Pacific Ocean become a new theater of international competition with never a thought of the Latin-American interests involved. The English contemplated inauguration of a steamship service from Panama to New Holland and New Zealand by way of the Marquesas Islands. This line would join with another to India and the Red Sea. The promoters of this project hoped to establish the first round-the-world system of communication, which, with the new steam navigation, would provide unequaled regularity and speed. Alvear observed, "That which one looks upon as possible would not have passed ten years ago—perhaps five—as the dream of a delirious man." The new republics should observe cautiously, he warned, the course which the big nations give to the politics of either hemisphere. This interest should mount when the powers turn their attention to South America, for though they come with modest appearances, they cannot be disregarded, especially with South America strategically located for world trade.[33]

These schemes of world-wide transportation had quickly aroused the French. Their newspapers, emphasizing the potential importance of the Marquesas Islands, called for advancement of eastern commerce by a canal through the Isthmus. Alvear quoted the French press as saying, "When the Isthmus of Panama shall have been conquered by the commercial activity of Europe, once the indolence of the Spanish race has been overcome, there will be no doubt that all the commerce of Europe and of the archipelago of the Southern Sea will be taken in that direction." He saw clearly that once the French had established themselves in the far Pacific, construction of "what is called the Panama Canal" would be the logical development.

He reported, too, that the United States did not intend to be a laggard nation in the newest race. With the project of the canal in mind, Senator Buchanan from Pennsylvania presented to Congress a petition signed by Philadelphia businessmen, asking that the United States acquire possession of land between Chagres and Panama. The merchants wanted a line of packet ships regularly plying between Panama and the principal cities of the United States. Previously, the minister wrote, the Secretary of the Navy had taken steps to secure establishment of such a line.[34]

These great nations, in the conflict of ambitions, were not satisfied only to develop their existing possessions. None of them would hesitate to take possession of the areas they found most desirable. He declared that what they wanted was not only a new route to China, but also a monopoly of its advantages. France felt that she must seize the island of Tahiti if she expected to control crucial points in the great race for commerce in the Far East. The United States was establishing bases in Panama. "All of them," he moaned, "overlook the Spanish race"; yet he seemed to be hurt most by the attitude of the North American nation, for "thus one American republic once considered until now the protector of the others, converts itself quickly into the most terrible enemy, for all of its plans of expansion are based upon devouring the rest of Mexico when it is most convenient."[35]

By the Treaty of Guadelupe-Hidalgo the Mexican Republic possibly had bought a respite, but Spain had nothing to offer in place of Cuba. Therefore Alvear, finding no hope of succor, looked upon the seizure of that island as a foregone conclusion. England wanted the island also; but in addition to the clear opposition of the United States, she could count on the resistance of the Cubans themselves, who would then have to free their slaves. France had not the naval power to prevail over either nation. He presumed that if the United States took possession, Cuba would become a state, and its people would be received not as colonials, but as citizens. The Cubans would count themselves fortunate at the prospect of enjoying an immense and free market for their goods. Besides they could buy much more cheaply as citizens of the United States than they could as citizens of Spain.[36] Alvear outlined such potent advantages to annexation that he could not have opposed that act on account of injury to the Cubans. Nor did he suggest that such action would constitute a threat to his own country. He based his opposition solely on grounds of attachment to his race. And Spanish loss of empire he appeared to feel as keenly as that of a sister republic.

The Argentine minister considered the filibustering expeditions against Cuba as preludes to ultimate conquest. Repeated failure of these untimely groups only postponed Cuba's certain fate, yet he was happy at every delay in the American road to conquest. Nothing that the United States could do changed his opinion one whit. Presidential proclamations prohibiting the organization of hostile expeditions he regarded as evidences of hypocrisy. When he reported honest and effective disruption of the raiding parties, he bitterly observed that with a spirit of conquest rampant in a democracy the hand of torment could not long be restrained.[37]

After the failure of the first López expedition to Cuba, Alvear talked with the Spanish minister, Calderón de la Barca, about the episode. To his surprise, this minister expressed satisfaction at the conduct of the United States. The expedition had been frustrated; the individuals involved had been disarmed and dispersed. But Alvear remained unsatisfied. Instead of confiscating captured property, government authorities had returned to the original owners all their arms and ammunition as well as the ships they would have used as transports. Neither American citizens nor Cubans had been tried for violating neutrality and, as he had previously observed, punishment for offenders seemed out of the question, "for these laws protecting nations with whom the United States is at peace were passed when the nation was not yet dreaming of conquests and seizures, and when its political morality was preserved." As he feared, the malefactors suffered no real punishment.[38]

Departure of subsequent expeditions served only to intensify Alvear's conviction that these schemes enjoyed the favor of a majority of the people, especially in the Southern states. Prompt destruction of the second López expedition by the Spaniards pleased him and he eagerly waited to see how the United States would punish the returning stragglers as violators of its neutrality. He presumed that the men would be freed; he supposed that Spain, in righteous anger, would then break off diplomatic relations; he thought this act would call for war; and he predicted that Spanish privateers would destroy North American commerce.[39]

All predictions fell wide of the mark. Spanish release of the prisoners banished the possibility of the war he had so lately prophesied. Some said that Spain had demonstrated generosity; others that she had been politically sagacious in order to avoid offense. He explained the officially correct conduct of the United States on the basis of the honesty of the President and the talent of the Secretary of State, Daniel Webster. The Secretary, he reported, came from Massachusetts, the most civilized and industrious state in the Union, an area into which plans for conquest had not penetrated. In the following year when he reported other arrests and frustrations of would-be Cuban liberators, he grudgingly admitted, "The United States appears to be acting in good faith,"[40] yet threats of Southern zealots to make another raid aroused his former suspicions. He did not deny that separatist sentiment existed among Cubans, but he believed that the Spanish armies could control creole ambitions for independence. Fearing that Cuban independence would lead to annexation, he preferred to see it remain a Spanish possession.

Dismayed at the disastrous end of the second López expedition, sympathetic adherents held a mass meeting in New York City: a meeting to which Alvear gave disdainful attention. The speaker, Thomas N. Carr, once a consul at Tangier, flourished extravagant promises, as speakers on such occasions are wont to do, and these promises Alvear reported as typical of public feeling. Carr began by quoting false reports which indicated overwhelming success of the expedition in Cuba, and the spread of "liberating sentiments" to Mexico itself. He continued: "No power on earth can stop the Cuban revolution . . . and I predict, my compatriots, and stake my private and public reputation on it, that before a year is out all the land from Hudson Bay to Patagonia and adjacent islands will belong to the United States."[41]

Alvear recognized the wildness of such predictions, but instead of attributing it to misplaced enthusiasm, he saw in it a revelation of true expansionist sentiment. "He who expressed such thoughts was listened to with tremendous applause by a meeting of 10,000 people in the most civilized and commercial city in the country. . . . I must report that the more extravagant and ridiculous appear these opinions, the more they are nourished and are popular in the hearts of North Americans." Such was Manifest Destiny as he saw it: extravagant and ridiculous, cheered by the futile fury of a mob; a sentiment boding ill to Latin-American people. He challenged his government to awake to the danger, to unite with sister republics for safety against the encroachments of an overbearing race. His was a voice in the wilderness: his own countrymen languished under a dictator; the other republics spent themselves in factional disputes. None, it seemed, attended the Northern fury.

While Alvear saw all Latin America as the ultimate prey of the aggrandizing United States, he logically picked the Caribbean area as the next field of action. The fate of Texas was sealed; Mexico would never survive the next conflict. Exploratory bands of adventurers were feeling out Cuban resistance, while the southern section of the country was openly committed to its capture and annexation. Beyond those countries lay Central America, divided into small, heedless republics whose leaders possessed little education or statecraft. Their territory grew more important to the United States as its interest in the Pacific developed and the construction of a canal through an isthmus became an eventual certainty. These countries he marked for national extinction under the advancing Juggernaut of the North. Yet the opposition to this rolling mightiness could come, not from the menaced states themselves, but from another zealous exploiter, England, equally foreign, and equally heedless of Latin-American peoples. He desperately hoped that in the inevitable conflict of interests between the two great powers both sides would temporize before resorting to war, and that in the period of grace perhaps the victims would grow strong enough to fight for themselves, and wise enough to play the two powers against each other. While such a solution may have been possible, he did not entertain real hope of its success.[42]

Conditions in Central America received Alvear's attention as early as 1842, when he sent to Arana an account of a British blockade of El Salvador. This action aroused in Alvear no expression of resentment or distrust. He merely commented that it would be useful to the new republics to be conversant with everything which takes place in reference to European powers.[43] He wrote no more, so far as his existing letters reveal, on the problems of power in Central America until aroused by a crisis in 1849. At that time the United States was bent on securing control of the Isthmian canal routes, while

England also aspired to dominance. Alvear bore witness to the popularity of the issue:

> This question gets to be popular in this country and promises to bring strong discussions and debates between this country and England, a discussion that ought to be of great interest for all America, and very particularly for the republics which find themselves nearby.

He reported in December, 1849, that Honduras had ceded to the United States the island of El Tigre. This act seemed to confirm his previous statements that the great republic wished to rob the Spanish race of its strategic land areas. At the same time he saw little possibility of the Central American countries attempting to resist. Rather, they seemed to acquiesce in the plan. The states, divided among themselves, resisted centralizing control and enthusiastically continued their destructive civil wars. Painfully he concluded that the dangerous procedure of ceding possessions would lead to loss of independence.

The somewhat ungraceful efforts of England and the United States to outwit each other in the race for control of any Isthmian route had recently demonstrated the Nicaraguan officials as perfect puppets.[44] These gentlemen, agreeable to all persuasions, negotiated treaties for canal construction with both nations. Thus they avoided unpleasant refusals, and in the subsequent struggle of each side to preserve their especial rights the private interests of individual negotiators surely would not be forgotten.

When the Nicaraguan chargé, Señor Carcache, arrived in Washington in January, 1850, the Argentine minister promptly visited his fellow-Latin. This worthy gave such devious reasons for signing a treaty with the United States that he came away fortified in his poor opinion of Nicaraguan statesmanship. Alvear discovered that the aggressive American chargé to Central America had convinced the governments of Honduras, El Salvador, and Nicaragua that liberal grants to the United States would guarantee strong resistance to England. Señor Carcache ignored the General's suggestion of a possible war between England and the United States and of the retribution that, in the event of an English victory, would be visited upon the Central American governments. The Nicaraguan believed that the United States supplied England with essential foodstuffs without which she must starve. The American chargé had thought of every argument for Señor Carcache, and Alvear left the conference sadder, if no wiser.[45] He reported without special comment the agreement between the two great powers whereby both repudiated the brash actions of their representatives in securing rights-of-way. Presumably he found advance and retreat a part of the game which he had predicted. Through no virtue of their own the intended victims had won a respite.

The Clayton-Bulwer Treaty resulted in an official adoption of the type of action Alvear had predicted. Both countries formally ratified their intention of constructing a canal from the Atlantic to the Pacific Ocean, and both countries surrendered any pretensions to superior influence in Central America. As Alvear remarked, neither was moved by generosity toward Central America, but by a mutual desire to avoid hostilities.[46] He saw in the treaty no change of purpose by the United States, no weakening of resolve to dominate the Caribbean. That Democrats had waged a war for northern Mexico or that the Whigs had compromised with England was simply an historical accident. Mexico had shown herself a weak antagonist, England a strong one. He considered aggrandizement the more certain because the Compromise of 1850 had apparently ended domestic issues on the one divisive factor in national politics. He failed to realize that compromises at home and abroad indicated that councils of state were uncertain about the nation's progress.

When a situation parallel to the Nicaraguan affair developed in El Salvador in 1851, the General felt that he had already foreseen its causes and ultimate solution. With bitter humor he foretold the routine procedure that ensued. England first moved to protect her interests. The United States followed suit for fear that its preferential rights would be jeopardized. There would be conflicting newspaper reports: Rosas would have to wait until the issues had clarified before deciding where justice lay, "for the ease and ability with which periodicals of this country carry all sorts of notices and events that afterward turn out to be false have made me delay in communicating the matter. . . ." Public disorder would cease, Alvear predicted, when the two countries realized that only through mutual agreement could they undertake the great project of a canal.[47]

From whatever angle Alvear viewed the expansion of the United States, he resented its growth. A mob in New York yelling for the whole of Latin America within a year, or international agreements made by suave diplomats—all were moved by desires of national aggression. Because he hated this heartless advance, yet saw no way to prevent it, he grew increasingly resentful toward the American people. Among this people, whose national policies he found so repellent, he was forced to spin out his mature years, and among them he died. During his long residence he referred, time and again, to the changes in habits and thoughts he had witnessed in a quarter of a century, to new national leaders, to the spirit of a new day. The American scene as viewed by the first Argentine minister to the United States occasionally won his admiration—more often he warned his countrymen of the sweeping tide of public opinion.

6. The American Scene

General Alvear's report of the American scene represents contrary points of view: official relations of great cordiality, and private opinions of constant hostility. Even his private opinions are not free from contradiction. Alternately he condemned and admired, and favored his home office with his latest estimates. Probably Rosas disregarded the adulatory comments; certainly he paid no attention to criticism of the United States government or of its people. The United States had enough power and influence to cause abandonment or sharp modification of the blockade if it chose to exert its full weight. This fact Rosas clearly understood, and he never permitted national policy to reflect his minister's personal animosity.

Conflict between his opposing attitudes does not seem to have restrained Alvear from expressing contrary sentiments with equal vigor. When the United States saw fit to meet Argentine claims, then dispatches to Rosas swelled with assurances that the North American republic had at last shown some measure of understanding for a Latin-American nation: for example, the reluctance of the United States to recognize Paraguay without the approval of Argentina. When a special agent whom President Polk had commissioned to Asunción sent an imprudent letter to Rosas, the young man was promptly recalled, and Alvear was given official apologies that smoothed the Dictator's ruffled sensibilities. Cancellation of a United States Navy survey of the Paraná River after Rosas had prohibited all passage up the stream again illustrated consideration for Argentine nationalism.

But such consideration was not to last. With the French and English fleet based on Montevideo blockading Buenos Aires, and Rosas, in turn, declaring a counterblockade of Monvideo, American shipping found itself at odds with one side or the other. It would have required diplomatic finesse to avoid a rupture with either side; but subtlety the American naval officers lacked. When a small Montevidean boat, fleeing a Rosas pursuer, took refuge behind an American ship stationed in the estuary, the American captain protected the anti-Rosas craft and roughly ordered the Argentine ship away. Both officers reported their versions to their respective superiors, and in due time Alvear was presenting his case to Secretary of State Calhoun and to his successor, Buchanan.

In the meantime an American commodore had reached the estuary and after hearing of the unpleasant incident, had sent the offending American officer, Captain Voorhees, home for trial. The courtmartial of Captain Voorhees occasioned much publicity, and his conviction on five counts satisfied the Argentine minister that the United States government had tried to act impartially in the controversy.[1]

Since the Voorhees trial aroused a great deal of comment in naval circles, Alvear set himself to secure as much attention for his country as possible. Popular sympathy lay with the captain, and predictions had run that a naval courtmartial would never condemn actions done in the name of American interests. Besides composing reports of his own for various New York newspapers, the minister engaged a correspondent of the New York

Herald to send to his paper a daily account of the trial with a summary of the charges and the prosecution of the captain. He vainly sought a similar arrangement with the *National Intelligencer*, a popular Whig paper, which had given but brief reference to the affair, "without doubt," declared Alvear, "on account of the repugnance which they all have in this country to confess their errors."

The Washington *Daily Union*, the Democratic administration paper, would accept extensive reports of the Voorhees trial only after a gratuity of $170. Payment of this sum greatly reduced Alvear's propaganda funds. He consoled himself with invidious reflections upon the chicanery, intrigue, malice, and mercenary designs common to newspaper men,[2] but he counted the money well spent. Naval personnel and the diplomatic corps could read in the American press that Argentina on a point of national honor had secured satisfaction from the United States.

On the pretext that he did not understand the exact procedure which Secretary Buchanan would adopt in tendering regrets for the Voorhees affair, Alvear called upon him a second time. The Secretary assured him that the "satisfaction" would meet his every wish and that an official transcript of departmental records would follow as soon as possible.

The conversation shifted to the continued troubles in La Plata with the English and French fleets. Alvear declared that it was the duty of the United States to assist his country with all its moral strength, and that the critical situation developing between England and the United States over the Oregon territory furnished an additional reason for mutual assistance against the intervention. The possibility of an alliance between two New World republics intrigued his fancy. He promised that if the United States and England should come to war over Oregon, the United States would find Argentina a faithful ally. Glancing at a wall map nearby, he called attention to the favorable geographic position which his country occupied: it faced the South Atlantic not too far from the Cape of Good Hope and was ideally situated for privateers who could raid English commerce and then find protection in Argentine ports. These privateers would be able to destroy an immense amount of English traffic from India, China, and the Pacific.[3] Buchanan made no verbal reply, but nodded agreement. Nor did he take the Argentine offer of assistance seriously, for he made no memorandum of the interview. Each country could meet its conflict with England separately: Buchanan intended there should be no war with England if he could prevent it.[4]

This attempt to secure an agreement between Argentina and the United States on the basis of "general principles of American interest" scarcely conforms to Alvear's usual attitude toward the northern republic. In general, he disliked the American people because he believed that they considered all Latin Americans barbarians incapable of self-government and unable to raise themselves to the level of civilized nations. The newspaper campaign of 1845 he embraced as an opportunity to raise American opinion of Argentina. Resenting the "Black Legend" of Spanish cruelty and treachery which throve on the difference in religion, culture, and language, he took great pains in his propaganda activities to stress the fact that Argentina, largely populated by Europeans, was neither of Indian nor of Negro stock. Quite forgetful of his long acquaintance with Poinsett, he remarked that he had met no man who had traveled in South America. Even Congressmen and others in responsible positions knew nothing of its history, climate, or people.[5] For this low popular esteem the General thought that Mexico was largely responsible. Its government, he admitted, had been so weak and timid that Mexicans must have become a degenerate race, "and because [Mexico] is of Spanish origin, they think that we are all alike."[6]

Sometimes the disillusioned envoy thought that Americans were jealous of all Spanish-speaking people. He noted that California mining laws of 1850 permitted mining only to citizens or to Europeans who had declared their intentions of becoming naturalized. Defenders of the law had declared it their purpose to exclude the Latin peoples, and Alvear believed that more skilful Mexican, Chilean, and Peruvian miners could amass greater fortunes than Europeans or Americans. He urged his government to remember this discrimination when, in future negotiations, the United States should demand that its citizens be put on a footing of equality with those of the most-favored nation.[7]

The American people possessed a tremendous national pride which would permit them to stand second to none. They were quick to resent injuries. As individuals they were willing to make war on a country without regard to their own laws. In contrast, the proud General confessed that he maintained toward all citizens of the United States and especially toward diplomatic and naval agents what he called "a very moderate and circumspect manner." Even the Voorhees case, which had closed so triumphantly for Argentina, gave him small grounds for inner satisfaction. The conviction had stimulated outbursts of popular bitterness and aroused the vindictiveness of American sailors.

> I think that this example will not keep some other American captain from doing the same thing if he wished to do it or thought that he should. . . . If you will remember the acts committed by American diplomats and sailors in various parts of the world and in various nations, you will see that my reflections are based upon positive acts as well as the knowledge I have of this people.[8]

The major characteristics Alvear noticed about the American people were their pride in their country and confidence as individuals. In their pride they seemed to think that "to the strong everything is permitted." Their reckless bravery—Alvear's type of bravery—irritated him. They were inordinately confident of their ability to defeat any number of people under any circumstances. With no little satisfaction he commented upon the failure of the first López expedition to Cuba: "Many of the expedition declared that it would have succeeded if its members could have set foot on land. Such is the concept which these men have of their valor."[9]

Although Alvear frequently wrote in terms of alarm at American advances, he betrayed at times considerable admiration for those who win great prizes. He told of the race westward by caravans and by ships around the Horn to California, and of the rich discoveries there. Although he felt that this land had been ill-won from Mexico, he regarded the discoveries of immense treasure as the reward of "an active, laborious, illustrious race." These spectacular results showed the superiority of knowledge over ignorance—the great advantage of labor over indolence. Its former Mexican masters had left it so poor that the rest of the world had forgotten it, yet under its new government it would have a population of 4,000,000 whites within ten years.[10]

Knowledge, labor, boldness—these traits win fields of gold. Economic gain advertises its own importance, and Alvear often discussed the basis of American advancement. Yet the political machinery through which the bold Americans governed themselves he never really understood. Nor did he feel it important that he should. And Rosas never objected: there is no record that the Dictator felt any lack of information on the political organization of the United States. Occasionally Alvear referred to political parties and to public issues of the period. Never did he set forth a serious account of the political programs of his time. In some of his references to the machinery of American government he showed himself surprisingly ignorant. After eight years of residence, he still believed that Congress had the power to grant or refuse recognition of Paraguayan independence.[11] Between the political parties themselves he made no real distinctions. The Democrats and Whigs he sometimes designated *Conservadores* and *Liberales*. He had particular difficulty with the term "Whig." Sometimes he translated it for his government with the Spanish *pelucas* meaning "wigs"; on other occasions he called them "Washingtones." He identified the Democrats with the expansionist movement, but ultimately concluded that the process must be continued under the Whigs or else the Democrats would regain control. National expansion, he reasoned, would continue more slowly under the Whigs, and perhaps the delay might give the Latin-American republics time to halt the menace. Always he hoped for a Whig victory in the national elections.[12]

Alvear first saw a presidential inauguration on March 4, 1841, a celebration attended by the Diplomatic Corps, civil clubs, military organizations, and university groups. The orderliness of the spectators, the simplicity of the ceremony, and the unaffected manner of President Harrison deeply impressed him. The President, he noted, addressed the audience from a raised platform and wore only the ordinary frock coat of a countryman, and during the course of the day attended only two social functions and those for very brief intervals. With frank admiration he spoke of the "democratic magnificence of the event."[13]

The Argentine minister made no pretense of understanding the moving power behind the government. He seems to have regarded the political organization of the United States as a curious arrangement hit upon by accident and quite unintelligible to others. "The United States form an exceptional people among all the nations," was all that he could write after six years' observation. "There is too much government," he frequently heard people say, yet in moments of exasperation he felt that the reverse was true: no central government at all, but only a collection of individuals so guided by prudence and reason that they lived without either laws or leaders. "These people build without being directed and destroy in the same manner, so that in a national panic their borders are those of a torrent without a dyke." He marveled at a government lacking the centralizing personality of a chief or dictator; an administration devoid of the trappings of force, of martial proclamations, of a standing army, or of abundant policemen to enforce the decrees of the administration. As a result of the absence of organized forces Alvear found that every city in the United States lay at the mercy of a mob that could do irreparable evil before being dispersed.[14]

Alvear considered this tendency to group violence a dangerous portent of the future. The phenomenon of rolling mobs divorced from political revolution seemed inexplicable, and he duly reported this persistent American trait. He saw how the Irish Roman Catholics in Philadelphia were attacked by "Native Americans" on July 4, 1844, and for three days were subject to persecution because the small police force could not stop the riot.[15] He wrote in meticulous detail of an actor who became the precipitating agent of a great riot in New York City.

This unfortunate individual had abandoned his efforts to please his audience after being run from the theater with rotten eggs, but at the ill-advised solicitation of friends he tried a second performance. Again his detractors became violent; stones began to fly; the police fired first into the air, and then into the mob which numbered some five to seven thousand people. Twenty-one were killed and one hundred and twenty-seven wounded before the demonstration was over. The Argentine was amazed when no repercussions—except that of news interest—were heard in the rest of the country.[16] By 1851, when mobs destroyed the Spanish consulate in New Orleans, he had learned that such action represented no official attitude, and he brushed aside the incident as a regrettable American habit in a country where the constitution rests only on the good faith of the people.[17]

The people of the United States, he observed, laid greater stress on the general right of making laws than they did on the responsibility of the people to obey their statutes. Alvear had reason to condemn such lopsided thinking when he became the victim of a disastrous fire in New York caused by the explosion of gunpowder stored illegally in a near-by provision and wholesale house. The fire spread with incredible rapidity to paint and paper shops, and from one wooden structure to another. For almost a week it raged before burning itself out, leaving a whole section of the city devastated.[18] The minister was caught in the initial outburst but managed to reach the door. His sons, forced to jump to lower roofs and clamber over walls, barely escaped, and at 3:30 in the morning they stood in the streets watching their economies of seven years rolling skyward.[19] In his exasperation at the loss, Alvear laid the blame to "a country like this where there exists neither police nor government and every man does what seems best to him."

The liberty of every man to do exactly as he pleased Alvear called "the purest democracy," "a government by the masses," "control from below," and he did not like the results of such an administration. He had seen how Manifest Destiny, under the impact of mass desires, had shaped the statesmen of the period. When the revolutionary European movements of 1848 won popular favor in the United States, Alvear grew disdainful of national leaders who praised the revolutionary outburst. He heard Senator Cass, a potential candidate for the Presidency, win applause by making a motion in the Senate that the United States break relations with Austria as a sign of favor toward the Hungarian patriots.[20] Cass also wrote an approving letter to Garibaldi, and its publication in the New York *Herald* caused a popular outburst which disgusted the General. It seemed to him that men who aspired to political power would adopt any issue, regardless of its justice, which they thought would influence the voters.

The "masses," in Alvear's opinion, were frequently moved by meretricious or positively unmoral appeals, yet by the power of their votes they controlled the policy of a nation. He resented the popular sensation caused by the arrival of Garibaldi in 1850. All Argentines had good reason to be familiar with the Italian hero. Before beginning his fight for unification of Italy, he had been a colorful and effective filibuster against Rosas, and had roamed the Uruguayan plains pursuing adherents of the Argentine dictator. In the privacy of his diplomatic correspondence Alvear bitterly denounced Garibaldi as a pirate, and sneered at the "frantic joy" with which the Italian residents of the city received their hero. He lamented that a man who had carried on an unjust revolution against the Pope and who had brought down upon himself the condemnation of decent and moral men of the world should win applause of anarchists and demagogues.[21]

Italian revolutions which ran counter to Papal desires aroused in Alvear an intense hatred. His reckless and reforming zeal of 1812-1814 had vanished. The sinful escapades of Bolivian days were behind him, and the Church had become dear to the audacious soldier who once had flaunted its sacred tenets. There remained only the middle-aged diplomat reviling the crudeness of revolutions. He considered it ironical that His Holiness Pius IX should have started reforms which spread over Europe and that he, in turn, should be destroyed by the fire of his own kindling. "There is in all this an eloquent lesson, a proof that everywhere the cause of revolution rises up and destroys even those who raised it from the abyss; that everywhere anarchy is worse than despotism."[22]

At least the despot would keep order; "the masses" could not have their uncouth way. And a free democracy verged on anarchy when it reflected the popular will. He considered a democracy where "the majority govern" as a nation blown to any course by the shifting winds of mass opinion. This mass opinion he found formidable and difficult to control. Since each individual had particular interests he would see advanced, it followed that the majority on any one issue found many other matters competing for attention. Therefore, at any one time the government of the United States might be ready to engage in an infinity of projects. The administration would try to choose those issues which would satisfy the most people.[23] Logically, a government moved from below would make a series of spasmodic gestures toward varying policies, and in the end would accomplish nothing except public confusion.

Yet, as Alvear admitted, the United States in spite of its democratic institutions had shown good judgment and had devised a method of action admirably adapted to the creation of a great country. He pointed out that the federal system of autonomous states surmounted all the obstacles which differences of climate, of customs, and of necessities could impose.

> The inhabitants of Louisiana and Texas with their hot climates are completely distinct from snow-covered Massachusetts. The states of the South with slaves, the East without them and by their industry and civilization very superior to all the rest, as well as the half-savages of the West, are all governed locally by their laws adequate to their situation and necessity. . . . At the same time steam employed on the railroads and in ships has cut distances and overcome the difficulties this factor can exert.[24]

By virtue of the provision which their federal Constitution made for local differences, Alvear considered that the American Union was based upon the greatest interests of the majority. By means of discussion and pacific measures the voters sought decisions on political matters. He noted how this tradition had developed a great respect for the opinion of the majority, once it had been pronounced in established, legal methods. Because he found such political principles basic to the existence of the United States, he did not, like some of his contemporary critics, believe that the great expanse of territory or increase of population would automatically cause the Union to break into smaller units. Use of steam in railroads and in ships was largely overcoming the separatist feelings which great distance normally encouraged. Local government through state organization would minimize the chances of political cleavage. Perhaps, he agreed, Oregon or California might at some future date break away, but he saw no prospects of such action within the recognizable future. Rather, he predicted growth so amazing that by 1871 the nation would reach a population of 40,000,000.[25] Not a bad estimate—the census figures for 1870 gave a total of slightly more than 38,500,000. Alvear's figures for 1850 showed the United States with slightly more than 23,000,000.

Thus, with full confidence in his judgment, he prophesied that the next twenty-one years would see the nation grow ever stronger and stronger. Popular agitation over the Compromise of 1850 he brushed aside as routine debate. The question of slavery might under certain conditions have been a precursor of separation, he admitted, but this question would lose its seriousness for those who knew the country well. From the press notices some foreigners might conclude that the Union was on the point of breaking up, but one—such as himself—more familiar with the background of the country did not see the least danger. Once Congress had reached a decision, there could be no question of its acceptance by the country. The Union, doubly fortified by majority agreement, would continue its march with greatness and prosperity toward its early destiny: the greatest and strongest nation in the world.[26]

The attitude of Alvear toward the American people is to be contrasted with that of Domingo Faustino Sarmiento, an Argentine exile who fled to Chile while waiting the downfall of Rosas and there won distinction as an educator. He won so much distinction, indeed, that in order to evade Argentine wrath the Chilean authorities sent him abroad in 1846-1847 on an extensive international tour of educational institutions. While on this junket Sarmiento traveled widely in the United States. By contrast, Alvear lived for a time in Washington, then for the rest of his life in New York City. Once he retired to Boston to escape an outburst of yellow fever, but he soon returned. He moved little, saw little. He subscribed to newspapers of the Atlantic seaboard in order to report only political debates—fulsome, torrid harangues without perspective and true only after making allowances for party fervor.

Alvear made no allowances; but Sarmiento knew better. He traveled over the greater part of the country by train, river-boat, and carriage. He became familiar with many cities: with New York, of course, but with Boston and Providence too, and with the New England villages in between. Albany, Buffalo, and the Erie Canal; Pittsburgh with a future prosperity beyond compare; St. Louis and down the Mississippi to New Orleans, the city with a hotel whose cupola reminded him of St. Peter's! The hotel for the teeming travelers or the American home with its excellent iron stove in the kitchen—all gave evidence of a national genius for adapting itself to its environment.

This adaptive capacity gave to the United States a superiority which enabled it to overcome all other nations. And Manifest Destiny had nothing to do with it.

> I do not propose to make Providence an accomplice in all usurpation, nor in its bad example which, in more or less remote periods, may attract to it politically, or annex to it, as the Americans say, Canada, Mexico, etc. Then the union of free men will begin at the North Pole and for lack of territory, end at the Isthmus of Panama.[27]

Alvear found the secret of national advancement in wicked machinations and unjust usurpations. Sarmiento took a different view: the recent victory over Mexico showed the result of natural superiority—superiority in education, in work, and in use of natural resources. Americans dared to travel, to use new products, to test the latest invention. They had coal without stint for the railroads which were continuously probing the wilderness and no lack of food for the streaming immigrants from Europe. Although he and Alvear both predicted a tremendous growth for the United States, Sarmiento saw nothing malevolent about it.

However, the Argentine-Chilean educator was not blind to national defects, or, as he called them, "its bad examples." Incivility and rudeness he perceived as clearly as Mrs. Trollope, but he saw deeper: "Europeans make fun of this rudeness, more apparent than real, and Yankees out of stubbornness persist in it and try to put it under the aegis of liberty and the American spirit." Americans felt themselves of one class. In their own estimation, all men were gentlemen. While a great many gave a lie to the word, there was a leavening of worthy conduct through the whole society in a way Sarmiento had never seen elsewhere. Alvear condemned the national arrogance; Sarmiento tempered his judgment: "Their defects, therefore, must be those of the human race at any given period of its development."

American government exhibited these defects clearly enough. Frequently riots got out of hand; yet they were not to be taken too seriously, he learned. The rioters themselves, having homes, property, and families did not intend to upset the whole of society. Even if it became necessary to call out the militia, the disturbance would subside completely; at the state capital the legislature could meet in peace and its measures would be obeyed. He found nothing suave about this American democracy but called it a blunt and crude instrument for enforcing popular rule. "Yet," he observed, "it is effective; it is solid in its structure, and its basis is strong."

This strength Alvear tended to interpret in terms of armed might which would become the instrument of violent usurpations. He considered the military forces of the United States formidable. The General particularly admired the academy at West Point, but he praised the training of officers for all branches of the service. In proving the excellence of the Navy, he reminded his superiors of the remarkable showing it had made in the last war against England. Already the republic was provided with sufficient military might to carry out ambitious projects and to give the country great security. Its national armories he considered models of efficiency and adequate for war.

Ambitious projects—security of the country—national armories adequate for war—here the General spoke as an authority. And his government had no reason to question the might of the republic whose support it had often needed so badly. Because he considered the personal independence, initiative, and industry of the Americans quite malevolent, his recognition of vigorous traits is generally coupled with doleful predictions on the use of these abilities to the hurt of Latin America. So frequent are these disparaging comments that they might easily appear to reflect his most private opinion about the American people. But in the last months of his life he left his son, Emilio, a long political testament in which he referred to the United States in terms even of admiration.

The exiled General saw his end approaching. He wanted a last word which would be heard only after his death. Neither Rosas nor the new leader, Urquiza, could deny him that. He may really have felt that he had acquired special wisdom which he should share with his countrymen. He reasoned that long residence abroad had brought a better perspective on domestic issues; the advent of death itself would free him from charges of personal aggrandizement. But not even the presence of death could overcome the love of approval. Self-righteously he wrote of foolish ambition, of the unfailing "justice of History"—the justice for which—so many years ago—he had not possessed the patience to wait. While asserting the dying father's privilege to speak without reserve to his son, yet he remembered the scene of his triumphs, and asked the young man to publish the testament in order that his countrymen might learn his inner convictions.[28]

Abjuring the usual expressions of hatred or alarm, he now professed that residence of fourteen years in the bosom of the American people had shown them to be the only truly free and democratic republic in the world. He now accepted the United States as the standard by which his own country and all Latin America should be judged.

By comparison with the United States Alvear discovered that his countrymen had failed to set up institutions providing for genuine freedom and self-government. He had known few

Argentines who realized that political independence alone would not greatly improve their condition. Like all civilized cultures, free institutions must provide channels for human betterment. But in Argentina their vaunted independence had brought only submission to the will of a ferocious man who took power into his own hand. "Of all people," he wrote, "the Spanish race has shown itself the most incapable of self-government," and of all the former Spanish colonies he thought that Argentina had shown the least capacity. The other large Spanish-American nations had lived for long periods under established constitutions. Although they had suffered revolts and revolutions, they had always returned to a constitutional regime, while the Argentine Confederation in its forty-two years of independence had not succeeded in putting into effect a single constitution.

Without a constitution Argentine unity could never achieve full expression. Stunted national pride had permitted Bolivia, Paraguay, and Uruguay to secede. The United States, on the other hand, had handled matters differently: by 1852 the thirteen states had grown to thirty-one.

> Among us there is a tendency to divide and form independent nations, and among these people, on the contrary, is the tendency to grow and increase daily in strength. Excepting Rhode Island and Delaware, each of the North American states has greater population, wealth, commerce, and industry than those which had separated from the Argentine Confederation. If the United States had held to the necessity of dividing themselves into nations, would they be where they are? NO! Are the Americans the people who do not know what they have done and do not recognize their best interests, or are we the wise ones?

As proof of the lack of national feeling in his countrymen, Alvear mentioned their failure to celebrate national triumphs. None of the victories of the revolution—Tucumán, Maipú, or Ituzaingó—was recognized by holidays or other festivities. He blamed the ignorant ambition and envy of dictators only in part. The fault lay, rather, in the apathy of the masses, who could have made a dictator heed their desires. No laws prevented citizens from preparing commemorative celebrations of past victories. Argentines never organized themselves to do honor to fellow-citizens who were distinguished by their eloquence, by their wisdom, or by their services.

Again Alvear contrasted this sorry situation with the practice in the United States where groups regularly gave a testimonial dinner, a sword, or a cup to their esteemed citizens. Generals, returning from Mexico, were received in triumph in whatever towns they stopped, he had noted, although many communities had opposed the Mexican War. Local authorities rendered these tokens not only to generals, but to subordinate officers, and even to civil officials of their city and state. The minister cited particularly the acclaim given to men high in civil life, the awards made to Clay, Benton, Calhoun, John Q. Adams, and, as he said, "to thousands of others" in literature, science, and other professions. Furthermore, Americans had not hesitated to honor spontaneously the liberal leaders of other nations. They had given to Lafayette, hero of two revolutions, a national welcome in 1824. They had done scarcely less for Kossuth, the Hungarian leader, and for General Páez, champion of Venezuelan independence. All these demonstrations honoring merit and high service Alvear considered

> a testimony to the moral qualities and high intelligence of North Americans, who recognize that in a democratic government it is more necessary than in any other to esteem good actions and to present to the masses the models for which they should strive. By this means they block the ambitions of the worthless or evil persons who aspire to power.

The father anticipated a protest which his son, or other reader, might make: namely, that Argentina had not produced men of as superior qualities as had the northern republic. In reply he entered an emphatic denial. His country had produced men distinguished in many fields. Even the famous North Americans who earned popular acclaim had been guilty of a thousand faults common to all humanity, and some possessed real vices. But the citizens of the United States were sufficiently intelligent to realize that no man is perfect. They felt it sufficient to be superior in one field in order to merit popular acclaim. Only ignorant countries thought that their heroes should be perfect in all things; yet the ignorant had no standard of "perfection." As a result of this faulty judgment no man in Argentina had been able to gain a national reputation by sticking to the good road. Instead, men of no service to their country, those of the most unworthy intentions, had enjoyed the most popularity and had received the greatest demonstrations.[29]

As he reflected on the history of his country he presented a terrible indictment. Ignorance and apathy in the higher classes and brutish tendencies among the lower groups had been responsible for misfortune. No leader had known how to use republican principles to save the people from great calamities. The United States, by grace of better leadership and by use of sound democratic practices, had enjoyed a far happier and more prosperous history.

The last message of Alvear to his son expresses genuine admiration for the country in which he lived for so long while his native land lay silent under the iron rule of a red-shirted dictator. None of the Argentine leaders was more acquiescent under this harsh rule than Alvear. As a citizen he made no recorded gesture against it. He accepted employment under it, and as a representative abroad, he served its interests without stint for thirteen years. His lengthy service, his profound silence call for explanation. As we seek an answer to this problem, we must bear in mind General Alvear's birthright of great wealth which he lost in the revolution. And then the paradox: his generalship was marked by two clear victories, but robbed of public benefit by political machinations; his promising political career was promptly frustrated by rebellious military chieftains. Taken together these experiences shaped the man whose loyalty to Rosas has left for his countrymen a recurrent question.

7. At the Service of a Dictator

For fourteen years, from 1838 to 1852, Carlos de Alvear represented the Rosas regime in the United States, but before he had been in the country six months he was asking for another assignment. When he discovered the unwillingness of the government at Washington to negotiate on the Falkland Islands problem, he promptly suggested that his mission be abandoned. He complained of the climate, of the cost of living, of his poor health. He had received no salary since his arrival and his funds were running low. Alone, in a strange country, he feared the embarrassment of debt and in addition he protested that the small salary of his post at Washington made it difficult to provide for the large family God had given him. While flattering Rosas, he pled for a transfer to London or to any place besides the United States, a country cursed with hot summers and bitterly cold winters.

But he expressed no desire to return home. It would have been painful for him, considering the state of his fortune, to face his creditors there. After stressing his new ties of gratitude to Rosas (perhaps for rescuing him financially) he sought a new position, but in vain.[1] Arana acknowledged receipt of the request, but year followed year without change of duty. Rosas had few foreign stations at his disposal, and when they were made vacant by death he ignored his Washington representative.[2] The Dictator did not neglect the request on account of dissatisfaction: he occasionally praised his envoy and publicly commended him for his service to the country. And Alvear was careful to please his master by courtly flattery, a practice which he continued with increasing frequency in later years.

Alvear experienced, at certain periods, great difficulty in collecting his salary. In part this irregularity was the fault of the uncertain system of international exchange,[3] but also it was due in part to Rosas' inability or unwillingness to complete payments on time. The blockade interrupted the dispatch of funds, and for over a year after Alvear's arrival in the United States he received no salary. His plight was extremely hard to bear and his appeal for relief very strident. He asked in vain for a raise in salary. He complained that the Congress of Buenos Aires had set a higher scale for European than for New World legations. The Washington post, he declared, should be excepted from this general rule. The United States was as alien as any country in Europe and the most expensive in the world: a nation which charged high prices for necessities and to these necessities added luxuries in keeping with its immense prosperity. In great despair he cited his own modest layout: fifty pesos per month [the gold peso was then equivalent in value to the dollar] for a small furnished room for himself and his son, Emilio, fifteen more for heat, and five for light. Board cost him forty-four pesos, and to this account he added a charge of five hundred pesos annual salary for the secretary.[4]

To his living expenses Alvear added the comparatively costly item of postage. Twenty-eight dispatches to Buenos Aires had cost him ninety-nine gold pesos, besides the cost of forwarding his mail from New York to Washington—a total of one hundred and twenty-two pesos. These expenses he had paid in advance, and the long delay before remuneration could be made to him caused much inconvenience. Repeated requests for a prepaid allowance for postage and his lengthy explanations of the postal regulations in the United States show that the matter was never settled to his satisfaction. His later requests grew more complaisant: he would remind Arana that he spoke of no rights of his own, but considered the problem from the point of view of the Confederation and the proprieties of diplomatic usage. Without funds, he reminded Rosas, he could not influence the press to publish articles of national interest. As in Europe, nothing could be done without money. No person offered free publicity, and the influence of the press in constitutional countries was well known. Correspondence on the sums due him from his appointment in 1838 continued until August, 1843. At that time Arana ordered full payment.

Hectic and irregular as were financial arrangements under the Rosas administration, Alvear had no choice but to remain on good terms with the man whom he had once opposed. He soon acquired the art of fawning, courtier fashion, of composing long and fulsome praises of the Dictator. In part these discourses may be discounted as a necessary excess of verbiage demanded by a vain leader. But beyond this apology the frequent and laudatory panegyrics force one to conclude that Alvear had abandoned whatever opposition he had once entertained for Rosas.[5]

Praise of Rosas carried abuse of the Unitarians as its concomitant. In this denunciation Alvear showed himself proficient. When the first English-French intervention came to a close in 1841, he hailed the triumph of justice and order and condemned the Unitarians as a blind faction which, ignorant of lessons of the past, sought the ruin of their country while ignoring Rosas' generosity to his opponents. Alvear made his position crystal clear. He congratulated the Dictator on the splendid victories "against the anarchical, savage Unitarians commanded by the assassin, Lavalle, and the fool [*zopenco*], Lamadrid." He voiced hopes for the perpetual disappearance of the Unitarian band, cause of so many troubles and disasters, and congratulated Arana on his privilege of being an assistant permitted to labor so close to General Rosas in his illustrious and glorious tasks.[6]

Alvear's eager acceptance of the assignment to secure for Rosas favorable press comments in the United States was accompanied by another essay of unrestrained flattery:

> I shall employ myself with greatest zeal in fulfilling the order, not only as an individual in the employ of the government, but also by the sympathy of recognition and gratitude that, as an Argentine citizen, I profess to an administration whose worthy chief has known how to elevate the credit and splendor of our country to a height hitherto unknown.[7]

The press releases which Alvear published in the United States were usually somewhat objective and detached, but occasionally lapsed into an encomium which must have sounded extravagant to American ears:

> Rosas is the most remarkable man on the continent. . . . For Rosas there is no rest or recreation—he devotes even hours of rest and refreshment to public service. The country has improved under his guidance so much better than when under the mad Unitarians.[8]

Rosas' anger was easily aroused and his praise hard to win. He would order the strongest condemnation for a salutation which displeased him, for failure to acknowledge receipt of newspaper packets, or for terse summaries of received correspondence. But in matters of greater import the Dictator was satisfied. His Secretary of Foreign Affairs occasionally sent word of approval for Alvear's handling of diplomatic questions: for the Voorhees affair or for his activities in behalf of the Confederation in the second intervention. The Dictator gave evidence of being pleased with the service of the erstwhile Unitarian: he considered him both zealous and faithful.[9]

When Alvear, an appeased and perhaps repentant Unitarian, came to the United States in 1838, he left his former partisans badly disorganized. All their schemes had failed. Alvear himself had led the first, secret machination against the Federalists: an ambitious scheme the authors referred to as "the Big Job." As ringleader in Buenos Aires, he directed the gathering Unitarians in Montevideo, and he had reached an agreement with the Bolivian dictator, Santa Cruz. This ambitious rival promised to invade the Argentine northern border on some pretext, and, when joined by Unitarians infiltrating from Uruguay, he would lead the united forces to victory over Rosas.

In some unexplained way Rosas learned of the Big Job and seized all the leaders save Alvear. Thereafter the surviving Unitarians were never sure whether Alvear's immunity was due to genuine luck or was the result of a double-cross.[10] While they could prove nothing, they would not trust him again. They found a bitter explanation for his continued good fortune: he was of no further use to Rosas once the Unitarians had dropped him, but in return for his former services the Dictator could not cast him aside. So accomplished a conspirator as Alvear was dangerous, and so Rosas sent him out of the country on a tour of duty.

Still the anti-Federalist plots continued. Within a short time leaders of Unitarian bands reorganized with secret names, simple codes, and mystic passwords. Again Rosas got wind of the intrigue and eliminated the leaders.[11] However, there is no indication that after Alvear left Buenos Aires for the last time that he was ever associated with these plots; certainly his name is not found in all the extensive correspondence which Señor Gregario F. Rodríguez collected during his patient study of this period. The General seems to have divorced himself from his former associates: they seem to have regarded his acceptance of a high position in the Rosas administration as tacit acknowledgment that he had abandoned them.

Besides this negative testimony of Alvear's loyalty to Rosas, we have the positive evidence of his former colleagues. From Valparaiso, Chile, in April, 1846, José Bautista Alberdi (then in exile) wrote to his former compatriot in Washington. Don Manuel Carvallo, whom the Chilean government was sending to the United States, brought the letter. Alberdi introduced the bearer, who, he declared, would bring details "which you will be pleased to hear." The group in Chile contained many of Alvear's good friends of whom Carvallo could give news "for he is a friend of us here." Writing as if the Washington envoy were one of them, Alberdi thought that the happy day would not be remote when their common friends dispersed over the whole world would have the pleasure of embracing Alvear once more in their homeland. Alberdi expressed regret that he had not heard from his friend of earlier days. Only from occasional press notices and travelers from Buenos Aires did he learn of Alvear or his family. This letter bears strong testimony of Alvear's separation from his former party, and plainly Alberdi was hoping to discover whether the exiles could count him one of their number.[12]

Carvallo brought still another letter from an old revolutionary in Chile, General D. Z. Benavente, who was gaining a livelihood as a schoolmaster.[13] Carvallo and his wife were accompanied by three young students whom the former general commended to the care of the General in Washington. Benavente wrote in terms of strongest friendship to his dear friend, from whom he had not heard in so many years. Witnessing to the efficiency of Rosas' detective system, Benavente declared that each day relations with Buenos Aires became more tenuous; more and more rarely did word of events in that city slip through. For two years Benavente had been isolated in unbelievable fashion in a country adjacent to Alvear's. All the old companions of the War for Independence were scattered. "When we meet, how many things we will have to say! What sad memories will draw our tears! At least if we may not see each other we can write, you arousing yourself from the lethargy that has come with age."[14] Both letters from Chile make it clear that Alvear had long since separated himself from the anti-Rosas party, and these communications sought to enlist his support once more. The young and impetuous conqueror of Montevideo had slipped in the scale when he had to be aroused from the lethargy of age. He had made an end to revolution.

While former associates in Chile were seeking the favor of their departed leader, active opponents of Rosas in Corrientes and in Montevideo were making bids for Alvear's assistance. Joaquin Madariaga, Governor of Corrientes, urged him to accept leadership of a new revolt against Rosas. The Governor declared that he and his brother had planned a campaign which could gain a final victory within thirty-six days if led by a man of talent. He felt sure that if Alvear had been leading the calvary in the earlier campaigns they would not have suffered cruel defeat. As an old companion of the war against Spain he pledged the support of forces from Corrientes where memory of Alvear was still vivid. "Knowing the noble thoughts and elevated ideas which you possess, I invite you with all that I have and value to accept the leadership of our revolution and free the country from the evils it suffers."[15]

José María Pirán of Montevideo seconded Madariaga's invitation. In greater detail he explained the difficulties which beset them because of inept leadership under General Paz. So completely had General Urquiza outmaneuvered him that his army of thirteen thousand (not counting Paraguayans) either had deserted to the able general or had disbanded. The rioting and looting which the soldiers had committed while retreating to Paraguay gave the Unitarian cause a bad name. Again the fond hopes of the patriots had become a barroom joke. Don Joaquin, in the bitterness of failure, had wished for Alvear! With his help the Republic would have been freed. The revolutionary leaders joined in sending a call for him to make a glorious sacrifice and to lead them to early victory.[16]

An older and wiser Alvear resisted this call to "glorious sacrifice." In his earlier days he would have responded with alacrity, but he now preferred the bare comforts and the barren honors of diplomatic security to the hazards of campaigning against the undeniably capable Urquiza. In all Alvear's papers there is no record of a reply to these entreaties. Pirán, like the Chileans, speaks of old friendship, of long separation, and of the joys of returning his *abrazo*. All of these letters show that Alvear had taken no part in revolt against Rosas. His support was desired, and his neglect of the offers indicates that he had abandoned his opposition to the Dictator.

Until the end of Rosas' Federalist regime, Alvear's correspondence continues flecked with praises of Rosas and of his government.[17] The Dictator, after sixteen years, had exhausted the country. The city grew destitute, and his counterblockade of La Plata had paralyzed river traffic. Over the whole republic business came to a standstill. Public services ceased; private credit vanished. In his determination to unite the nation against the European intervention Rosas brooked no opponents in the other states of the Confederation: his control was more centralized than any the Unitarians ever achieved. Eventually, some of the governors of the other provinces objected to his domination, and Urquiza of Entre Ríos led the dissidents. Exiled Unitarians enlisted in his cause; disgruntled Federalists supported the revolution. A quick descent from the north, one battle at Monte Caseros: Rosas fled to a British warship and into exile.

As the revolt gathered headway, Alvear hastened to disavow any connection with the movement. He was sorry to see an Argentine who had been honored with the governorship of a province commit such black, perfidious treason and show base ingratitude toward the Illustrious Chief of the Argentine Confederation. Breathing assurance that Rosas would emerge triumphant, he trusted that God would reward the virtuous and curse the evil ones whom he also labeled "enemies of order, traitors, and perfidious ingrates."[18]

From this mounting evidence we would have no reason for questioning Alvear's ultimate loyalty to Rosas if one of the great leaders against Rosas had not declared otherwise. Two years after Alvear's death his remains were transferred to Buenos Aires and there laid to rest amid tributes to his memory from the country's leading citizens. Alsina, in his oration praising the deceased hero whose bier rested before the emotional throng, declared that Rosas had hated Alvear's presence; he had feared his soldierly past, and for that reason had condemned him to an honorary exile. Alsina gave to Alvear the major credit for accomplishing the eventual fall of the Dictator. To prove this astounding statement he gave details of early plotting against Rosas. The orator recollected that on the night of April 10, 1835, prior to Rosas' second inaugural, he and Alvear discussed the fate of their nation. The General freely predicted the public turmoil, dictatorship, and sorrow yet to come. As their conversation lengthened into the morning hours they planned to overthrow the rising order. They agreed that Alsina should emigrate to Montevideo (as he did), where he could work openly and that Alvear was to inaugurate secretly a vast, ingenious plan. This plan, said Alsina, was accompanied by great danger. It was often delayed, sometimes wrecked, but was continued with admirable perseverance until an indiscretion revealed the plot. When Rosas got wind of the proceedings, he sent the dangerous General into exile. He dared not kill him.

Alsina declared that while in Montevideo he had received secret correspondence from Alvear through private agents. For three years he followed the risks the brave General took as he kept his council and laughed off his danger. His departure into exile in 1838 upset their calculations and destroyed their organization. But at long last the hateful dictator was overthrown. Their final success was accomplished according to the broad outline the two men had planned that April night before the blight of dictatorship had first settled upon the city. Modestly effacing himself, Alsina flatly asserted that Alvear was the first man to work actively and risk everything to bring about the overthrow of the cruel, hateful regime.[19]

Thus the tribute stands and none can flatly deny the word. These things may have happened exactly as Alsina stated. The private conference may have taken place; the secret correspondence over the three-year period before Alvear's departure to the United States may have been destroyed upon receipt. Perhaps Alsina never wrote to his friend in Washington; certainly no record remains in Alvear's files. Even the stimulus to pay honor to a revolutionary hero may not have loosed his tongue. Alsina may not have realized that great honor to Alvear would inevitably reflect credit on his surviving collaborators. But today there exists no documentary evidence to prove any part of Alsina's contention. Although he collected many codes and secret messages from others, Señor Rodríguez found no anti-Rosas correspondence from Alvear's pen. None of these letters mentioned Carlos de Alvear. Many plotters against Rosas were alive in 1854, when Alsina made his astounding claim. They neither affirmed nor denied what he said. If the deceased Alvear had been in truth their mentor and chief, they would not have been silent when all were doing him honor. Their silence indicates that Alsina's revelation was news to them; unwilling to challenge a tribute to the dead, they said nothing.

If Alvear was other than a latecomer to the ranks of Rosas' flatterers, those who believe it must prove their contention. Alsina's unsupported word has run from pen to pen. It has gathered authority by repetition: it has become a part of the folklore of Argentine history. On the contrary, evidence of Alvear's loyalty to Rosas abounds. The fire of 1845 may have destroyed correspondence with Alsina as well as other proof of the General's hidden hatred of Rosas. Documents showing his zeal for the regime survived it.

Alvear's written record gives no clue to his inner convictions —if he entertained any after fourteen years abroad. One may say that Rosas demanded of his subordinates the extravagant praise with which Alvear clogged his dispatches. Yet he praised Urquiza just as elaborately when that General won leadership of the Confederation. Sugared words for victorious Urquiza meant as little as the assurances, even then in transit, which had pledged loyalty to the old regime. Such testimonials (*adhesiones*) are commonly expected from government employees of Latin-American countries when a revolutionary change of administration is impending or has recently occurred.

In part the General doubtless desired to stand on the side of the administration in power; in part he may have come to accept Rosas as the best leader for his people. To this day Alvear's own countrymen have not been able to judge the relative sincerity of his protestations to Rosas or to Urquiza. The truth is that Alvear could and did write with two minds on many issues. He could hate the loser and love the winner, and was prepared to serve any man with whom he could find profitable employment.

After sending his protestations of loyalty to Rosas, the envoy to Washington discreetly awaited the outcome of the inevitable battle between Rosas and the rising Urquiza. But the soldierly enthusiasm of the Dictator, which Arana eloquently described to Alvear, had no existence in fact,[20] and after a brief engagement at Monte Caseros which was marked by large desertions to the enemy, Rosas departed into a long exile like that which he had forced on so many others.

Alvear heard news of Rosas' defeat from returning merchantmen and presently he received official notice from Luís José de la Peña, whom Urquiza had appointed as temporary Secretary of Foreign Affairs to succeed Arana. At the same time Peña gave Alvear his official notice of recall. He said that if the minister wished to stay in the United States, he could do so; but he must notify the Ministry to suspend his salary. Otherwise, the government would expect him to take the next packetboat for Buenos Aires. Peña explained that the provisional government had no authority to represent other provinces; therefore, representatives abroad had no function since they could not deal with any subject presented to them. He enclosed for the President of the United States an official letter which would explain the reason for the end of the mission.[21]

The most interesting part of this communication is the assumption that Alvear, in all probability, would not care to return home. In fact, he was in no hurry to depart. He answered that he might be delayed for some time pending the departure of a safe and reliable ship. There was no direct passenger service to Buenos Aires in those days: vessels departed at the wishes of the shippers, and many had no accommodations for passengers. In the meantime he kept in his possession the official notice of his recall addressed to the President.[22]

While this exchange was taking place, the provinces of the Confederation had reached an agreement at San Nicolás del

Arroyo. By these terms they granted to the governor of Corrientes, General Urquiza, control of their foreign affairs. The new administration reappointed Alvear and his son to their former positions. This gesture was proclaimed as a mark of confidence in them and satisfaction with the patriotic and dignified course which had always characterized their conduct.[23]

In the meantime Alvear had been engaged in the embarrassing task of changing loyalties without too apparent haste. Within three days after official report of Urquiza's victory reached him, he promised the new leaders that he would inform the United States of the liberal policies about to be inaugurated. With courtly ease he expressed his joy at the restoration of security and liberty—the ideal for which the War of Independence had been waged. This graceful adhesion was only the beginning of his tribute. In the middle of July he sent to the new leader a more extended acknowledgment:

> As a man who has served the grand cause of American independence and as an Argentine citizen I cannot do less than send to you the most sincere thanks for the noble resolution you took and knew how to carry into effect for bringing our country back into the road which it should never have left. . . .
>
> Señor General, you have the immense glory of having placed our beloved country in the true path of its laws and institutions, . . . making it in this way acceptable to all our citizens.

He protested that Urquiza's services were too great for any person to show black ingratitude or disgraceful envy. As an experienced commander of troops in the field, Alvear declared himself qualified to praise the masterly handling of men, as, with zeal and speed, the army made safe progress southward to victory over Rosas. He praised the new leader for foregoing retribution on his political enemies. By this means he had shown a notable example of good character and had vindicated the Spanish race from the charge of being cruel and insatiable in revenge.

The envoy justified his expressions of tribute by referring to the practices of the people of the United States, who freely and promptly recognized men worthy of public esteem. "Thus,

General, on giving you my recognition and accepting the justice of your merit . . . I fulfil the sacred duty as an Argentine and as an individual I have ever been prompt to give to any citizen who by his talents or patriotism has known how to make himself notable among us."[24]

With his firm tribute duly inscribed, Alvear next considered his relationship to the new administration. His reappointment to the United States had not yet reached him, and he faced the unpleasant prospect of an early return home. He reminded Urquiza of his promise to his wife, Señora Quintanilla de Alvear, that he could consider himself "a friend of her heart." Taking advantage of this friendly declaration, Alvear ventured to ask for another diplomatic appointment. He wanted a change. The United States, while one of the greatest nations of the world, endured one of the worst climates. The winters he found long and horribly cold—worse than Poland: the summers were hotter than those of Río de Janeiro! In any season the temperature might vary from twenty to thirty degrees in one day. At his advanced age and with the pulmonary troubles which the odious climate had given him, he must leave soon or die. He would count it proof of friendship if Urquiza could assign him to another station blessed with moderate temperatures. England had a bad climate, even for a healthy man; France would be much better, and so he asked to be sent there.[25] He seems not to have considered the temperate climate in Buenos Aires. If he had been the exile from Rosas that some of his contemporaries supposed, he would have embraced the first opportunity to return after his long absence from home and family. On the contrary, both Urquiza and Alvear understood that he would not care to return to Buenos Aires.

Perhaps it was only a matter of common prudence. An old friend, Tomás Guido, suspected the public calm after the departure of Rosas. He acknowledged that within the short space of four months incredible changes had taken place. The revolution had been almost bloodless! Yet, he warned, the end was not in sight; a Constituent Congress must determine the place of Urquiza in the government and set up a stable administration. The city of Buenos Aires was growing restive. As one cautious man to another he advised the absent envoy to stay out of the country: in the existing circumstances experienced council and cold reason would not be heeded. He, too, assumed that Alvear would not be recalled if he did not ask it; and he hoped that the new assignment would be a pleasant one.[26]

With Guido's letter in hand and with death now indisputably near, Alvear addressed another letter to the new Argentine executive. For two full pages his hand struggled to the end before he laid it aside. The letter itself contained no new message: a farewell to Urquiza and a word of thanks for the favors given his two sons, Emilio and Diego. His final paragraphs he devoted to praise of the new leader: he sent congratulation for the support given to him by the other governors, and the hope that he would be chosen for the Presidency. Urquiza, he said, had shown himself worthy of this honor by his eminent services, distinguished capacity, noble sentiments, and liberal principles.[27]

As age and disease weighed down the once buoyant adventurer, he seemed to stand detached from his country. When he surveyed its history, he was saddened at many mistakes of its leaders. Of his own errors he made no mention. To Emilio, who had returned to Buenos Aires in order to take part in the new administration, Alvear penned his final meditations: ignorant ambition to dominate everyone had been the besetting sin of Argentine public life. Dorrego had forced out Rivadavia; Lavalle killed Dorrego; Lavalle was overthrown by Rosas; Rosas in his turn had met his conqueror, Urquiza. "Would it not have been better," he mused, "if all had united to form a constitution and govern according to law?" To prove the point he referred to the United States, where two political parties, Whigs and Democrats, divided power. These parties, agreeing on major matters, differed only on secondary points, and elected first one leader and then another to the Presidency. "This confirms my opinion of the foolishness to pretend that one party or one man should have the power all the time."

As evidence of ignorant ambition, Alvear cited the revolt against Belgrano by Bustos and Paz, and the declarations against San Martín. None of the men who had led the revolts proved anything except their own incapacity. And the army which he formed and with which he had triumphed at Ituzaingó . . . "Lavalleja, Lavalle, and Paz thought themselves capable of everything. It must be confessed that they had an ability at ineptitude to have been defeated by such soldiers as Rosas at Buenos Aires, as Quiroga in Tucumán, and López in Santa Fé."[28]

To the very end we see the Alvear of old—proud, opinionated, disdainful, unconscious of his own ignorant ambition or ineptitude. He thought that he had been hamstrung by little, bungling men. After a lifetime devoted to political action based on the arbitrary decision of a single individual, he vividly proclaimed his faith in a truly democratic government as the great anchor of salvation—Power under a Constitution!

Vicente F. López made the final political gesture. On October 5, 1852, less than a month before Alvear's death, López sent the old leader a plea to return home rather than accept another foreign post. López had discussed the matter with Alvear's family and at their prompting he had decided to write.

He remembered Alvear's Unitarian principles of a centralized, national government. As López witnessed a second rise of provincialism, he turned from Urquiza to the revolutionary founder: "The republic needs you in a vital way, and we have all commenced to turn our eyes toward you as the only person who can lead us from the labyrinth in which we have lost ourselves." Referring to Alvear as "one of the most conspicuous actors of the revolution," López reminded him of the revolt of the chieftains against Rivadavia when they believed that their local control was threatened. This revolt had ended with the installation of Rosas. López declared that Alvear, living at a distance, could not imagine how Rosas had eliminated all ideas but his own—even down to the clothes which the Terror had imposed. The noble Urquiza had freed the country from tyranny, but beyond this he had accomplished little. People had no constructive ideas and did nothing but talk. Urquiza stood for "fusion."

Let any man shout loudly enough that he is a Rosita and Urquiza will give him a job in order to prove his fusion. Urquiza has lost his grip. The Constitutional Convention has failed; we need a Constitution and peace. All this has been defeated by the Revolution of September 11, a provincial affair, where each section builds a wall around itself.

With magnificent crescendo López continued: "There is no man here able to unite the country in a national cause as did Rivadavia, you, and your friends of that time."[29] López acknowledged that Alsina had won a temporary popularity in Buenos Aires, but he pronounced him a man of narrow vision surrounded by incompetent followers. General Paz was a man of small mind and skimpy ways. To rescue the nation from nullities, López and his friends had turned to Alvear, a progressive man of good family, a wise leader who had directed the war for independence. Although of provincial origin, he had suffered from provincial revolt in 1815; therefore he could be depended upon to provide a national organization.

In ringing phrases López called on him not to hesitate. "Come to our help. Build up a following. Your friends are prepared. The interior will rise for you. All men of intelligence, all young men—except a few *gauchos*—will support you. With your talent and experience you cannot fail."[30]

With your talents. . . . You cannot fail. . . . How sincerely the dying General had once believed those words! He had rejected a call like this six years ago. Would he have accepted this new summons to defeat the conqueror of the Dictator? Probably not. Already a final decision had been made for the revolutionary hero and victor of Ituzaingó: long before the offer reached him death had brought release from exile.

Even while his life was spinning out its last days, new honors were accorded to the seasoned diplomat, but he died before they reached him. Urquiza granted his request for the French post. This appointment was decreed on August 23, 1852, with salary to begin on his acceptance; but he was ordered not to leave for Paris until a treaty with France had been signed. Undoubtedly Alvear won the post as a reward for his years of diplomatic service.[31]

With surprising suddenness the General's illness took a turn for the worse. He had been ailing for a long time. As early as 1841, he wrote of the lamentable and dangerous state of his health which prevented his attendance at diplomatic functions in Washington. The following year he gave as his reason for not residing in the capital that he could not secure proper medical treatment there. Recurrent attacks of asthma almost prostrated him. In 1843 he excused himself twice from the customary diplomatic functions on grounds of poor health.[32] On some of these occasions his ailments may have been "diplomatic" rather than physical, but by 1851 his health was unquestionably failing. An obstinate sore which threatened to spread to his eyes kept him from attending social or public functions. Secretary of State Webster invited him to come to Washington for an interview, but he could no longer travel. He wrote that a painful and cruel infirmity which proved almost stronger than his will prevented him from keeping the appointment.[33]

During the months of September and October, 1852, Alvear was prostrated with what his son described as chronic asthma and "inflamation [*sic*] of the lungs," but as the fall season advanced he seemed to improve. His official correspondence had accumulated rapidly in the interval, and with obvious determination he set himself to put his business in order. His young son, León, assumed the task of secretary after Emilio had departed for Buenos Aires. Under the young man's expert pen the letters rapidly took form, and on October 27 and 28 his father signed many documents. The pen quavered in his hand and skipped half of the concluding flourish, but the papers were done.

As his last official act, he dictated a letter for León. The father composed the rough draft on scrap paper, an old sheet which a scribe had blotted when writing to Rosas a few months earlier. Below the old heading, with its Federalist curse on "the crazy traitor, savage Unitarian, Urquiza" the onetime Unitarian began his last request of Urquiza's government. The state of his health had prevented him from performing his duties after his secretary had returned to Buenos Aires. Because he needed some reliable person who could speak Spanish and

English—a very rare individual in the United States, and very expensive to hire—he had engaged his son, León, for this work. León had abandoned his regular occupation, and since March 14 had been employed at the rate of 70 *pesos metálicos* per month. The minister requested that the government honor his draft totaling 490 pesos for seven months' service as secretary.[34] With these words Alvear closed his diplomatic correspondence and his diplomatic career.

The letter was never signed. The ailing father collapsed and León, hovering at his parent's bedside, had no chance to copy the communication. Although too ill to speak, his determination was strong. His unfinished correspondence—he must have the letter to Urquiza with its mention of Diego[35]—and the note about León's salary. He motioned for pen and paper. His hand bore down heavily to shape ill-formed letters:

León, it is necessary for you to copy this note it is probable that you will receive this money. I am giving you a letter of Peña's so that you can copy his name. It serves in the heading. Bring me at the same time the letter You will also need to copy for me a letter to Urquiza.

Gone now was all ambition. Gone the cares of diplomacy. Gone everything except the father's determination to care for his family. He took the pen and paper once more: this time he wrote more feebly—the spaces between words and phrases were wider, the lines shorter.

> León in the office instead of putting seventy
> pesos per month put one hundred and make the
> total in proportion[36]

He could do no more. They would not question his deathbed correspondence. He knew that. On the morning of November 2, 1852 he died.

. . . .

León took charge like a veteran. He notified the Secretary of State, Baron Bodisco, Dean of the Diplomatic Corps, and representatives of the Latin-American governments. On November 5 he advised his own government, telling of the minister's last illness and of the interment at St. Patrick's Cathedral to be held the following day at four in the afternoon.[37] He secured the archives of the legation, placed them in order and sealed them. As his father had directed, he sent the draft for seven months' salary at 100 pesos per month rather than the original 70. He notified the family by a letter to his American brother-in-law, Henry Tomkinson, then residing in Buenos Aires.[38]

Alvear's remains rested at St. Patrick's Cathedral little more than a year. In 1854 the aged Captain William Brown, first commander of the Argentine navy, sailed to New York to claim the body for his government. Alvear had appointed Captain Brown to his first Argentine command—the little fleet before Montevideo in 1814—and now he was bringing the former President to his home with honor.

The Argentine man-of-war bearing the deceased hero stopped first at Montevideo. In the great cathedral Uruguayans extolled the name of Alvear as their liberator from Spanish power. They draped the casket with two flags captured at Ituzaingó, and Tomás Guido hailed him as the victor over the Brazilians. "With all the demonstrations of respect and gratitude that a kind and noble people could pay" his remains were placed on the ship once more and the next day were deposited in the cathedral on the Plaza de Mayo. Newspapers carried fitting tributes. Officials vied with one another in expressing their admiration of the long absent diplomat. In order that he might be buried in a style befitting one of the highest rank, the army paraded with flags draped in mourning. Mitre proclaimed him as the founder of Independence; Alsina called him the earliest opponent of Rosas. Both Uruguayan and Argentine assemblies voted to his widow the highest pension permissible under the statutes. He was laid to rest in the lot he had purchased at La Recoleta cemetery in 1829. The ceremony was worthy of a hero.[39]

The process of forgetfulness began early. Guido in his Montevidean address had confessed that "all men are not perfect" and "the sun has its eclipses," but he insisted that if Alvear had been in a position of power, the Rosas tyranny would have disappeared. Alsina recognized that Alvear was not free from the charge of having served a tyrant. But the military glory of Montevideo and Ituzaingó promptly erased from popular memory the political errors of youth and the long service to Rosas. By 1860 Alvear, no less than San Martín, had become a legendary figure. In congressional debates the former diplomat was regarded as a national hero so far above local jealousies that his memory was cited to call men from petty bickering and into the larger citizenship of the nation. Such was the transforming power of a pious tradition.

APPENDIX

Reply of Carlos de Alvear to George Canning's Questionnaire on Conditions in the United Provinces[1]

1. The state of Buenos Aires includes all the old viceroyalty of that name. The census before the revolution gave it 3,000 persons, but it has more, because it was to the advantage of the province to reduce its official population reports. By this time a new census for Congressional representation is surely completed.

2. The population as well as the type of people varies sharply in the provinces. In the provinces, Buenos Aires, Montevideo, Paraguay, Córdoba, Mendoza, Tucumán, Salta, Santa Fé, Corrientes, La Rioja, Catamarca, Santiago de Estero, and Entreríos, the population must be about 4 to 100 of people of color to white. The people of color are Africans or descendants. The Indians have disappeared except for groups in some forests. The province of Missiones was founded by Jesuits, and there the Indians have accepted Christianity and have settled down to civilized life in thirty-one towns. These towns have been decreasing for twenty years and now average about thirty inhabitants, and the whites here are about 4 to 100.

3. A partial answer has been given in the second section. The present state of Buenos Aires consists of all the territory once under the viceroyalty of that name and includes the establishments of Patagonia.

4. All the provinces in the second question have reunited and obeyed the central government of 1820. They meet this year—excepting Paraguay and the Banda Oriental, who find themselves unjustly occupied by the troops of Brazil, and thus their sacred rights are violated.

5. Answered in sections one and two.

6. The election of representatives has been explained. Congress is to meet soon and consider: a) the Brazilian invasion of the Banda Oriental. What steps to be taken depend upon the judgment of the Secretary of Foreign Affairs who has principal charge of these matters for the country; b) installation of a permanent form of government; c) nomination of an Executive Power for the State.

The provinces recognizing the Congress are: Buenos Aires, Córdoba, Mendoza, Tacumán, Salta, Santa Fé, Corrientes, La Rioja, Catamarca, Santiago de Estero, Entreríos, Missiones. Members from the Banda Oriental cannot come on account of Brazilian occupation; Paraguay, on account of its isolation, will send no representatives.

The Congress will meet after fourteen years of actual independence—since May 25, 1810. Montevideo was the only city held by royalist forces and it surrendered to the Liberating Army in 1814. Buenos Aires has not had to defend its borders, but instead has carried the war beyond its boundaries. In a brilliant march over the Andes, its army united with patriot forces and drove out the Spanish power. Its forces helped capture Lima and Quito.

If Buenos Aires has not sent an agent to England heretofore, it is because of the conviction that the English cabinet will act in a favorable manner spontaneously in favor of the rising states of America.

[General Alvear concluded this section with a peroration on English virtue and morality and a note on the menace to peace induced by Brazilian occupation of Buenos Aires.]

7. The military forces are set by law annually as determined by the House of Representatives of each province and according to the necessities that may arise. As for the navy, since there are no Spanish forces in our seas, it has been disbanded on account of expenses, and only enough ships to patrol the coasts have been kept.

8. Since there is no opportunity at this time to check on the exact figures, the undersigned can only say that the income has exceeded expenses.

(TRANSLATION)

Conference . . . between His Excellency the President of the United States and the undersigned Minister Plenipotentiary in Washington, the 14th of October 1824

The President said:[1] that fearing that France after her fine success in Spain would try to send an expedition over to South America, he had made the solemn declaration that was contained in his annual message of 1823 by which he had obligated himself in an unequivocable manner to protect the cause of the new States of America in the situation to which the same message referred. He had further asked the British government to declare what would be its conduct if any power other than Spain should wish to intervene in the subjugation of the former colonies, asking it to state openly and frankly in reference to its ultimate conduct in such a hypothetical case. The British government, by means of the declaration and speeches of Mr. Canning in Parliament, had answered in a completely satisfactory manner, adopting the principle established by the government of the United States, a principle which upset the hostile desires of France. Having seen the success which this suggestion had enjoyed, he advanced another step and invited the English government to recognize the independence of the new States, a step entirely suitable and consistent with the good dispositions which had been shown in the foregoing statement, and by which that country would place itself entirely in accord with the government of the United States in order to co-operate more easily and to agree on the means which ought to be employed if it should ever become necessary to take a stand in order to fulfil the promises made in favor of the new American Republics, and to oppose the principles of the Holy Alliance, of which the two countries, united, would have nothing to fear. This proposition was made through the minister of North America in London, who, on interviewing Mr. Canning received the answer that it was not yet time to ratify the recognition which he sought. The English minister had not entered into any previous explanations of the motives which his government might have for judging that as yet the period for making such recognition had not arrived.

In North America there had been a very zealous party which was desirous that the government should have taken a more decided part in favor of South America in its dispute with Spain. But he, more prudently, had believed it better for the new American governments to conduct themselves within the limits which he had set, because if he had interfered in the above question, other nations would have pled identical rights, which, naturally, would have originated a great war whose effects it was not easy to foresee. Then the very same party undoubtedly would have attacked the government for its imprudence. He had believed this procedure particularly favorable to South America since he was firmly persuaded that the most he could win for them in their fight with Spain was to keep any other European power from mixing in the fight in a manner which would be hostile to America, it being understood that the weakness of Spain was so obvious that the outcome could not be doubtful while this nation should be the only one to maintain the war against her former colonies.

The government of the United States, on formulating the declaration, had taken all means possible for making it effective—fortifying its coasts, increasing its [naval] armament, and sending a part of it to distant seas—and that in making this show of force its object had been to show to the other nations that it was prepared to work if necessary.

At this time the undersigned, seeing the frankness with which the President had proceeded, believed that he had found a good opportunity to ask him if he would be willing to inform him, if he had no reason to the contrary, what was actually the real manner of thinking and the interests which animated each one of the different nations which compose the Holy Alliance, and likewise the reasons or motives which his countrymen might attribute to the government of Great Britain for not having decided to recognize the independence of the new American states, adding that His Excellency would easily understand how interesting this knowledge would be to the government of Buenos Aires.

To this request the President answered that it would be a great pleasure to do it. He had never ceased to recommend to his ministers in the various courts of Europe, that, according to the distinct desires and inclinations which they should discover, they were to moderate the evil disposition which they should note toward the new republics of America, and that they should contribute to the good disposition in others, influencing them whenever possible to speed up the greatly desired moment of recognition. When he had recognized the independence of the new states, the Emperor of Russia had shown his satisfaction because the said recognition did not alter the system of neutrality. To which the President had answered that neutrality ought not to be understood except in case no other power excepting Spain became involved in the question. He was pleased to assure him who writes that there existed the closest friendship between the Emperor of Russia and the government of the United States. He had reason to believe that the Russian government would not enter into any plan that should have hostility against America as its direct object. This same attitude had been confirmed through the medium of the Russian minister, Baron de Tuyll, who lived in Washington; and when the government of the United States invited some of the governments of the continent to recognize the independence of South America, it encountered in the cabinet of St. Petersburg less resistance than in the rest.

In respect to England, he had recently—and for a second time—invited its government to recognize independence and had received the same reply as formerly. He was not able to attribute to the Court and its indecision any other principle than the aristocrats who dominated the cabinet of the King. Mr. Canning should be considered as between the people who desired recognition of independence and the aristocracy which appeared to resist it. The dominant opinion of the People in favor of independence placed the new States in a situation where they had nothing to fear from the English government. On the contrary, they should hope that—this opinion mounting from day to day—the government would decide at last to yield to it, especially as this procedure was linked to the commercial interest of Great Britain.

In respect to France, its government had known that Spain was incapable by itself of resubjugating its colonies and it felt this so strongly that it had wished to aid her in order to facilitate the success of the enterprise—a thing which would have taken place if the message of which he had made mention and the declaration of the English had not stopped the Cabinet of St. Cloud. This government believed that republican principles had not been well fixed in America and even, on the contrary, the majority of the inhabitants are well inclined toward monarchy. This same idea had prevailed in another European government—a thing which was greatly prejudicial to the new republics, because with rising hopes of establishing monarchies in America, recognition was postponed. He would always continue making the greatest efforts in favor of the new States but it was also necessary that their respective governments should try for their part. . . .

Since, on arriving at this part of the conference, the undersigned noticed that the President hesitated to continue, exhibiting—it seemed—a certain embarrassment in explaining the subject, the undersigned took the liberty of pointing out to him that there were not in the range of the undersigned any events which could have contributed to those things on which the indicated governments of Europe should found their hopes on the ease of establishing monarchial governments in America. On the contrary, things being as they are, everything conspired in the new American nations to implant the republican system, the only one that the general opinion admitted, and which the circumstances of the people made indispensable and necessary, etc., etc., etc. . . . adding that nothing could be more pleasing to him who speaks, and equally to his government, than that the President, speaking with frankness, should be willing to communicate to the undersigned the wisdom of his advice over all those things which in the judgment of the President could interest the government of Buenos Aires. Then the President answered that he would do it with pleasure and with all the frankness and cordiality of sentiments which inspired him to favor America.

It is indubitable, he continued, that all the new governments of America have not progressed in the course of the revolution equally in a firm and regular manner. Some have fluctuated in the system of government they should adopt and others have proclaimed in certain periods for the establishment of monarchy, a thing which has fomented the hopes of the government of Europe. This is an obstacle which my ministers have encountered in the old world when they have wished to persuade their governments that America did not wish and was not able to have any other form of government than a republic. But they argue that American opinion is not set, as they say, in favor of such a system of government.

If America is decided, as you tell me and as I am persuaded by the information which I have, to establish the republican system to the exclusion of any other, why not have it declared always in a categorical manner that would not give room for any other contradictory interpretation? When my minister in Russia explained for the first time to the Emperor Alexander that in Spanish America nothing except republican governments could be established, the emperor was alarmed but in the end his reason prevailed and the President was able to assure the writer that this prince was at present convinced that the republican forms are the only ones adaptable to the new nations of America.

As long as in some of the powers which compose the Holy Alliance the opinion prevails that the establishment of monarchies is practicable, a hostile attitude toward America will be preserved, and this active hostility will not cease until they become convinced of the impracticability of their ideas and only you are able to produce this conviction.

He who writes, as was his duty, and as may be supposed, did everything possible in order to overcome some sinister impressions that, as above expressed, the President showed that he had with respect to the ambiguous conduct which certain States in America at certain times had maintained in reference to the system of government that ought to rule them, the writer exerting himself, for his part to make him see by means of the merit of certain acts how incorrectly the conduct of the American governments had been censured on certain occasions by means of false interpretations and also because many times the opinion of a small number of individuals had been taken for that of the majority, etc., ...

His Excellency said that the privateers established by the government of America had caused him a great deal of trouble, and that by the means by which it had been conducted was prejudicial to the American cause. Some of his own citizens of North America with patents from the new states had committed atrocities and that many North American ships had suffered much; but that he, out of interest and inclination toward the new states had employed all means in his power to calm the people who were exasperated by the vexations that such violent acts executed by the pirates had produced. He had given orders to the naval commanders that they should pursue to extermination all ships which they should encounter exercising privateering [commissions] but in case that some of these ships should belong to any of the governments now independent, the commanders should conduct them to any of the ports of their respective countries and there should present their complaints in order that they should be punished.

He had endured this conduct in order not to give grounds for argument to the government of Europe and in order that they should not be able to found hopes in the supposition of poor understanding between the government of the United States and the rest of the American continent. The President was here interrupted by the undersigned. . . .

I do not say this, he replied, of Buenos Aires. I know that your government has prohibited privateering. That which is desired is that all the other governments should follow this judicious conduct. I understand all the evils that through lack of experience and other circumstances the new governments suffer. I am a man of the Revolution and I know those things which we ourselves passed through when it began, but it would be desirable if ideas against privateering should become general in America and I am working with Colombia in order to get her to follow the example of Buenos Aires. Recently there has occurred a notorious atrocity with a ship and citizens of Baltimore occasioned by one of the corsairs of Colombia, and I have brought to bear all my influence in order to calm these men, assuring them that they would be indemnified by the government of Colombia. I have been obliged to act in this manner because this and other similar acts, once published, would produce an about-face in the public opinion of this country: an opinion that today is completely favorable to the cause of the new states and that if it should change would make it impossible for the government to display its resources in case it should be necessary to employ them in the aid of South America.

At this stage of the conference the undersigned brought the conversation around to Brazil and the conduct that unfortunately its new emperor observed in respect to the United Provinces by his occupation of the Banda Oriental, an integral part of their territory, etc., etc. . . .

The President said that he had recognized the independence of Brazil. When he had announced this resolution to His Most Faithful Majesty [King of Portugal], he had shown himself greatly surprised and querulous, but had no other result. He had recognized the independence of Brazil because it was not in the principles that rule the United States to meddle in the system that other States would wish to adopt, but that his private wish, and that of all the North American nation, was that Brazil should establish a republic. This could not help but come to pass sooner or later by the influence of the example which the rest of America in its established form was giving to it, and particularly if one paid any attention to the imprudent manner with which the emperor of Brazil conducted himself and to the unjust and hostile desires which he had displayed with respect to his neighbors.

His Excellency concluded by saying that the States of America would be able to secure from the United States all the supplies in arms, munitions, and ships which they might need in order to continue the war—just as Colombia and others had done. In reference to this matter he had received several remonstrances from Spain but that he had always found honest and honorable means of evading them.

The undersigned thanked His Excellency for the frankness with which he had deigned to favor him during the course of the conference whose details, he explained to His Excellency, he would bring to the attention of his government. The President reminded him of the risks to which communications were subject—as much from privateers as from unforeseen accident—and he took the liberty of recommending that he entrust the said communications, on account of their importance, only to the very safest means of conveyance.

The undersigned believes it opportune to add as proof of the good faith of the President that this conference took place in the presence of the Secretary of the Legation, Don Tomás de Iriarte, a circumstance that according to diplomatic usage gives to it the character of an official declaration, although reserved.

—Carlos de Alvear
(rúbrica)

Diplomatic Comment

We would have no reason for questioning the nature of Alvear's first interview with President Monroe (which the minister says was very brief) if the Argentine Secretary of Legation, Tomás de Iriarte, who was present at the conference, had not published a version of it over forty years later in the *Revista de Buenos Aires* in 1866.[1] And his account of the first interview has significant variations from those prepared by his chief. According to his report in the literary publication, Monroe conducted a monologue of considerable intensity. Vociferously and in poor taste the President commented upon the hostility of Europe to the "germ of republicanism." "It is our character," he is quoted as saying, "to do good without talking about it." According to Iriarte, Monroe reminded Alvear of commercial considerations which guided England's foreign policy: she dared not interfere with the recent declaration of the United States for fear of losing her trade with India. But financial arrangements did not warp the policy of the United

States: despite Spanish protests she had continued to supply the colonies with all the articles of war "because in this country they are considered as simple objects of industry. By this means we observe our international system of not interfering in the armed dissensions of other countries."

Next, Iriarte quotes Monroe as turning to Spanish affairs. The President, he says, declared that Fernando VII had been quite disgusted on hearing that the United States had recognized the independence of South America, but that he had written his minister in Madrid to pay no attention to it. Years before, said Monroe, when he was in Spain as representative of the United States he had known that monarch as the Prince of Asturias, and was convinced that he was "an ignorant sovereign with a perverse heart."

Iriarte declares that the conversation next turned to Brazilian affairs. The President branded the existence of monarchy in that country as a black page in the history of the republican system and assured him that North American relations with Brazil were merely matters of courtesy. He warned the republic of La Plata to be watchful in relations with this misplaced monarchy. The interview ended curiously:

> An occurrence of the moment suspended this conference; President Monroe said to us that he had to attend to other matters that were urgently pressing, but he insisted that we should return for a second visit as soon as possible.

This account bears no similarity to the official reports which Iriarte drafted and Alvear signed over forty years earlier. Señor Carlos Correa Luna, a modern Argentine historian, generously suggests that the later account represents the "confused memories" of an old man made forty years after the event. And yet when Iriarte chose to report the second conference for the *Revista,* he suffered no confusion. Word-for-word agreement between his and Alvear's reports of the second interview show that the former secretary was painstakingly copying a document laid before him—not writing from memory. Clearly, Iriarte had access to Alvear's official report long enough to copy accurately all that he desired of the text of the second conference. The report of the first conference is in the same file.

Only recently has the matter been cleared up. Those portions of Iriarte's memoirs which have been published since 1946 reveal the source of the variant text. While living in Uruguay as an exile from Rosas the former amanuensis composed his recollections of the mission to the United States, and he did it without recourse to his files in Buenos Aires, of course. In these memoirs written twenty years after the event he declares that the first interview was notably short—they did not even have time to sit down—and that there was time only for an exchange of official speeches. And then, he says, they returned later for a two-hour conference in the President's private office. In his memoirs he summarized the long conference as he remembered it, and the passing years had played tricks on his memory. He had forgotten about the conference with Secretary Adams on Brazil, and he telescoped the two conferences as one and added elaborative material which does not appear in the official record.[2]

When he began to prepare an article for the public twenty years after he had composed his memoirs, Iriarte consulted the files of the *Misión Alvear* in the National Archives in Buenos Aires. There he found his official report prepared in 1824. But he could not forego the temptation to use his picturesque version which he had drafted during the days of his exile. Monroe's first reception had been so brief and colorless that Iriarte apparently cast aside the contemporary record and used, instead, his version of the second conference of 1846 as the *first* for his magazine article for 1866. There were enough variations to make the two accounts appear to have been different interviews.

While we may not excuse Iriarte for his distorted version of an historic conference, his presumptive reasons for reporting the conference in 1866 are clear. During the course of the American Civil War, Spain had become involved in a war which eventually engaged the former colonies of Chile, Bolivia, Peru, and Ecuador. Secretary of State Seward filed a protest through the United States minister to Spain. The Spanish replied with bland disclaimers of any intention to reconquer Peru or to annex any territory of the former Spanish Empire; but hostilities continued. Chile and Peru, in the name of the Monroe Doctrine, then appealed to the United States to protect them from attack. Seward replied that the Doctrine did not prevent Europe from waging war against the republics of the New World: so long as Spain did not attempt to set up a monarchy or to destroy existing republicanism, the United States would not intervene. This interpretation disappointed the South Americans, who wanted the United States to serve as their protector.

The war continued in a desultory fashion until 1866, when Spain seized the Peruvian guano islands of Chincha. The Spanish representative then argued that since Spain had never recognized the independence of Peru, she was not violating the Monroe Doctrine in attempting to recover her former possessions. On Seward's second protest the Spanish declared that they were not acquired territory, but would reimburse themselves for war expenses by selling guano. Again the old specter of Spanish intervention haunted the former colonies.

By this time Tomás de Iriate had become an elder statesman. He fondly recalled the impressive policies as President Monroe had explained them forty years before. Unfortunately, the United States, after its exhausting Civil War, appeared to him to be in no mood to fight beyond its own borders. A suggestion might prove useful. Perhaps he could remind the great republic of its former policy that had been so effective in preventing aggression, so beneficent to the southern republics.

During this period of attempted Spanish aggression, therefore, he wrote for the *Revista de Buenos Aires* two long articles which he hoped would alert the New World to old monarchial tricks and to their unprincipled actions. The first consisted of his account of the two conferences with President Monroe; the other told again of the sinking of the *Mercedes* when so many of the Alvear family were lost. Iriate's father had been the commander who became ill and for whom Don Diego de Alvear had taken over on that fateful crossing. The son remembered that horrible episode and from it drew a bitter lesson: the attack proved that God favors the side with the biggest cannon, not the best right, and His favor had not changed. In a world ruled by deed, not law, Mexico, Santo Domingo, and the republics of the Pacific furnished "recent and vibrant examples" of the usurping tendencies of the Old World. Help would come, not from on High, but from a republic whose big cannon supported liberal principles. President Monroe's two interviews with Alvear had indicated a fine determination of the United States to repel such aggression. Without it the two continents would have been the theater of prolonged war against Spain and France.

Presumably Iriarte believed that publication of his two articles would encourage the South Americans to believe that the United States might again stand between them and the European storm. Unfortunately he sought to confirm this hope by altering radically Alvear's original report so as to attribute to the President abusive remarks about European and American monarchies which it appears he never said.

Hopes of securing assistance of the United States in the Spanish war were soon realized, but not as a result of articles in the *Revista*. After Spain had occupied the islands and had begun to justify the seizure, Seward prepared for the United States minister to Spain instructions which declared in the veiled language of diplomacy that the United States could not be expected to maintain its neutrality even if the occupation were only temporary. The communication was read to the Spanish minister in Washington, and he reported its contents to the home government. The Spanish withdrew from the islands so promptly that it was never necessary to deliver the warning officially.[3] Perhaps Iriarte never knew that the United States had again exerted its influence in favor of the Spanish-American republics.

Unfortunately there is no American version with which we can check Argentine reports of the conference. The State Department has no memoranda of these interviews. An investigation of Monroe's papers reveals no reference to Alvear. The President probably considered his conferences of such a routine nature that he did not feel it worth while to refer to them again. John Quincy Adams completely omits the whole period in his diary. Just at this time there occurs one of the rare breaks in his daily record: a skip from October 8 to November 10. The famous Secretary, facing his election for the Presidency that fall, found himself too busy to keep his journal. But he did make extremely terse record of Alvear's appointment for interviews in his office Day Book—entries that may have been clear to him, although they are not free from ambiguities to us. Yet these notes, brief as they are, establish the fact from an American source that Alvear was presented to the President on two occasions and that he had a long conversation with either Adams or Monroe—perhaps with both.

An accurate version of Alvear's conference with Monroe has never been published. Iriarte, who first publicized the interview, had other purposes than accuracy in mind when he presented his account in 1866. Sr. Carlos Correa Luna printed the interview in 1926 in his study, *Carlos de Alvear y la diplomacía de 1824-1825*. On that occasion he edited and modernized the original version. He expanded abbreviations, changed the capitalization, and added accents as well as harmonized the spelling. Neither Alvear nor Iriarte appear to have exercised themselves over the mechanics of composition.

Mechanical changes to facilitate understanding of the text are surely legitimate, but beyond this point the editor must proceed with greatest caution. In his zeal to freshen Alvear's report, Señor Correa Luna has made changes in the wording of the text which do not alter the total import of the dispatch, but do change the original meaning of particular sentences. After a close comparison with the original version, the following summary can be made:

In Señor Correa Luna's version of Alvear's report there are five changes in word order, seven additions of one or more words, eleven changes in verb tense, fifteen omissions of one or more words, and thirty-nine substitutions of one or more words. In all there are seventy-seven textual variations, some of a minor nature while others change the "color" of a sentence if not its whole meaning.

Examples of some of these alterations and emendations are:

Alvear	*Correa Luna*	*Alvear*	*Correa Luna*
exigió	requirió	hacer	formular
previas	ulteriores	combidado	pedido
cuestión	contienda	vinculado	unido
parte	actitud	ingeniar	inmiscuirse
el mismo	idénticos		

Alvear—del ministro del Norte America en Londres.
Correa Luna—del ministro de los Estados Unidos en Londres.

Alvear—esperanzas creyendo que reinaba mala intellegencia.
Correa Luna—esperanzas en el supuesto de mala intelligencia.

Alvear—que a los aristocráticos.
Correa Luna—que al influjo de las personas aristocráticas.

Alvear—no tener que temer nada.
Correa Luna—no tener nada que temer.

Alvear—sus gobiernos respectivos trataran por su parte.
Correa Luna—sus gobiernos respectivos ofreciesen a la Europa pruebas prácticas del error de su juicio y del espíritu democrático de las masas.

Alvear—y así es que bien persuadido de esta incapacidad había querido asistir a la España.
Correa Luna—y tan era así, que hasta había pretendido ayudarla.

Alvear—creyó hallar una bueno oportunidad para exigir de Su Excelencia se dignarse informarle, sino tenía embarazo, cual. . . .
Correa Luna—aprovechó la oportunidad para pedirle se dignase informarle cual. . . .

In October, 1932, Señor Carlos Ibarguren published a series of historical studies on certain relatively unknown phases of Argentine history. These articles originally appeared in the literary section of the once great Argentine newspaper, *La Prensa*, and later were issued in book format. Señor Ibarguren explained in the preface that in spite of the casual manner in which the material first appeared, he had tried to subject his work to the most rigorous documentary verification. The chapter entitled "Confidencias del Presidente Monroe al General Alvear" falls somewhat short of this laudable aim. The author ignored Alvear's version on file in the archives of the nation. Rather, he accepted Iriarte's version of 1866, and then spiced the account to suit his literary taste. Making no attempt to reprint the whole interview, he omitted passages altogether (without indicating the omission) and then summarized them in his own words. He added descriptive comments which neither Alvear nor Iriarte provided—comments presumably designed to make the scene more vivid. He has further flavored his account by throwing the conversation between the two men into direct quotation. Whereas Iriarte used the colorless "nos dijo," Ibarguren says "recalcó Monroe." On another occasion he felt justified in adding the descriptive comment "agregó con energía el Presidente."

As examples of the gradual changes in the text as given first by Iriarte and then by Ibarguren, we note the following passages:

Alvear—A lo que el Señor Presidente contestó que tendría un gran placer en hacerlo.

Iriarte—Contestó el presidente que tendría gran placer en satisfacer la justa curiosidad del Ministro Argentino.

Ibarguren—"Con mucho placer"—respondío Monroe—"voy a satisfacer la justa curiosidad del Señor Ministro."

Or again:

Alvear—Como al llegar a esta parte de la conferencia el que suscribe notase que el Señor Presidente titubeaba en continuar, manifestando al parecer cierto embarazo en explicarse sobre la materia.

Iriarte—Como al llegar a este período de la conferencia el Ministro Argentino notase que el presidente vacilaba en continuar, revelando al parecer cierto embarazo y retracción de explicarse abiertemente.

Ibarguren—"Yo por mi parte"—Monroe decía esto con visible embarazo y vacilación—"temo que pueda no existir el espíritu republicano en las masas."

And so the original draft of Alvear's conferences with Monroe has been subjected to changes with each printing. Señor Correa Luna, although he made many small changes in Alvear's text, has not altered its general tenor. For a political reason

Iriarte inserted drastic alterations in the portion of the interview which he published. Why Señor Ibarguren further altered and embellished Iriarte's version is unknown. The story of the publication of this manuscript illustrates again those historical maxims: that a careful student should consult original documents rather than the memoirs of elder statesmen or casual reprints; and that historical documents, when reprinted by careless or biased persons, may be altered so greatly as to become valueless for accurate citation.

BIBLIOGRAPHICAL NOTES

MANUSCRIPT COLLECTIONS

The sources for the study of General Alvear's diplomatic career are found almost wholly in manuscript collections in Buenos Aires and Washington. Most of the relevant archival material in the United States has been published under William R. Manning's capable supervision. That in Buenos Aires still lies unnoted, save for the perusal of occasional scholars who seek material for some special study. Two archives in Buenos Aires contain almost all the manuscript material relative to Alvear's diplomatic activites:

Archivo General de la Nación

The extensive collections in this archive include most of the papers relating to Carlos de Alvear and his family. The documents referring to the mission of 1824 are filed under the title "Missión Alvear." Collections for the second assignment to the United States, under the heading "Ministro Alvear, 1833, y 1837-1852," are quite incomplete, particularly after 1846. Fortunately the immensely valuable documents donated by the General's grandson, the late ex-President of the Republic, Don Marcelo T. de Alvear, have filled many gaps. This acquisition is known as the "Donación Alvear." Photographic reproductions of this collection—except the undated manuscripts and rough drafts without headings—are now in the Library of Congress in Washington. This material was secured for the Library through the intercession of Professor Samuel Flagg Bemis, who in 1938 saw the originals in the Archivo General de la Nación.

Archivo del Ministro de Relaciones Exteriores y Culto

In two boxes (cajas 12 y 41) are preserved many dispatches from the second mission of Carlos de Alvear to the United States. In general these documents do not duplicate those found in the Archivo General. They largely deal with the minister's comments on the expansion of the United States under the impulse of Manifest Destiny. Caja 12 contains correspondence from 1838 through 1846; while caja 41, with its dispatches from 1847 through 1852, includes the letters outlining Alvear's opinion of the foreign policy of the United States.

The collections in these two archives embrace some 75 per cent of Alvear's official dispatches. The hazards of the voyage, uncertainties of the hostile blockade, and the ravages of time or carelessness of clerks may account for the loss of the remainder. No personal letters of General Alvear are found in either archive. Those not destroyed by the New York fire of 1845 should have been preserved by some member of the family. A personal visit by the author to Don Marcelo T. de Alvear in August, 1941, revealed the fact that the Alvear family possesses no further documentary collections of its distinguished ancestor.

Señor Gregorio F. Rodríguez had access to the collections owned by Don Marcelo T. de Alvear before the donation was made to the Archivo General. By his own research Señor Rodríguez unearthed a few private letters from Alvear, and these he printed in his excellent *Contribución histórica y documental*, which will be referred to somewhat later.

Publication of the diplomatic correspondence of the United States with Latin-American nations has included all the official correspondence which Alvear directed to the Department of State. Mr. Manning omitted some routine correspondence, which, except for the special purposes of this study, would have been valueless. Search in State Department files for material omitted from Manning is an unrewarding task, but in the interest of thoroughness, the following collections were surveyed:

Notes to Foreign Legations, V.
Instructions to United States Minister, IX, X, XIV, XV.

Argentine Republic, Instructions, XV.
Notes to Argentine Republic, VI.
Notes from Argentine Republic, I, pts. 1 and 2.
Argentine Republic, Dispatches, II, and V through IX.
Notes to Legations, III through V.
Consular Letters, 1832-1854.
Miscellaneous Letters, 1838-1853.

The manuscript collections of American political leaders of the second quarter of the past century make no reference to Alvear's presence in the United States. Caleb Cushing's Papers (Miscellaneous Papers, 1839-1840; Anglo-American Relations, 1839-1842; nonmilitary correspondence, 1846-1847) contained nothing relating to Alvear, although Cushing was probably the best informed man in the United States on the intervention in La Plata.

Unprinted Monroe papers in the New York Public Library, like the President's printed papers, carry no mention of the Argentine minister. President Polk's papers (First Series, February 15, 1845, to January 1, 1846, and the Second Series, volumes VII through XX) do not refer to Argentine problems. John Quincy Adams' papers are not open to general historical research, but the custodian of the collection could find but the very briefest mention of Alvear's visit to Washington in 1824. Published collections of Daniel Webster's papers as well as those of Buchanan ignore the presence of Alvear, although he frequently conferred with them on matters of national policy. Joel R. Poinsett knew Alvear better, probably, than any other American, but a catalogue of his private papers carries no mention of the Argentine minister. Not only is General Alvear unknown in the United States today, but he was, one must conclude, also unknown—certainly obscure—in his own time. The Argentine minister had very good reasons for wishing to remain unnoticed in the United States, and in this endeavor he enjoyed, for once, exceptional success.

The British archives contain no copies either of the questionnaire which Alvear said that Canning gave him or of the replies which he drafted so hurriedly. Canning left no memorandum of the conference, and for its conduct we are dependent wholly on Alvear. A search through the papers of the British Foreign Office, Buenos Aires and Argentine volumes for 1824-1825, as well as through the Embassy and Consular Archives, revealed nothing beyond that indicated in Professor Charles K. Webster's *Great Britain and the Independence of Latin-America.* Perhaps the "easy and unostensible" communication to which Rivadavia once referred implied an absence of documentary records.

BIBLIOGRAPHICAL AIDS AND DICTIONARIES

The citations in Miss Adelaide R. Hasse's *Index to United States Documents Relating to Foreign Affairs* (Carnegie Institute, Washington, D. C., 1914) combine error and fact in about equal proportion. Alvear's presence in 1824 and 1838 is duly noted, but, guided by official announcements in the *Gaceta Mercantil* of Buenos Aires, she mistakenly records Alvear's presence in the United States from 1832 to 1835.

The best bibliographical guide to the literature of Argentine history is the very excellent work by Romulo D. Carbia, *Historia de la historiografía Argentina* (La Plata, 1925). This analytical evaluation of Argentine historical writing should serve as an invaluable guide for every research student, but especially for the foreigner.

Of these general bibliographical aids to which the research student quickly turns, one of the earliest and best is that by Haywood Kenniston, *A List of Works for the Study of Hispanic-American History* (New York, 1920). The great mass of material, both documentary and monographical, published since 1920 limits its usefulness today. The bibliographical aids begun under the editorship of Lewis A. Hanke, *Handbook of Latin-American Studies* (Cambridge, 1935-), are indispensable to research in Latin-American history.

Every student of diplomatic history must seek the assistance afforded him in the bibliography of Professor Samuel F. Bemis and Miss Grace G. Griffin, *Guide to the Diplomatic History of the United States* (Government Printing Office, 1935). This work does double service: it provides an excellent list of materials available for any study of Argentine-American relations, and at the same time it reveals how scanty are scholarly works in this field.

Antonio Zinny made a major contribution to Argentine bibliography when he published simultaneously a catalogue and a summary of articles appearing in the early newspaper, *Gaceta de Buenos Aires*, and a list of historical material appearing during the late colonial and revolutionary eras. This second work, *Bibliografía histórica de las provincias del Río de la Plata, 1780-1821* (Buenos Aires, 1875) is particularly valuable in showing the sources available for study of Alvear's full revolutionary career.

Not until many years later did another significant bibliographical work appear in this field. Carlos I. Salas offered two titles, *Bibliografía al General don José de San Martín y la emancipación sudamericana* (5 vols.; Buenos Aires, 1910), and *Bibliografía del Coronel don Fredrico Brandsen.* The exhaustive bibliography on San Martín consists largely of listed titles, without critical evaluation, relating to San Martín's military career. Material relative to Alvear occurs only in the sections referring to the early days before San Martín made his Andean crossing. The work on Colonel Brandsen, a secondary figure in the War for Independence, is likewise devoted to military affairs. Colonel Brandsen fought through the war with San Martín and met his death at Ituzaingó while leading a charge at the command of General Alvear. Especially is the work valuable in making any study of the war with Brazil and in evaluating Alvear's by no means small contributions to victory.

An American scholar, Lewis W. Bealer, has published under the modest title, "A Contribution to a Bibliography on Artigas and the Beginning of Uruguay," *Hispanic American Historical Review,* XI (1931), 108-34, an extensive but uncritical collection of printed materials available in some of the larger libraries of the United States. The citations to Alvear refer to his fateful struggle with Artigas, and as such provide only background material for the General's diplomatic career.

Argentine biographical dictionaries represent a low standard in national historiography. None of them are based upon thoughtful or critical research; all are undocumented, laudatory sketches which refer to the obvious events and dates in the lives included in this discussion. As far as the essays on General Alvear are concerned, editorial interest centers exclusively on his work as leader of the revolution and his military success. His break with San Martín, his career as an exile from 1815-1820, and his long service in the United States receive no real consideration, either through oversight or ignorance. The following may be considered typical biographical dictionaries:

Adolfo P. Carranza, *Los héroes de la independencia* (Buenos Aires, 1910)
José Arturo Scotto, *Notas biográficas* (Buenos Aires, 1910)
Enrique Udaondo, Dictionario biográfico argentino (Buenos Aires, 1910)
Jacinto R. Yarben, *Biográficas argentinas y sud-Americanas* (5 vols.; Buenos Aires, 1938)

MANUSCRIPT COLLECTIONS (*printed*)

A natural result of Argentine nationalism has been the extensive publication of manuscript collections relative to national origins. In these publications Carlos de Alvear the general and revolutionary leader is frequently cited, as in the *Documentos relativos a la guerra de independencia americana* (4 vols.; Buenos Aires, 1903), which contains governmental and military notes and orders from the beginning of the Revolution to the year 1829. General Mitre had projected a biography of Artigas on the same masterly scale of his studies of San Martín and of Belgrano, but the work was never realized. However, some of these papers were extracted from his extensive files and published by the Museo Mitre under the title *Contribución documental para la historia del Río de la Plata* (5 vols.; Buenos Aires, 1913). This collection covers, in large part, the same period included in an earlier collection by Clemente L. Fregeiro, *Artigas: documentos justificativos* (Montevideo, 1886), but it is wider in scope and seeks a more balanced judgment than "justification."

Of general interest is the monumental collection *Documentos para la historia argentina* (Buenos Aires, 1920), Volumes VIII, XIII, XIV, which relate to the period from 1815 to

1824, both for domestic and foreign policy. The latter volume carries several documents relating to Alvear's nomination to the United States, his instructions, and his recall; there are, however, no communications from General Alvear to his government.

Facsimile editions of early publications have proved quite popular in Argentina, three of them being *El Redactor de la Asamblea de 1816-1820* (Buenos Aires, 1913), *Actas del Cabildo de Buenos Aires* (Buenos Aires, 1912) and the *Gaceta de Buenos Aires, 1810-1821* (5 vols., Buenos Aires, 1910). This latter publication, under the sponsorship of the Junta Histórica y Numismática, contains important material relative to Alvear's political and military life, but does not cover his diplomatic years, which began in 1824. Adolfo Saldías, first of the Rosas biographers who wrote without vituperation, published two folio volumes of *Papeles de Rosas* (2 vols.; Buenos Aires, 1907). This collection includes no appreciable fraction of Rosas' correspondence, but it does carry one letter from Alvear while he was serving as minister to the United States.

Gregorio F. Rodríguez projected a multivolume work on General Alvear, but realizing that he could not live to complete his study, he published selected documents which related to General Alvear or revealed the political and social life of the times. Of the printed manuscript materials this *Contribución histórica y documental* (3 vols.; Buenos Aires, 1921) is the most important. It includes but few documents found in the government archives, and therefore supplements these unprinted collections in a most fortunate manner. This exceedingly valuable material on Alvear as well as other subjects related to Argentine national life from 1812-1852 is important out of all relation to its modest title, and must be consulted in any study of the Rosas regime or of personalities of that period.

A catalogue of the files of the Diego de Alvear mission to survey the Spanish-Portugese boundary of Brazil has recently been published by the Instituto de Investigaciones Históricas as volume seventy-five of its series, *La colección de documentos de Pedro de Ángeles, y el Diario de Diego de Alvear* (Buenos Aires, 1941), Teodoro Becú and José Torre Revello, editors.

The diplomatic mission of General Alvear and Díaz Vélez to Upper Peru to confer with General Bolivar involves use of manuscript material quite distinct from those related to other phases of General Alvear's diplomatic career. The earliest published collection of documents related to the mission to Bolivia was that by Manuel Odriozola, *Documentos históricas del Perú* (10 vols.; Lima, 1874). The documents were published in chronological order with no editing and are accompanied by a table of contents, but have no index. Volume VI of this series contains a few official reports on the mission as sent to the foreign office at Lima. Either the Peruvian officials were poorly informed as to proceedings of the mission or else the editor has omitted valuable material relative to it: the collection is quite incomplete.

The Colombian Academy of History, under the editorship of Ernesto Restrepo Tirado, published the *Archivo de Santander* (24 vols.; Bogotá, 1918-1932). This collection includes not only the letters from Bolívar relative to the Alvear mission, but also the replies of Santander. The correspondence demonstrates the restraining influences on Bolívar and reveals Santander's hostility towards Buenos Aires. One of the most important compilations for the study of the Missión Alvear-Díaz Vélez is that arranged and edited by Ernesto Restelli, Subsecretary of the Argentine Ministro de Relaciones Exteriores y Culto, *La gestión diplomática del General Alvear en el Alto Perú* (Buenos Aires, 1927). The work purports to be a complete publication of the official files of the Argentine government on the subject. Portions of this correspondence were printed earlier, some of it in a centenary publication, *Documentos del Archivo de San Martín* (12 vols.; Buenos Aires, 1910), but the material given in Volume X has now been completely superseded by Restelli's work. Official correspondence printed by Rodríguez in his *Contribución* also has been rendered obsolete by Restelli's later publication. However, Rodríguez' collection of private correspondence furnishes valuable points of view not available to the Ministry. He reprints, also, one official document on the negotiations in Upper Peru which Restelli omitted—a document that a later generation would consider discreditable: perhaps the collection by Restelli is not as complete as it appears to be.

The correspondence of Bolívar has gone through several editions and has been variously published. The latest, best, and most usable edition is that by Vicente Lecuna, *Cartas del Libertador* (10 vols.; Caracas, 1929: vol. 11, 1947). Presumably these are all the letters from the Liberator which are known in northern South America. Rodríguez adds a few from Bolívar to Alvear, and somewhere in Argentina a fortunate historian should one day encounter additional letters from Bolívar to Dean Funes.

Under the curious title *Memorias de O'Leary* (Caracas, 1884) Simón O'Leary has published twenty-six volumes of documents and two of narration which his distinguished father, Daniel F. O'Leary, the Liberator's adjutant, prepared. The correspondence of Sucre and of Funes and a few letters from Díaz Vélez are of particular importance and, in addition, General O'Leary's narrative of the Argentine mission to Upper Peru. O'Leary is the only historian in all South America who has deemed the mission worthy of more than passing comment.

Vicente Lecuna has edited a manuscript collection, *Documentos referentes a la creación de Bolivia* (2 vols.; Caracas, 1924) which, while including some Argentine documents now more completely assembled by Restelli, print valuable archival material from Bolivia in reference to the mission. The work was published as a centennial publication in honor of the Generals Bolívar and Sucre, and although it lacks an index for ready reference, it presents new material on the history of Bolivia and the Tarija dispute with Argentina.

Few manuscript collections printed in English relate to diplomatic negotiations with Argentina. William R. Manning edited two series of diplomatic correspondence of the United States with Latin America: *Diplomatic Correspondence of the United States concerning the Independence of Latin-American Nations* (3 vols.; New York, 1925). Volume I prints the exchanges with Argentina and indicates how very well informed was the United States on Latin-American affairs at the time of Alvear's interview. This collection offers no documentary evidence that the Argentine minister had other than official conferences with President Monroe or with Secretary Adams. The second series, *Diplomatic Correspondence of the United States: Inter-American Affairs*, pt. 1, Argentina, 1831-1860 (12 vols.; Washington, 1932-1939) carries the correspondence of the State Department well beyond Alvear's period. The official exchanges of Alvear with the various Secretaries of State give no clue, of course, to the bitterness of the Argentine minister's feelings on American expansion nor to the extent of his propaganda activities.

England has no published series on Latin-American relations which parallel Manning's great compilation. Probably stimulated by the appearance of the series in the United States, Charles K. Webster edited a notable collection, *Great Britain and the Independence of Latin America, 1812-1830* (2 vols.; London, 1938). The editor has published select documents from the archives of the British Foreign Office which, he believes, show that Great Britain played a greater part in the establishment of the independence of Latin America than any other nation. For the period and the subject this is the finest collection of archival material so far published, but one must take into account the author's private conviction and the large number of documents necessarily omitted.

Finally, there is James D. Richardson, *Messages and Papers of the Presidents, 1789-1897* (20 vols., Washington, 1897). This compilation reprints the presidential messages which defined the Latin-American policies of the United States.

BIOGRAPHIES, MEMOIRS, AND COLLECTED WORKS

Alvear's diplomatic career in the United States was relatively unknown to his contemporaries. Save the fact of his residence abroad, his activities were seldom mentioned because Dictator Rosas kept public attention upon himself; and Alvear, no tyro in political intrigue himself, preserved no memoirs nor personal papers except those of a most innocuous nature. Argentine historians have preferred to study those phases of his career when he was an active participant in shaping the nation. Therefore biographies, memoirs, and collected works relate to

Alvear's early life or to his times. Practically nothing directly concerns the General's diplomatic activity.

The *Writings of James Monroe* (7 vols.; New York, 1898-1900) edited by S. M. Hamilton, Volume VI, covers that period when the presidential doctrine was in the process of formation. In the long list of Monroe's letters and addresses Alvear's name does not appear. As much may be said for the *Writings of John Quincy Adams* (7 vols.; New York, 1913-1917), edited by Worthington C. Ford, or for his *Memoirs* (12 vols.; Philadelphia, 1874), edited by Charles F. Adams. Two later Secretaries of State, James Buchanan and Daniel Webster, knew Alvear well, but their collected papers and writings reveal nothing beyond official exchanges as preserved in the files of the State Department. No biography of President Monroe mentions Alvear's early appearance in the United States. *James K. Polk* (Berkeley, California, 1922), by Eugene I. McCormac, scarcely mentions the foreign interventions in La Plata at the period when Alvear was working faithfully to direct the attention of the administration toward the plight of his country.

Two Englishmen, J. P. and W. P. Robertson, who lived long in Argentina during its formative years, published their reminiscences, *Letters on South America* (3 vols.; London, 1843), in the form of letters. They furnished a lively account of Alvear's career as Director; and though they were aware of his residence in the United States, they had nothing to say about his diplomatic services. An American, J. Anthony King, who spent twenty years in La Plata and who fought through almost the whole of the Argentine war for independence, published his memoirs under the title *Twenty-four Years in the Argentine Republic* (New York, 1846). The author's lively narrative style and his innocence of Argentine politics lend an air of credibility to his tale of personal adventure. Alvear criticized King's condemnation of Rosas' Federalist regime, yet almost any North American of 1830-1850 would have taken the position which the author assumed.

A didactic novel by Paul Haro-Harring, *Dolores* (New York, 1846), gave a sorry account of the Rosas administration.

It won the Argentine minister's censure, although his comments on the details of the text are so general as to indicate that he had not read the book.

General William Miller, who served the cause of Spanish-American independence so well, returned to England just before Alvear and Díaz Vélez arrived in Upper Peru, and therefore his account, *Memoirs of General William Miller* (2 vols.; London, 1829), edited by John Miller, unfortunately contain no reference to the second phase of Alvear's diplomatic services. However, a young officer in Bolívar's staff, José María Rey de Castro, remembered well the brilliant social gatherings which characterized the meeting between the Liberator and Alvear, and these he has preserved in his memoirs entitled *Recuerdos del tiempo heróico* (Guayaquil, 1883). General Daniel O'Leary, in two narrative volumes of his *Memorias*, wrote an account of the Bolivian meeting after fortifying his memory with documents from Bolívar's files.

Alvear's uncle, Gervasio Antonio Posadas, who first held the position of Supreme Director, wrote his *Memorias* (Biblioteca Ayacucho, Madrid, 1920) which contain an embittered defense of his own administration and justification of his nephew's short service as Supreme Director. These memoirs relate, as do so many others, to the period of Alvear's leadership in Argentine politics. A memorial publication by Juan E. de Alvear, *Corona fúnebre* (Buenos Aires, 1890) contains, besides extravagant eulogies, a reprint of General Alvear's final political testament.

Several of Alvear's contemporaries have been the subject of competent biographies, and in so far as these studies relate to the national scene, he receives due attention. Classic biographies to which the student of Alvear's period must refer are Mariano A. Pelliza, *Dorrego en la historia de los partidos unitarios y federales* (Buenos Aires, 1878), and Bartolomé Mitre's *Historia de Belgrano* and *Historia de San Martín,* both three-volume works and best presented in the Buenos Aires edition of 1887. Pelliza contends that it is erroneous to say that the terrible partisan conflicts which plagued Alvear's generation represented the contest between civilization and barbarism; they should be viewed rather as the conflict between the rural *gaucho* and the urban *porteño*. He shows that Alvear, taking no such statesmanlike view, sought through personal intrigue to gain ascendancy. General Mitre, in his monumental studies of two great military leaders of early Argentine life, found in General Alvear an object of criticism and disparagement.

A later historian, Gregorio F. Rodríguez, in what he intended to be a definitive biography of General Alvear, sought to restudy the General's work as a political leader and to rescue his military reputation from the limbo to which Mitre had consigned it. This work, *Historia de Alvear* (2 vols.; Buenos Aires, 1913), reached only to the period of Alvear's exile when the author was forced to relinquish his study.

Following the lead of Señor Rodríguez, another distinguished historian, Carlos Correa Luna, began to study General Alvear's diplomatic career and published a series of short essays entitled *Alvear y la diplomacía de 1824-1825* (Buenos Aires, 1926). This work was based on a preliminary survey of documentary material in the Archivo General de la Nación. He reprinted with minor changes Alvear's report of his interview with President Monroe. Carlos Ibarguren published a series of popular sketches, *En la penumbra de la historia argentina* (Buenos Aires, 1932), in which he drastically altered a version of the Monroe interview published by Tomás de Iriarte a generation earlier. This later study compounded confusion.

Juan Manuel de Rosas, who dominated so completely the last twenty years of Alvear's life and under whom Alvear served for so long, has never been the subject of a satisfactory biographical study. Immediately after the fall of the Dictator all accounts of his work burgeoned with vituperation. Adolfo Saldías in his *Historia de la confederación argentina: Rozas y su época* (5 vols.; Buenos Aires, 1892) sought a less prejudiced appraisal of the man's life. The whole library of Rosas biographies, whether laudatory or condemnatory, tends to concern itself with the minutiae of Argentine life and party politics, and in these discussions Alvear does not figure. Saldías made passing reference to Alvear's propaganda activities in the United States, but his citations on this subject are so erroneous as to discredit his whole discussion of Alvear's work. No biographical study of Rosas, therefore, throws any light on Alvear's diplomatic career.

Biographies of Rivadavia likewise scarcely mention Alvear's diplomatic activity under that great leader because they, too, relate themselves to the first titular President of Argentina and to his domestic concerns. This generalization applies even to Ricardo Piccirilli's *Rivadavia y su tiempo* (2 vols.; Buenos Aires, 1943), best and most scholarly work on the great Argentine leader, though it is notably weak in its study of Rivadavia's foreign policy.

In 1930 Alice S. Pylman prepared a biographical study of the life of Carlos de Alvear as her master's thesis at the University of California. This work, being limited to the printed materials available at the Bancroft Library, includes almost nothing on Alvear's diplomatic career.

For many years Iriarte counted himself an admirer of General Alvear and was one of his closest associates until the end of the Argentine-Brazilian War. In the civil strife that followed the advent of Rosas to the leadership of the nation, Iriarte found himself allied with the Unitarians and fled to Montevideo. There he took part in the long struggle to depose the Dictator in Buenos Aires. Besides saving his own life and assisting in the overthrow of a determined tyrant, he found time to compose an amazingly detailed account of his public and professional life. Seven volumes have so far been printed: not all are equally useful to this study. (Tomás de Iriarte, *Memorias*, 9 vols.; Enrique de Gandía, ed., Buenos Aires, 1946- , Sociedad Impresora Americana.)

Volume I deals with the latter period of the Argentine wars for independence, and with the bitter anarchical struggles that swept La Plata from 1819 to 1822. General Alvear appears in this account as one of the rebellious chieftains who made war on the government of Buenos Aires.

Volume III recounts Iriarte's experiences as Alvear's secretary on the mission to the United States by way of England in 1824-1825. Here appeared first a version of the Monroe conference which Iriarte used again in 1866.

Volumes IV through IX trace the Unitarian-Federalist struggle for control of La Plata. In these volumes Alvear is but seldom mentioned, for he took no active part in the attempts to overthrow Rosas and Iriarte had brought their long friendship to an end. This contemporary evaluation of Alvear in the history of the nation is of great importance.

These *Memorias* are basic to any study of the life of Alvear from 1817 to 1838, and Iriarte's testimony composed more than a century ago carries the ring of truth.

SECONDARY MATERIALS: GENERAL STUDIES

At the time of the Spanish-American Wars for Independence the people of the United States knew little about their southern neighbors, although they wished them success in their struggle. One publication aimed at informing the public on southern affairs was printed in the form of letters to Henry Clay, who was championing loudly if not successfully the recognition of Latin-American independence. The writer, Vicente Pozas, in his *Letters on the United Provinces of South America* (New York, 1819) posed as a native of Upper Peru, and presented a readable narrative of social life of whites and Indians, as well as a summary of Argentine political questions. While purporting to be the work of a native South American, the author's obviously bitter opposition to the Roman Catholic Church and his confessed ignorance of its rites make one suspect that the translator may have interpolated a great many comments of his own.

The better part of a century passed before trained historians superseded the traveler's relation. A publication by Frederic L. Paxson, *The Independence of the South American Republics* (Philadelphia, 1903), marked the beginning of a long series of studies on Latin-American history by scholars in the United States. This early and sound survey of relations of the United States with South America has been widened, re-enforced, and expanded by later studies. Several of the outstanding works which contain background material on the diplomatic career of General Alvear are:

William S. Robertson, *Rise of the Spanish-American Republics as Told in the Lives of Their Liberators* (New York, 1918).

———, *Hispanic-American Relations with the United States* (New York, 1923).

———, *France and Latin-American Independence* (Baltimore, 1939).

This latter work represents a major contribution to the study of the diplomatic relationship of Latin-America with Europe. It details the French monarchial schemes which President Monroe found so disturbing and about which he talked so earnestly with Alvear.

J. Fred Rippy, *Rivalry of the United States and Great Britain over Latin-America* (Baltimore, 1929) emphasizes with the detachment of a later generation a point which Alvear as a contemporary recognized and bitterly condemned. Charles C. Griffin, *The United States and the Disruption of the Spanish Empire* (New York, 1937) stresses the relationship between the United States and Spain during the course of the Latin-American revolution. Arthur P. Whitaker, *The United States and the Independence of Latin-America* (Baltimore, 1941) offers a modern and thorough restudy of the problem Paxson had first presented in 1903. This latest research, including material found in the archives of the Latin-American countries, emphasizes how incomplete must be any study of New World problems which does not avail itself of southern archives. Of particular interest is a study by Edward H. Tatum, *The United States and Europe, 1815-1823* (Berkeley, Calif., 1936), which furnishes a fresh approach to the background of the Monroe Doctrine by studying the world problems from the materials available to the statesmen guiding the destiny of the United States in those days.

Mention should be made of several useful general studies such as *American Secretaries of State* (New York, 1927-1929), Samuel F. Bemis, editor. Three scholars, J. Fred Rippy, P. A. Martin, and Isaac J. Cox have collaborated in a general study, *Argentina, Brazil, and Chile since Independence* (Washington,

1935), which offers general but brief accounts of the national life of three major countries of South America. The conclusions are sound and the citations furnish guides for further study. A similar work is another collaborative publication, *South American Dictators*, Alva C. Wilgus, editor. The word "dictator" is used loosely when Rivadavia's name is included in this list.

For an introductory account of La Plata affairs no better one-volume survey exists than that by Frederick A. Kirkpatrick, *History of Argentina* (Cambridge, 1931). The major emphasis in this general survey is on the period of the revolutionary governments. The author wrote to prove to the Argentine people that England had taken great interest in their welfare and to show English readers the contributions which their country had made toward Argentine development. The painful story of the Falkland Islands episode, being unsuitable for this double-barreled objective, has been relegated to the appendix and there abandoned. Except for this national bias, the book is both readable and reliable.

Latin-American scholars have not been attracted to the problems involved in the composition of a general historical survey. If one is attempted, it tends to become a life-time chronicle for author and reader alike; or else a series of faintly related essays. Yet the first writings on the Latin-American revolution appeared as general studies. The earliest account appeared in Spain where regret at loss of the colonies must have been very keen. Mariano Torrente in his *Historia de la revolución hispano-americana* (3 vols.; Madrid, 1829) tried to report impartially the struggle for independence, but his work ultimately reflected peninsular hostility to the colonial cause. While he possessed no systematic, documentary collections such as are available to the modern scholar, Torrente took advantage both of contemporary accounts and of personal contacts with participants.

Yielding somewhat to standards of elegance, Carlos Calvo published his study of the revolution with a French title, *Annales historique de l'Amerique latine* (5 vols.; Paris, 1864), but he retained the Spanish text. At the slightest excuse the author quoted whole documents, so that his composition by current standards is slow; but absence of documentary collections seventy-five years ago made this treatment less laborious than it appears today.

Three general histories of Argentina are worthy of especial note. Mariano A. Pelliza, *Historia de Argentina* (2 vols.; Buenos Aires, 1910), being uncritical and undocumented, serves only as an introductory narrative of arms and politics on La Plata. A great Argentine historian, Vicente F. López, began a monumental *Historia de la República Argentina* (10 vols.; Buenos Aires, 1910) which was to have run through the period of Rosas, but the death of the author left the work incomplete. As far as he progressed, his study is as thorough and well-rounded a survey of domestic affairs as any Argentine has attempted single-handed. Under the general editorship of Ricardo Levene, the prominent Argentine historians and men of letters have collaborated to write a definitive history of their country, *Historia de la nación argentina* (10 vols.; Buenos Aires, 1936-). This ambitious project includes phases of Argentine life from the geological past and the prehistoric Indians to the postrevolutionary development of the provinces. The latest volume, showing markedly lower standards than the former ones, appears to have been written for the approbation of provincial pride. Earlier volumes, however, offer the best study yet made of the work of Alvear in the formation of the nation.

When Argentine historians have invaded the field of diplomatic controversy, they have appeared, apparently, as national champions. Many works are heavily biased, weighted with nationalist arguments, and are based on uni-archival investigation. The product is disappointing. Typical of this nationalistic school are:

Carlos Oneta y Viana, *La diplomacía del Brazil en el Río de la Plata* (Buenos Aires, 1903).

Vicente G. Quesada, *Historia diplomática latino-americana* (2 vols., Buenos Aires, 1918).

José León Suarez, *Diplomacía universitaria americana, Argentina y Brazil* (Buenos Aires, 1918).

Norberto Piñero, *La política internacional argentina* (Buenos Aires, 1924).

SECONDARY MATERIALS: SPECIAL WORKS

During Alvear's residence in the United States, Rosas permitted publication of a laudatory sketch of the public honors which he had accepted and this text, *Rasgos de la vida pública de Su Excellencia, el Señor Brigadier General Don Juan Manuel de Rosas* (Buenos Aires, 1842), Alvear translated into English and used repeatedly in articles which he offered to the North American press.

Argentine historians have by no means presented a balanced survey of their national development and only separate phases have been subjected to more than a cursory survey. Rosas' policy in foreign affairs they have preferred to leave to polemical writers. Some of the special topics related to this study of Alvear on which Argentine historians have worked include a study of the boundary disputes over the province of Tarija. Juan Martin Leguisamon and Mariano Zarreguieta prepared an historical essay and a documentary appendix on *Los límites con Bolivia* (Salta, 1872). These published materials represent Argentine sources only, and the authors approach the problem from a strictly legal point of view. Bolivia, however, won the province. Gabriel Rene-Moreno extracted a section from his larger work, *Bolivia y el Perú* (Santiago, Chile, 1907), and published these portions relative to the creation of Bolivia under the enigmatic title, *Ayacucho en Buenos Aires* (Madrid, 1917). He protested Bolívar's right to foster creation of Bolivia. This study is not based on archival research, and it totally ignores the Alvear-Díaz Vélez mission. The historian, Vicente Fidel López, began his long historical composition on Argentine history in the columns of a literary and historical journal, *La Revista del Río de la Plata,* and Volumes XI, XII, and XIII (1875-1877) carry excellent surveys of "The Terrible Year" (1820) and a detailed study of the War against Brazil. Dr. Manuel M. Cervera, in his well-known work, *Historia de la ciudad y provincia de Santa Fé, 1573-1853* (Santa Fé, Argentina, 1907) reflects local reaction against centralist aristocracy emanating from Buenos Aires. Alvear, the exile, appears in these pages as the malcontent leader of the rabble, a very unlikely person for national recognition as Argentine minister to the United States.

Francisco V. Silva of Córdoba, Argentina, prepared a life of Dean Funes for the series "Biblioteca Ayacucho" and to it he appended the Funes correspondence found in O'Leary's *Memorias*. The study begins as an historical survey, but gradually loses itself in bitter invective against the capital city. The author attributes everything which he regards as a national misfortune to the influence of Buenos Aires. Dean Funes stands as the type of political leader who resisted the blandishments of the new Sodom. Sr. Silva believed that his biography and reprints, *El Libertador Bolívar y el Dean Funes en la política Argentina* (Madrid, 1918), would reorient Argentine history so as to present the provinces and not Buenos Aires at the dominant factor in national life. A less polemical work is by Martin V. Lazcano, *Las sociedades secretas, políticas y masónicas en Buenos Aires* (2 vols.; Buenos Aires, 1927), a discursive study of the secret societies in Buenos Aires during the revolutionary period. The author belives that all the early political organizations such as the Lautaro were essentially non-Masonic, although they had Masons in them. The obvious lack of documentary materials in dealing with secret organizations blocks all attempts at reaching a definitive conclusion. Marío Belgrano in his *La Francia y la monarquía en el Plata* (Buenos Aires, 1933) has made an excellent study from Argentine sources of French attempts to install a monarchy in Argentina.

Loss of the Falkland Islands has come to be regarded as such a reflection on Argentine sovereignty that national historians have lost their professional reserve. Typical of Argentine publications on this inflammable subject is Juan G. Beltran, *El zarpazo inglés* (Buenos Aires, 1934). In a burst of Argentine impartiality, he divided his generous indignation equally between the United States and England. A more temperate work is Paul Groussac, *Las islas Malvinas* (Buenos Aires, 1936). This study, based on Argentine sources, naturally sustains the national cause and regrets that Alvear won only a postponement of the dispute with the United States. The latest and most nearly definitive Argentine study of the Falkland Islands controversy is by Ricardo R. Caillet-Bois, *Una tierra Argentina: Las Islas Malvinas* (Buenos Aires, 1949). This impressive work, based on archival research in Europe and Argentina, traces the history of the islands from their discovery to the seizure by the English. The author devotes more attention to Alvear's presentation of the case in Washington than have any preceding scholars.

The extensive bibliography of the Monroe Doctrine need by no means be repeated, yet certain special works are important in furnishing a background for evaluating Alvear's report of his conference with the author of the Doctrine. In particular, one should notice the personal influences which were believed to dominate the President:

Worthington C. Ford, "John Quincy Adams and the Monroe Doctrine" in the *American Historical Review*, VII (1902) 676-696, VIII (1903) 28-52; T. R. Schellenberg, "Jeffersonian Origins of the Monroe Doctrine" in the *Hispanic-American Historical Review*, XIV (1934), 1-31, and William A. McCorkle, *Personal Genesis of the Monroe Doctrine* (New York, 1923).

The study of the relations between the United States and Latin America has attracted the attention of many American scholars. Some of the articles of William S. Robertson which are pertinent to the study of Alvear's period include "The Beginning of Spanish-American Diplomacy" in *Essays in American History* (New York, 1910); "South America and the Monroe Doctrine" in the *Political Science Quarterly*, XXX (1915), 82-105. In his article "Foreign Estimates of the Argentine Dictator," *Hispanic American Historical Review* X (1930), 125-137, Robertson quotes extensively from French sources in order to emphasize the importance of material available in French archives on the history of La Plata. A study by William R. Manning, "An Early Diplomatic Controversy," in the *Hispanic American Historical Review*, I (1918), 123-145, shows how Adams' hope of standing as mediator in Latin America was frustrated, in part, by poor agents. Mary Williams' *Anglo-American Isthmanian Diplomacy, 1815-1915* (Washington, 1916) affords a sound and scholarly study of isthmanian diplomacy at the time when Alvear was inveighing against the avariciousness of the great powers and against the stupidity of the Central Americans.

Julius Goebel's *Struggle for the Falkland Islands* (New Haven, 1927) is an impressive study of the problem of the juridical basis of ownership of the islands. This work is not directly concerned with the involvement of the United States in the islands and therefore has little to say on this point. The references to the Argentine dispute with the United States are, therefore, incomplete. Paul D. Dickens "The Falkland Islands Dispute between the United States and Argentina," *Hispanic American Historical Review* IX (1929), 471-477, expands the phase so briefly considered in Goebel's work, but it is based upon printed manuscript materials available in the United States.

The only work of scholarly merit on the foreign affairs of Rosas' regime is John F. Cady's *Foreign Intervention in Río de la Plata* (Philadelphia, 1929). The account is based on extensive archival research in France, England, and the United States, but not in Argentina. Since Alvear played no active role in the tortuous negotiations in Río de la Plata, his presence in Washington is scarcely noted, and his activities, being recorded in Argentine archives, were unknown to the author. An article by Watt Stewart, "Argentina and the Monroe Doctrine, 1824-1828" *Hispanic American Historical Review*, X (1930), 26-32, provides a short account of an Argentine appeal to the United States for a ruling on their dispute with Brazil over the Banda Oriental. The author, drawing from United States sources, does not know of Alvear's interviews with Monroe or Adams. Another short article on "United States-Argentine Commercial Negotiations of 1825," *Hispanic American Historical Review*, XIII (1933), 367-371, discusses an interesting sequel to the Alvear-Adams conference. He shows that the Argentine commercial treaty of 1825 with England was not the blow at United States prestige which it was generally considered to be, for Buenos Aires was ready to sign a corresponding treaty with the North American republic. On account of

Forbes' insistence on reciprocal legislation the treaty was never signed.

Harold E. Peters, under the title *The Foreign Debt of the Argentine Republic* (Baltimore, 1934), made a brief study of the export of capital to the southern republic. He gives the best available account of the first loan which, in 1824, England closed with Argentina.

A Peruvian, Victor Andrés Belaúnde, made a thoughtful, interpretive study of *Bolívar and the Political Thought of the Spanish-American Revolution* (Baltimore, 1938). One should note, however, that either Alvear's conferences in 1825 with Bolivar were unknown to him or that he considered them of no importance, for he does not mention the meeting.

Three recent works are especially important if one is to understand the background of President Monroe's conversations with Alvear. General Alvear was the first official representative to the United States, but agents from the revolutionary La Plata were not unknown before his time. Professor Samuel F. Bemis has prepared an excellent study of these first agents in his *Early Diplomatic Missions from Buenos Aires to the United States* (Worcester, Mass., 1939). His account of the assistance the United States accorded the early missions from Argentina justifies somewhat the growing estimate of Latin-American assistance which President Monroe detailed to Alvear. Also of interest in the study of Monroe's conversation with Alvear is C. C. Griffin's "Privateering from Baltimore during the Spanish-American Wars for Independence" in the *Maryland Historical Review*, XXXV (1940), 1-25. This account, thoroughly documented from American sources, illustrates the piratical irregularities which Monroe and Adams faced, and the terms on which privateering was done. David C. DeForest, who gained wealth from the misty land of smuggling and privateering left his Letter Books from which Benjamin Keen in his recently published work, *David Curtis DeForest and the Revolution of Buenos Aires* (New Haven, 1947), has found additional information on the smuggling operations undertaken during the Spanish-American revolution. These two works by Professors Bemis and Keen trace diplomatic relationship between the United States and Argentina until the advent of Alvear and the assumption of official relations.

NEWSPAPERS AND PERIODICALS

Argentine newspapers published before the time of the Dictator bear a general resemblance to a popular press, but under the control of Rosas they became a projection of the Dictator's will. As such their columns were filled with the meticulous details of those phases of his negotiations about which he wished to make political thunder. The early press is best represented by the *Gaceta de Buenos Aires*. Excellent facsimiles for the years 1810-1821 were prepared by the Junta de Historia y Numismática Americana de Buenos Aires. Through the columns of this paper one may trace the rise and fall of Alvear's political fortune.

Rosas permitted the *British Packet and Argentine News*, an English-language newspaper, to continue as an organ for the English-speaking residents of the capital. Its editor quickly discovered how pleasant life could be if the Dictator were pleased. Always the *British Packet* supported every phase of Rosas' program with noisy acclaim, but on the fall of the Dictator it hailed the victorious Urquiza without an editorial qualm. The *Archivo Americano* Rosas used as an organ for reprinting annual messages, governmental reports, and the multitude of official notes occasioned by his constant diplomatic embroglios. Its wide columns and fine print present such a forbidding aspect that the publication never enjoyed a wide reading public. The *Gaceta Mercantil* of Buenos Aires, Rosas devoted to more popular forms of news reporting. American representatives in Buenos Aires greatly sympathized with Rosas' resistance to European intervention and in order to fortify their own opinion they enclosed for the Department of State many copies of the *Archivo Americano* and the *Gaceta Mercantil*, so that the files of the Department contain a substantial number of these two publications. Because Rosas did not permit any name but his own to appear frequently in the news columns, references to Alvear occur in the press but seldom.

During the revolutionary era the "newspapers" of the Pacific coast were exceedingly primitive. *El Duende* of Santiago, Chile, was no more than five by seven inches in size, yet such news as this and other publications carried was vital to the cause of independence. *El Duende* published Alvear's infamous Memorial to the Spanish monarch.

Only occasionally did European intervention in Argentine affairs become a matter for serious study in the United States. A Mrs. S. P. Jenkins presented her anti-Rosas opinions in an article "Buenos Aires and the Republic of the Banda Oriental" in the *American Whig Review*, III (1846), 160-167. This Whig publication affords a good example of the propaganda against Rosas as it appeared in the United States. *The United States Magazine and Democratic Review*, XVIII (1846), 163-184, 369-382, 480, carried two articles, one a whitewash affair based on material Alvear supplied to the author, and the other an excellent and nonpartisan survey as prepared by Caleb Cushing. Probably Cushing was the best informed American on the subject of European intervention in the Río de la Plata, and, without attempting to judge Rosas' domestic administration, he strongly approved his resistance to the English and the French. Alvear cited with indignation the article by Mrs. Jenkins, but no extant dispatch refers to Cushing's much more important article.

President Polk's special agent to Paraguay, a young, puff-headed fellow, Edward A. Hopkins, attempted to justify himself after the President had repudiated his gratuitous letters of disparagement sent to Rosas personally. The brazen young man prepared an article defending his highly irregular activities and he succeeded in obtaining its publication in two magazines: in the *Bulletin* of the American Geographical and Statistical Society, I (1852), 14-42, and in *DeBow's Review*, XIV (1853), 238-251. Young Hopkins could not forget La Plata, and after Rosas had been driven from power, he returned to Buenos Aires. Victor L. Johnson has prepared an excellent study of his later career, "Edward A. Hopkins and the Development of Argentine Transportation and Communication," *Hispanic American Historical Review*, XXVI (1946), 19-37.

Alvear very soon recognized that national news appeared first in New York and Washington, and that newspapers to the westward, lacking any other news source, copied material from the eastern metropolitan and partisan press. He rated first in importance the Washington *Daily Union*, and during the years when he was seeking to promote American intervention on behalf of his beleaguered country he was paying for published articles in this party paper. Next in importance Alvear rated the New York *Herald*, to which he devoted both time and money. The other New York papers he regarded as of secondary importance. However, he frequently forwarded copies of the *Daily Globe*, *Evening Post*, *Journal of Commerce*, *Morning Express*, and the *Sun*. Out-of-town newspapers he seldom sent, and only if they contained an article which Alvear claimed to have sponsored. He reported complete failure to secure publicity from the *National Intelligencer*, nor did he have contacts with another prominent paper, *Niles' Weekly Register* of Baltimore.

NOTES

Footnotes to Chapter I

1. Gregorio F. Rodríguez, *Historia de Alvear* (2 vols.; Buenos Aires, 1913), I, 3-27, 49-51. To his contemporaries the son was known as "Carlos María" and was so designated in official documents, but as an adult he used only the form "Carlos de Alvear." Probably he never knew his baptismal name of "Carlos Antonio José," for his little town was swept away during the Argentine Revolution and its records destroyed. Many years later a copy of the baptismal certificate, found among the father's documents in Spain, revealed these additional names.

2. *Ibid.*, I, 28-35, 54-56; Paul Groussac, *Estudios de historia Argentina* (Buenos Aires, 1918), p. 109; also an account by a survivor of the attack, Tomás de Iriarte, "Las cuatro frigatas," in *La revista de Buenos Aires*, X (1866), 192-244.

3. Diego de Alvear to José María Cabrer, December 31, 1805, "El diario de Alvear," in *Instituto de investigaciones históricas*, LXXV (Buenos Aires, 1941), xlii-xliii.

4. Gregorio F. Rodríguez, *Historia de Alvear*, I, 56-59.

5. *Ibid.*, I, 60.

6. *Ibid.*, I, 61.

7. Historians once believed that Francisco de Miranda organized widespread societies called collectively, the Gran Reunión Americana, with branches like the Lautaro in the larger cities of western Europe, and that through this secret order the creoles living in Europe were inspired to fight for independence. Bartolomé Mitre and Gregorio F. Rodríguez, two sound Argentine historians, accept this account; but William S. Robertson, editor of Miranda's diary and author of his biography, does not: "This story . . . in its most ample form . . . is at present hardly more than a legend" (*Rise of the Spanish-American Republics as Told in the Lives of Their Liberators*, New York, 1918, p. 53; also his *Life of Miranda*, 2 vols.; Chapel Hill, N. C., 1929, I, 199-200). For Argentine accounts of Miranda's secret societies, see Bartolomé Mitre, *Historia de San Martín y de la emancipación Sud-Americana* (Buenos Aires, 1887), I, 81-85, 134-37.

8. While in Cádiz, Carlos married Carmen Quintanilla, a native of Jeréz de la Frontera. Within the society of Buenos Aires she won high regard for her support of public charities.

9. *Gaceta de Buenos Aires*, March 13, 1812, no. 28.

10. Alvear's rank of lieutenant was much below that of San Martín, a lieutenant-colonel. San Martín had served for fifteen years in the Spanish armies. Between campaigns in Africa and in Spain he had carefully studied military science. He chose Frederick the Great of Prussia as his military mentor; the result of lessons in Prussian thoroughness is seen in San Martín's remarkable passage over the Andes.

11. F. A. Kirkpatrick, *The Argentine Republic* (Cambridge, 1931) and William S. Robertson, *A History of Argentina* (Chapel Hill, N. C., 1937), a trans-

lation of Ricardo Levene, *Lecciones de historia Argentina*, provide brief and reliable accounts of this formative period.

12. Vicente F. López, *Historia de la república Argentina* (10 vols.; Buenos Aires, 1910), VI, 265, declares that Alvear had no use for the Argentine Lautaro as a secret order, but that he valued it highly as a coherent machine for political purposes. He says that under Alvear's guidance its secrecy became nominal.

13. The story of this revolution is summarized in López, *Historia*, IV, 236-37; in Mitre, *Historia de San Martín*, I, 172-73; and in Rodríguez, *Historia de Alvear*, I, 160-76.

14. A summary of social reforms and of the political and administrative program of the Constituent Assembly of 1813 is found in López, *Historia*, IV, 294-317.

15. In June, 1813, Alvear resigned from the Assembly and resumed a military life again. See *El Redactor*, June 12, 1813. Also Mitre, *Historia de San Martín*, I, 197, and his *Historia de Belgrano* (2 vols.; Buenos Aires, 1887), II, 275.

16. Bartolomé Mitre, who generally finds little praise for Alvear, credits him with sufficient military acumen to sense, as did San Martín, the futility of advance through Upper Peru. Both men were searching for new avenues of attacking the Royalists on the South American west coast. See Mitre, *Historia de San Martín*, I, 274-75, 278.

17. Detractors of Alvear regularly repeat the accusation of Rondeau: that he was on the point of capturing the city when Alvear relieved him of command. Mitre repeats the claim, and since Mitre is the most widely known Argentine historian, his interpretations have been generally accepted. But Rodríguez, on the basis of material assembled since the time of Mitre, believed that a new estimate of Alvear should be made. In a most detailed manner he analyzed the Montevideo campaign and demonstrated that Rondeau was not succeeding in his mission; that he could not have taken the city without a naval squadron; and that Alvear alone was in a position to plan a new program and to put it into effect. He showed conclusively that Alvear planned the attack by land and sea and that he carried the program to its successful conclusion. López also agreed with Rodríguez on this point. See Rodríguez, *Historia de Alvear*, I, 349-456; II, 31-91; and López, *Historia*, IV, 411-44.

For Posadas's reasons, written in retrospect, for naming his kinsman to Rondeau's position before Montevideo, see his *Memorias* (Biblioteca Ayacucho, Madrid, 1920), p. 53-57.

18. Proclamations and letters relative to the occupation of Montevideo are given in the collection edited by the Museo Mitre, *Contribución documental para la historia del Río de la Plata* (5 vols.; Buenos Aires, 1913), III.

19. The *Gaceta* of Buenos Aires furnishes an accurate index of Alvear's rise and fall in public esteem. It bubbles with praise and boils with indignation. Reproductions of the *Gaceta* by the Junta de Historia y Numismática Americana have been excellently done. An index and an abstract of the *Gaceta* for the years 1810-1821 by Antonio Zinny (Buenos Aires, 1875) eases the toil of research.

20. Artigas never liked the Buenos Aires administration and he particularly hated Alvear. For examples of his abiding distrust, see Artigas to the *Junta* of Paraguay, Nov. 5, 1812. Also examples of secret information sent from Buenos Aires, Anonymous to Artigas, Dec. 4, 1812, in Clemente L. Fregeiro, *Artigas: Estudio histórico* (Montevideo, 1886) pp. 100-1, 105-6. See also Lewis Bealer, "Artigas, Father of Federalism in La Plata," in A. C. Wilgus, ed., *South American Dictators* (Washington, 1937).

21. Vicente F. López, loyal supporter of the Buenos Aires tradition, finds no valid excuse for the Rondeau revolt. He attributes it to Rondeau's hurt pride and to provincial jealously of the port city. See López, *Historia*, V, 149-65, and Rodríguez, *Historia de Alvear*, II, 256-65.

22. Rodríguez, *Historia de Alvear*, II, 295-97, 394; Mitre, *Historia de San Martín*, I, 390.

23. J. P. Robertson, *Letters on South America* (3 vols.; London, 1843), II, 229-35.

24. For terms of Alvear's surrender of the Directorate, see the letter written April 19, 1815, which Rivadavia received from his wife, as cited in E. Piccirilli, *Rivadavia y su tiempo* (2 vols.; Buenos Aires, 1943), I, 143.

25. Alvear to Colonel Terrada, Río de Janeiro, Nov. 19, 1816, in Rodríguez, *Historia de Alvear*, II, 489-90; also Luís V. Varela, *Historia constitucional* (4 vols.; La Plata, 1910), II, 453 n.

Tomás de Iriarte, who was close to Alvear during the difficult years that immediately followed, came to believe that Alvear did not tell the full truth about the disappearance of national funds. See his *Memorias* (9 vols.; Buenos Aires, 1946-), I, 164.

26. This *Memorial* was first published in *El Duende*, Santiago (Chile) gazette, in 1819. At the time of publication Alvear strenuously denied having written it. See his protest to Manuel José García, May 8, 10, 1819, in Gregorio F. Rodríguez, *Contribución histórica y documental* (3 vols.; Buenos Aires, 1921), I, 227-29.

The authenticity of the *Memorial* is now unquestioned. Señor Rodríguez, on the strength of Alvear's denials, had defended the luckless Director, but after seeing photographic reproductions, he frankly confessed himself in error. See his discussion of the *Memorial* in his *Contribución*, I, 214 ff.

Tomás de Iriate ultimately resigned himself to Alvear's treason, although at first he accepted the devious explanations that his friend offered. See his *Memorias*, I, 157-58.

27. Manuel José García urged him to take no part in further intrigue, but to remain in complete retirement with his family. If he should do this, his friends in the capital would have less difficulty in securing his remission of banishment (Rodríguez, *Contribución*, I, 232-33).

28. See the files of the *Gaceta* for Dec., 1819, and through 1820 for the strongest kind of invective against "the party of Alvear and Carrera." Also the recollections of a member of the Carrera-Alvear band, Tomás de Iriarte, *Memorias*, I, 170, 223.

29. A copy of the proscription against Alvear is given in Cervera, *Historia de Santa Fé*, II, Appendix. Files of the *Gaceta* of Buenos Aires for 1820 show the bitterness felt toward Alvear. His name aroused the citizens to a fury. They could be waiting behind barred doors resigned to the appearance of another revolutionary government, but on receiving word that Alvear was approaching, they would rally with one accord to resist this hated individual.

When the town council became fully informed of his activities, it appealed to López to rid the city of this proscript. Bitter experience had shown that a man of his ambitions could not be near the city if it was to enjoy peace (Cabildo of Buenos Aires to López, Governor of Santa Fé, Biblioteca Nacional, Buenos Aires, Document number 429).

30. *Gaceta de Buenos Aires*, July 19, 1820.

31. Manuel M. Cervera, *Historia de la ciudad y provincia de Santa Fé, 1573-1853* (Santa Fé, Argentina, 1907), II, 524; Tomás de Iriarte, *Memorias*, I, 230-397.

32. Rodríguez, *Contribución*, I, 242; Tomás de Iriarte, *Memorias*, III, 3, 9-14.

Footnotes to Chapter II, Part 1

1. Rodríguez, *Contribución*, II, 4; Tomás de Iriarte, *Memorias*, III, 21-63.

2. Forbes to Adams, Sept. 2 and 14, 1821 (William R. Manning, *Diplomatic*

Correspondence of the United States concerning Independence of the Latin-American Nations, 3 vols.; New York, 1925, I, 581).

Thomas L. Halsey, former United States consul in Buenos Aires, who had trafficked secretly with privateers, wrote General Winder of Baltimore that the new government would be both honest and just, but apparently he did not then anticipate an early end of the privateering business (Halsey to Winder, Sept. 30, 1821, Jonathan Meredith Papers, Library of Congress).

3. An informative account of Rivadavia's reforms during the years 1821-1824 may be found in Lewis W. Bealer, "Bernardino Rivadavia, Argentine Dictator and Institution Builder," in A. C. Wilgus, ed., *South American Dictators* (Washington, 1937).

4. Forbes to Adams, Sept. 11, 1828 (Manning, *Diplomatic Correspondence,* I, 582). President Monroe welcomed news of this drastic enforcement, for the menace of piracy to United States shipping was at its height. Many respectable citizens supplied ships for these privateers and reaped a large share in the profits from successful captures. See Charles C. Griffin, "Privateering from Baltimore during the Spanish-American Wars for Independence," *Maryland Historical Magazine,* XXXV (1940) 1-25. Benjamin Keen in his *David Curtis DeForest and the Revolution of Buenos Aires* (New Haven, 1946) has shown how one American citizen, serving as representative of Buenos Aires in the United States and at the same time retaining his American citizenship, profited extensively from the shadowland of law.

5. Marío Belgrano, *La Francia y la monarquía en el Plata, 1818-1820* (Buenos Aires, 1933), particularly on the candidacy of the obscure Prince de Lucca. Also William S. Robertson, *France and Latin-American Independence* (Baltimore, 1939); also Forbes's dispatches for 1821-1824 in Manning, *Diplomatic Correspondence,* I.

6. Several months after the Congress of Verona adjourned there circulated through the newspapers of Europe a purported "Secret Treaty" which the consulting sovereigns were said to have ratified. This ultraconservative "Treaty" condemned representative governments, demanded suppression of the liberty of the press, and called for support of the clergy, indispensable pillars of the old order. One article in the "Treaty" entrusted to France the suppression of the Spanish-American revolution by force of arms. Wide circulation of this "Treaty" indicated that many people believed that monarchial Europe still considered intervention in the New World. See Robertson, *France and Latin-American Independence,* pp. 248-50, for an account of this document and its publication in Europe and in the United States.

7. Forbes to Adams, Jan. 24, Feb. 24, Feb. 12, 1824 (Manning, *Diplomatic Correspondence,* I, 632-34).

8. Forbes to Adams, Feb. 12, 1824 (*ibid.,* I, 634).

9. The appointment was made on Dec. 23, 1823, and on Jan. 1, 1824, Alvear accepted it. On the following day Iriarte sent his note of acceptance. Tomás de Iriarte had been employed in the Department of Foreign Affairs, for his rubric is found on informal secretarial notes in the departmental files.

10. While holding the Supreme Directorship, Alvear had sent Manuel José García to Río de Janeiro on a mission whose purpose was never adequately explained. Alvear claimed that he authorized his envoy to present to Lord Strangford, British representative there, a request for English assistance in order to prevent the dispatch of an anticipated Spanish army for reconquest of La Plata, or else secure the promise of military aid to defeat it. His enemies said that the Director wished to secure British assistance, even at the cost of annexation to the Empire, so that he might maintain his unpopular administration. His detractors noted that he left inadequate records concerning the mission in the national archives. For accounts of this mission, see Rodríguez, *Historia de Alvear,* II, 299-

381, and his *Contribución*, I, 195 ff.; López, *Historia*, V, 207-8, and Appendix; Charles K. Webster, *Britain and the Independence of Latin-America* (2 vols.; London, 1938), I, 96-102; William S. Robertson (trans.), *A History of Argentina*.

11. Alvear to Rivadavia, June 20 (Ricardo Picirilli, *Rivadavia*, II, 288-89); Tomás de Iriarte, *Memorias*, III, 70-71.

12. Parish to Canning, April 25, 1824, from the section omitted in Webster's collection cited above, I, 110-111.

13. Records in the Archivo General de la Nación, Buenos Aires, for the Misión Alvear, 1824-1825, do not give Alvear's instructions on his conduct abroad. These instructions may be found in the excellent series of historical documents edited by Dr. Emilio Ravignani of the Facultad de Filosofía y Letras, *Documentos para la historia Argentina*, XIV, "Correspondencias generales de la provincia de Buenos Aires relativas a relaciones exteriores, 1820-1824" (Buenos Aires, 1920).

14. To private individuals whom he might meet, Alvear was to explain his public character as an emissary to the United States and to insist that he carried no European commissions. He was to account for his presence in England on grounds of convenience and private interest.

15. Alvear to Rivadavia, Feb. 18, 1824, Archivo General de la Nacion (AGN), Buenos Aires, S[ala] 1, A[mario] 1, A[narquel] 1, núm[ero] 10.

16. Alvear to Secretary of Hacienda, March 14, 1824, *ibid.* Since this sum was set by legislative enactment, the Secretary could not have increased the amount if he had wished.

17. The published message was sent to the Department of State and is found in the State Department, National Archives, Argentine Republic Dispatches, II.

18. Alvear to Rivadavia, June 15, 1824, Rodríguez, *Contribución*, II, 15; also his communication of June 29, 1824, AGN, S1, A1, A1, núm. 10. Tomás de Iriarte, the Secretary of Legation, was not at all impressed with the testimonial dinners; he was much more concerned with the London opera and theatre. See his *Memorias*, III, 122-23.

19. Alvear to Rivadavia, July 20, 1824, AGN, S1, A1, A4, núm. 10. This sum was intended for improving the waterfront at the capital, for establishing a municipal water supply, and for founding three cities at suitable harbors to the south. By the time this money was available, Brazil and the United Provinces were preparing to fight for the possession of the Eastern Shore, and these funds were used to finance Alvear's victorious campaign which culminated in the triumph of Ituzaingó.

Alvear took no active part in the closing of this loan with the Baring Brothers, although he believed that his publicity of Rivadavia's sound political principles induced a favorable frame of mind among the bankers. Credit for the details of the negotiation goes to Don Félix Castro (Alvear to Secretary of Foreign Affairs, July 20, 1824, AGN, S1, A1, A1, núm. 10). For an account of this loan, see Harold E. Peters, *The Foreign Debt of the Argentine Republic* (Baltimore, 1934), pp. 5-14.

20. Alvear to the Secretary of Foreign Affairs, June 29, 1824 (Rodríguez, *Contribución*, II, 31-35).

21. Alvear to Minister of Foreign Affairs, July 20, 1824; Ignácio Núñez to Alvear, AGN, S1, A2, A4, núm. 10.

22. Minutes of the conference held between Rush and the Señores García del Río and Paroissien on May 24, 1824, are found in Rodríguez, *Contribución*, II, 28-29. An indication of the royalist background of this Peruvian mission may be found in A. C. Wilgus, ed., *South American Dictators*, pp. 227-28. García del Río, as an associate of San Martín during the conquest of Peru, had encouraged the great General in his royalist leanings.

23. For Alvear's reports on his gleanings from the Latin-American envoys, see AGN, S1, A2, A4, núm. 10; also Tomás de Iriarte, *Memorias*, III, 129-31.

24. Parish to Canning, April 25, 1824 (Webster, *Britain and the Independence of Latin-America*, I, 111).

25. Alvear to the Secretary of Foreign Affairs, June 20 and 26, 1824, AGN, S1, A1, A1, núm. 10.

26. The questions to which Canning wished answers were:

1. What is the number of inhabitants of the state of Buenos Aires?
2. What is the population of each province, its tribes of Indians and colored persons?
3. What are the names of the provinces, and what actually constitutes the state of Buenos Aires?
4. Are all the provinces in complete subjection to the General Government, or with what exceptions?
5. What cities or considerable places are there in subjection to the present government and what is the population of each one?
6. What is the actual status of Paraguay and its relations, if any, with Buenos Aires?
7. What is the rating now in standing troops in the Army and Navy?
8. What is the income of the administration? Is it increasing or decreasing?

This is a translation of the Spanish version which Secretary Iriarte made for the archives of the mission now filed in AGN, S1, A1, A1, núm. 10. Canning's original paper is not on record. Alvear's written reply to these questions is given in the Appendix.

27. Alvear to Rivadavia, July 22 and 26, 1824 (Rodríguez, *Contribución*, II, 35-36, 45).

28. In June Alvear had written that according to reports Canning regretted Rivadavia's surrender of the ministry because another man would not likely retain such a high standard of administration. At that time Alvear expressed his personal regret that Rivadavia found himself unable to remain in office (Alvear to Rivadavia, June 20, 1824, in Piccirilli, *Rivadavia*, I, 502; II, 288-89).

29. In his written memorandum Alvear expressed the hope that England would induce the new state [Brazil] to respect former colonial boundaries and to take no populated territory [Banda Oriental] by force of arms. Rivadavia had assured the Legislature that Alvear would present this subject to the United States (Alvear to Rivadavia, July 26, 1824, and his memorandum in Rodríguez, *Contribución*, II, 35-44).

30. For all his lack of frankness Alvear did not convince Canning, because the British minister instructed Parish to verify the authority of Buenos Aires to bind the other provinces before promising that recognition would be forthcoming (Canning to Parish, Aug. 23, 1824, in Webster, *Britain and the Independence of Latin-America*, I, 114).

31. Rodríguez, *Contribución*, II, 46-49, provides Alvear's report of the conference with Canning and a memorandum, presumably prepared in retrospect. Other accounts of the interview are found in the relevant archival collections as cited in portions of this chapter.

The recollections of Tomás de Iriarte, written some twelve years later, do not agree precisely with the official version found in the National Archives. The Secretary says that a few days before leaving London, Alvear received a verbal invitation to call upon the Foreign Minister, Canning; and that when Alvear returned, he brought a sheet of paper with eight questions spaced for short answers between. Iriarte protested the gross exaggerations upon which his superior insisted. He also rationalized that the untruths which Alvear required him to draft for Buenos Aires should not be laid to the account of the scribe. Apparently

Canning was not the only one to receive the benefit of Alvear's generous composition.

It would appear that the picturesque phases of the Canning interview never occurred as officially presented. Presumably the Minister Plenipotentiary wished to impress his home office with his diplomatic skill and resourcefulness: even the wiles of the British Foreign Minister could not prevail against him (Tomás de Iriarte, *Memorias,* III, 127-29).

32. Robertson, *France and Latin-American Independence,* 300-301.

33. Foreign Office archives contain no report of this interview. Webster's collection of documents related to England and the independence of Latin America make no reference to the General's presence in England. A private search revealed nothing. Apparently Canning never mentiond to Woodbine Parish this interview with Alvear.

34. Harold W. V. Temperley, *The Foreign Policy of Canning* (London 1925), p. 144.

35. Canning to Parish, Aug. 23, 1824 (Webster, *Britain and the Independence of Latin-America,* I, 116). Manuel José García, Minister of Foreign Affairs under Las Heras, rejected the offer to bribe Spanish recognition as unworthy of the good faith of the South American states (Parish to Canning, Oct. 24, 1824, *ibid.,* I, 119).

36. Las Heras to Alvear, Jan. 19, 1825, AGN, S1 A1, A1, núm. 10.

Footnotes to Chapter II, Part 2

1. Alvear to Secretary of Foreign Affairs, Sept. 25, 1824, Archivo General de la Nación (AGN), Buenos Aires, S[ala] 1, A[mario] 2, A[narquel] 4, núm[ero] 10, and another of Sept. 26 in S1, A1, A1, núm. 10. Although he lacked official confirmation of the elections, Alvear knew its results through accounts which the business firm of Hullett Brothers had given him before he left England.

2. Presumably this member of Congress, whom Alvear did not name specifically, was John Gaillard, President of the Senate, *pro tempore,* on frequent occasions. The minister carried with him a cordial letter of introduction from C. A. Rodney, United States chargé in Buenos Aires, to that gentleman (Rodney to Alvear, March 5, 1824, AGN, S1, A1, A1, núm. 4; Tomás de Iriarte, *Memorias,* III, 142-43).

3. *Ibid.* This advice was more than a polite gesture to enthusiastic hosts. Earlier in the year Lafayette, while holding an interview in Paris with two representatives of Central America, offered the same advice. He gave them a letter of introduction to Monroe, which, in due time, they presented in Washington: "This letter will be delivered by two amiable Guatemalan Republicans, Messrs. García and Grazzio, who are on their way home by way of the United States. I hope that they carry long with them the conviction that on their own patriotism and American friendship they must solely depend, and that from European policy they have nothing to expect but hostilities, deceit, and seduction. . . . Your message of December, 1823, has been for European diplomats a seasonable check and an admirable lesson" (Monroe Papers, New York Public Library; also, Tomás de Iriarte, *Memorias,* III, 141-42).

4. This capable and ingenious Connecticut Yankee, while living in Buenos Aires, had made a comfortable fortune on wartime profits and privateering trade during the Spanish-American revolutionary period, and in 1818 had returned to his native state with a growing family and a competence. From New Haven, Connecticut, DeForest, who never surrendered his American citizenship, had continued secretly to issue privateering patents while holding a commission from the United Provinces. See Benjamin Keen, *David C. DeForest and the Revolution of Buenos Aires* (New Haven, Conn., 1947).

5. David C. DeForest to Rivadavia, Sept. 7, 1823, DeForest Letter Books, Yale University; Rivadavia to Alvear, Feb. 28, 1824, AGN, S1, A1, A1, núm. 5.

6 DeForest to Alvear, Sept. 14, 1824. DeForest had two reasons for not traveling to New York. His rheumatism had almost disabled him. Also, a judgment rendered in a Maryland court for $54,000 made him extremely reluctant to travel outside his own state for fear that he might be served with some legally binding process (DeForest to John Zimmerman, of Buenos Aires, November 18, 1824, DeForest Letter Book, Yale University Library).

7. DeForest listed 432 letters patent and commission for officers as issued by the Buenos Aires War Office, as well as the commissions of the privateers *Tucumán* and *Congreso*, but he included no diplomatic correspondence.

8. Instructions for the American phase of the mission are found in Carlos Correa Luna, *Alvear y la diplomacía de 1824-1825* (Buenos Aires, 1926), Appendix.

9. The dispatches from John Forbes brought up to date the information which the Department had received previously about Alvear. For years special agents of the United States had been penning notes which, in telling of vicissitudes in La Plata, had detailed the former Director's rise and fall in political fortune.

From 1820 to 1823 Alvear had dropped from official notice of the United States, and not until his appointment as minister did the government hear of him again. Forbes included all rumored information relevant to the mission as well as official notices given him by the administration. He wrote that in London the minister would settle long pending negotiations for a loan to the government and adjust a shipping dispute. Six weeks later he was not sure: some people were saying that the mission carried secret instructions concerning the search for a European prince, but men who claimed to know asserted that his journey to England would simply relieve Rivadavia of an opponent for the current year. Rivadavia himself, on receiving Caesar Rodney, explained Alvear's English detour as a visit to see an aged parent. Rivadavia's instruction on the English phase of the mission shows that this explanation was far from the truth. Forbes, who resumed correspondence after Rodney's fatal illness, gave Monroe the last word before the arrival of the new minister when he wrote that Alvear had gone to England to bargain for independence (Forbes to Adams, Dec. 17, May 22, July 5, 1824, National Archives, State Department, Argentine Republic, Dispatches, II; also Forbes to Adams, Jan. 3, Feb. 22, 1824, in Manning, *Diplomatic Correspondence*, I, 631-32, 638).

10. Notes from the Argentine Republic, I, pt. 1; Brent to Alvear, October 4, 1824, Notes to Foreign Legations, III, National Archives, State Department; *National Intelligencer*, Oct. 14, 1824; Alvear to Secretary of Foreign Affairs, October 11, 1824 (Rodríguez, *Contribución*, II, 55-56); Tomás de Iriarte, *Memorias*, III, 158-62.

11. Alvear to the Secretary of Foreign Affairs, Oct. 11, 1824, AGN, S1, A2, A4, núm. 10; Tomás de Iriarte, *Memorias*, III, 162-63.

12. For a divergent account of this first interview with Alvear, see the Appendix.

13. The manuscript of this letter is found in AGN, S1, A1, A1, núm. 5. It has been reprinted in Rodríguez, *Contribución*, II, 58-63.

14. See reports by J. R. Poinsett in Manning, *Diplomatic Correspondence*, I, 441; or in the same text, Forbes to Adams, March 2, 1823, Jan. 3, 1824, I, 617, 631. Also John Q. Adams, *Memoirs* (12 vols.; Philadelphia, 1875), IV, 498.

15. Professor A. P. Whitaker cited these interviews in his recent work, *The United States and the Independence of Latin-America, 1810-1830*. On learning that I was studying the diplomatic career of General Alvear, he generously left to me the presentation of this account.

16. Alvear to the Minister of Foreign Affairs, Oct. 14, 1824, AGN, S1, A2, A4, núm. 10. See the Appendix for the complete text of the interview.

We do not know precisely in what language Monroe conducted this interview. The men seem to have discoursed freely without recourse to an interpreter. We know that Alvear spoke English. Secretary Adams in his unpublished day-to-day notebook says of the official presentation on Oct. 11: "Speech in Spanish." The Secretary might well have noted this fact, for he considered himself unskilled in that language, yet on one occasion he attempted a general translation for the President. Adams's cryptic note for Oct. 20 reads: "Alvear—long conversation with him. Presented him and Iriarta to P[resident] U[nited] S[tates]." In the absence of any comment to the contrary we may presume that the long conversation was in English.

Mr. Henry Adams, custodian of the Adams Manuscripts, kindly supplied the citation to Secretary Adams's notebook.

17. Comments of Nov. 13 and Dec. 4, 1823 (Adams, *Memoirs*, VI, 185, 226).

18. Rush to Adams, May 8, 1824 (James Monroe, *Writings*, 7 vols.; New York, 1898-1903, VI, 435); Monroe to Madison, Jan. 26, 1824 (*ibid.*, VII, 2); Monroe to Jefferson, July 12, 1824 (*ibid.*, VII, 29-30); Monroe to Madison, Aug. 2, 1824 (*ibid.*, VII, 31). Also, Adams, *Memoirs*, VI, 314. The Secretary of State was particularly explicit in his statement that he feared no such intervention, and he made it equally clear that the President did. Monroe was not the only statesman who entertained such fears. George Canning secured his famous conference with Polignac because he believed "that France meditates and has all along meditated a direct interference in Spanish-America" (Canning to Wellington, Sept. 24, 1823, as cited in Harold Temperly, *The Foreign Policy of Canning*, pp. 109-110).

The Argentine Minister of Foreign Relations, Bernardino Rivadavia, in his instructions to Alvear, showed that he, too, believed French intervention on behalf of Spain not unlikely.

19. In cabinet meetings when the declaration was under discussion William Wirt had raised this same question and received from Adams the assurance that the policy did not actually commit the United States to a declaration of war (Adams, *Memoirs*, VI, 203-4). Monroe also accepted this comfortable assurance and as late as Aug., 1824, was writing in this vein (Monroe to Jefferson, Dec. —, 1823; Monroe to Jefferson, July 12, 1824; Monroe to Madison, August 2, 1824, in Monroe, *Writings*, VI, 343-45, and VII, 29-31).

20. Adams to José María Salazar, Aug. 6, 1824 (Manning, *Diplomatic Correspondence*, I, 225-26).

21. In a letter of instructions to the minister of Colombia, Adams, writing in 1823, described almost in Monroe's words to Alvear an offer made to England in 1819: "The British government declined accepting the proposal themselves without, however, expressing any disapprobation of it; without discussing it as a matter of principle, and without assigning any reason for refusal other than it did not suit their policy" (Adams to Anderson, May 27, 1823, and Adams to Rush, Jan. 1, 1819, in Manning, *Diplomatic Correspondence*, I, 195, 87).

22. In Dec., 1818, Secretary Adams had told David DeForest, then Argentine agent to the United States, of efforts to induce England to join in recognition of Buenos Aires. The President included this information in his address of 1819, and in the same year he filed a memorandum with the State Department recommending that the former colonies of Spain be notified of the proposal for joint recognition and of the European silence. The State Department did not heed the injunction (Adams, *Memoirs*, IV, 190; and Monroe, *Writings*, VI, 93-98).

23. The *Franklin* in 1824 was retired from the Pacific patrol and not replaced, so that a lone frigate sailed the Pacific ocean. A captain and his lieutenant stationed off the coast of Louisiana were discharged in July of the same year because their ship was no longer seaworthy, and the Navy had no other to replace it (Adams, *Memoirs*, VI, 337, 401; Monroe, *Writings*, VI, 169).

24. Monroe, *Writings*, VI, 331.

25. "He expressed firm resolution on what this nation is doing to sustain his message and it will not permit any other nation except Spain to make an intervention in our affairs. He explained how and when the United States had prepared the resources they have, the preventive measures they have taken, the increase of their navy, the fortification of their coasts" (Alvear to Rivadavia, Oct. 18, 1824, AGN, S1, A1, A1, núm. 5, and reprinted in Rodríguez, *Contribución*, II, 58-63). Alvear expressed identical sentiments to the Secretary of Foreign Affairs, Oct. 11, 1824, AGN, S1, A1, A1, núm. 10.

26. Adams makes explicit and sometimes sarcastic comments on his chief's impulsive, Spanish-American sympathies. See his *Memoirs*, IV, 15-16, 118, 461. Because of his strong, personal sympathy Monroe included in his annual message comments on the southern revolution, much to Adams's dismay (*ibid.*, V, 84, 109, 200; VI, 103).

27. Monroe to Jefferson, July 12, 1824 (Monroe, *Writings*, VII, 30).

28. Edward H. Tatum, *The United States and Europe, 1815-1823* (Berkeley, Calif., 1936) provides a fresh approach to the diplomacy of these years. He pays particular attention to the close relations with Russia. As late as Oct., 1824, Monroe had written, "Our accounts with Russia are favorable" (Monroe to Madison, Oct. 18, 1824, in Monroe, *Writings*, VII, 41).

29. That Monroe was not consciously mincing the truth about a "second offer" to England is seen in the President's letter to his confidant, Thomas Jefferson. In this letter written just after his famous declaration, he mentions the remarkable abatement of Canning's zeal after *an offer* of *joint recognition* of independence, and wonders if this new attitude proceeds from an unwillingness to recognize the new governments, or from seductive offers made to England by the European powers. Presumably by the time Monroe had sealed his resolve to deliver his message, he had convinced himself that England had rejected a late offer of the United States to recognize Spanish-American republics (Monroe to Jefferson, Dec. 4, 1823, in Monroe, *Writings*, VI, 342).

30. Diplomatic correspondence from Europe had repeatedly confirmed this estimate. See McRea to Monroe, Feb. 7, 1824, and Rush to Adams, Feb. 9, 1824 (*ibid.*, VI, 425, 427-28).

31. Alvear learned his lesson well, and he never forgot to give the United States prior credit for restraining monarchial interference in American affairs. Eighteen years later he embodied Monroe's teaching in an exposition on President Tyler's re-statement of American principles in 1842: "This principle was declared for the first time by President Monroe when France was preparing to help Spain in the fight against her former colonies and, adopted by Mr. Canning, freed us from this powerful enemy" (Alvear to Arana, Minister of Foreign Affairs, Dec. 16, 1842, Archivo del Ministro de Relaciones Exterioires y Culto [AMREC], Buenos Aires, Caja 12).

32. Forbes to Adams, Feb. 22, 1824 (Manning, *Diplomatic Correspondence*, I, 637-38).

33. We know that he had written quite the contrary to Jefferson (Monroe to Jefferson, June 2, 1823, in Monroe, *Writings*, VI, 310).

34. For evidence available to Monroe on monarchial tendencies in Buenos Aires, see Adams to Rodney, May 17, 1823 (Manning, *Diplomatic Corresponce*, I, 186-87); also Prevost to Adams, March 9, 1820; and a copy of a memorandum from the French Minister of Foreign Relations to Don Valentín Gómez (*ibid.*, I, 542, 545-47 n.); Forbes to Adams, Jan. 24, 1824 (*ibid.*, I, 632-33).

35. Adams, *Memoirs*, VI, 386.

36. See Secretary Adams's comments in his *Memoirs*, VI, 281-84, 308, 317-20.

37 Adams to Rodney, May 17, 1823 (Manning, *Diplomatic Correspondence*,

I, 186-92). See also Arthur P. Whitaker, "José Silvestre Rebello," *Hispanic American Historical Review*, XX (1940), 380-401.

38. As Secretary of State under James Madison, Monroe had given equal assurances to the first Buenos Aires representatives, Saavedra and Aguirre (Samuel F. Bemis, "Early Diplomatic Missions from Buenos Aires to the United States, 1811-1824," *Proceedings*, American Antiquarian Society, Worcester, Massachusetts, 1939). Richard Rush in 1817 stated a similar policy to Manuel Aguirre. See *Notes from the Argentine Legation*, I, pt. 1, National Archives, State Department; also Manning, *Diplomatic Correspondence*, I, 19, 31-32; Monroe to John Q. Adams, July 24 and Aug. 3, 1820 (Monroe, *Writings*, VI, 142-43, 147-50).

39. The formidable armament which Colombia had secured from the United States deeply impressed Alvear. He doubted the ability of the new republic to support such a large navy (Alvear to Rivadavia, Oct. 12 and 18, 1824, AGN, S1, A1, A1, núm. 5).

Footnotes to Chapter II, Part 3

1. For a brief survey of this chieftain's career, see William S. Robertson, *The Rise of the Spanish-American Nations as Seen in the Lives of Their Liberators*; W. H. Koebel, *Uruguay* (London, 1911); or Lewis W. Bealer, "Artigas: Father of Federalism on La Plata," in A. C. Wilgus, ed., *South American Dictators*.

2. See his private letters to Alvear while on this mission as given in Rodríguez, *Contribución*, II, 243-50.

3. This last principle Rivadavia told the Legislature he hoped to see added to President Monroe's message, but instructions to his minister, making no mention of the President's previous declaration, simply announced the principle of no expansion by force of arms. To Canning, Alvear had announced the principle, but neither to President Monroe nor to Secretary Adams did he make a clear exposition of this point.

4. These Spanish victories Alvear had deprecated to Canning, but he felt that they were really a serious obstacle to achieving national union (Alvear to Secretary of Foreign Affairs, Oct. 19, 1824, AGN, S1, A2, A4, núm. 10).

5. From the moment that the Argentine mission landed in New York the full details of the Presidential campaign were thrust upon them: Monroe's public career and high political achivements; General Jackson's famous bursts of temper; Adams's long diplomatic service. The chief topic of conversation seemed to be the election, and it appeared to Iriarte that the most vociferous were the recently arrived Irish (Tomás de Iriarte, *Memorias*, III, 157-58, 171-74).

6. Alvear to Adams, Oct. 18, 1824, National Archives, State Department, *Notes from the Argentine Republic*, I, pt. 1; Alvear to Secretary of Foreign Affairs (Oct. 19, 1824, AGN, S1, A2, A4, núm. 10).

7. Mr. Henry Adams, curator of the Adams' papers, reports that he found no note from Alvear in Secretary Adams' letter book. He presumes that it was a formal note of acknowledgment which was not preserved. Sometimes John Quincy Adams' records fell into arrears, and he could have easily mistaken a date when catching them up.

8. Alvear to Secretary of Foreign Affairs, Oct. 19, 1824, AGN, S1, A1, A1, núm. 10.

Iriarte, in his memoirs, does not detail a special conference with Secretary Adams on the Banda Oriental. He refers only to an interview when they informed him that both members of the mission were departing. However, in summarizing the work of the mission after its return to Buenos Aires, Iriarte lists "several conferences with the Secretary of Foreign Relations, Mr. Adams." We must remember that at the time he composed his memoirs (about 1846) Iriarte was living in exile and dared not attempt to secure his files in Buenos Aires. See his *Memorias*, III, 172, 210.

9. For the text of this interview, see AGN, S1, A2, A4, núm. 10; also an incomplete and somewhat edited version in Carlos Correa Luna, *Alvear y la diplomacia de 1824-1825*, 72-73.

10. Adams to Monroe, April 10, 1817 (John Q. Adams, *Writings*, 7 vols.; New York, 1913-1917, VI, 175). Alvear, in this period, had moved from Río de Janeiro to Montevideo, where he sought to use the confusion in the Eastern Shore to favor his party in Buenos Aires.

11. Aguirre to Adams, Dec. 26, 1817 (Manning, *Diplomatic Correspondence*, I, 365).

12. Monroe to Jackson, Dec. 21, 1818, *Monroe Papers*, New York Public Library.

13. Instructions to Middleton, Minister to Russia, July 5, 1820 (Adams, *Writings*, VII, 47).

14. Adams to Forbes, July 5, 1820 (Manning, *Diplomatic Correspondence*, I, 132). See also Forbes's correspondence, *ibid.*, I, 576, 610, 620, 622, 626, 628, 633.

15. Adams, *Memoirs*, VI, 359, 480.

16. Alvear to García, Oct. 19, 1824, AGN, S1, A2, A4, núm. 10.

17. Alvear to Secretary of Foreign Affairs, Sept. 30, 1824 (Rodríguez, *Contribución*, II, 53).

18. Alvear to Salazar, Jan. 1, 1825, AGN, S1, A2, A4, núm. 10; and quoted at length in Carlos Correa Luna, *Alvear y la diplomacia de 1824-1825*, pp. 65-69.

19. Minutes of Forbes's conference with García, March 24, 1825; Forbes to Secretary of State, March 30, 1825, National Archives, State Department, *Argentine Republic, Dispatches*, II.

20. Rivadavia to Alvear, April 25, 1824, AGN, S1, A2, A4, núm. 10. Alvear received the dispatch in London on July 19. In reply he declared that his health had been undermined by the rigors of the long voyage, but he would complete his assignment as soon as possible. Apparently Rivadavia had never planned carefully the Mexican phase of the mission and the projected journey to that capital seems to have been contingent on developments in La Plata. He did not intend to draft instructions on this assignment until the envoy had communicated with Mexico through its emissary stationed in Washington. In the meantime Rivadavia had announced the projected mission to the Mexican Minister of Foreign Affairs, Lucas Alamán, in a dispatch sent by way of Peru (Rivadavia to Alamán, Jan. 3, 1824, AGN, S1, A1, A1, núm. 6).

However, from London, where he had gone after surrendering his post in the government, Rivadavia wrote to Alvear, then in the United States, "I cannot help but advise you to make every effort to go on to Mexico and to establish with that government the first relations between it and our country" (Rivadavia to Alvear, Sept. 18, 1824, in Rodríguez, *Contribución*, II, 63-64).

21. Notice given on Oct. 21, 1824, National Archives, State Department, Notes from the Argentine Republic, I, pt. 1; Tomás de Iriarte, *Memorias*, III, 172.

22. Salazar to Alvear, Oct. 23, 1824, AGN, S1, A1, A1, núm. 10.

23. It took more than two months to secure even inadequate passage to Buenos Aires. In the interim the minister and his secretary spent an easy life in New York where they were well received socially (Tomás de Iriarte, *Memorias*, III, 174-97).

24. Valentín Gómez to Alvear, March 30, 1824 (Rodríguez, *Contribucion*, II, 252).

25. Valentín Gómez to Alvear, Oct. 9, 1824 (*ibid.*, II, 264).

26. Valentín Gómez to Alvear, Sept. 19, 1824 (*ibid.*, II, 261).

27. Dorrego had twice refused the Colombian assignment, once when Rivadavia

offered it and once when Las Heras tendered the same post, with Peru added. Presumably the administration thought that if the appointment were conferred on Alvear *in absentia* he would have to accept it. See Forbes to Adams, Aug. 13, 1824, National Archives, State Department, Argentine Republic, Dispatches, II.

28. Alvear to García, Jan. 1, 1825, AGN, S1, A2, A4, núm. 10. Señor Correa Luna calls the letter a "very curious document . . . not exempt from irony and even with a little heat which shows the exaggerated faith Buenos Aires placed in his patience" (Correa Luna, *Alvear y la diplomacía de 1824-1825*, p. 83).

29. Alvear's care that nothing should injure his reputation in the United States proved futile. The observant John Forbes accurately reported from Buenos Aires the returning minister's uncertain prospects (Forbes to Secretary of State, Nov. 30, 1825, National Archives, State Department, Argentine Republic, Dipatches, II).

Alvear purposely composed a rejection which would stop just short of personal insult, and not until he was nearing home did his secretary complete the final draft (Tomás de Iriarte, *Memorias*, III, 182).

30. García to Alvear, April 13, 1825, AGN, S1, A1, A1, núm. 5. An archival note dated March 28, 1825, consented to Alvear's refusal to go to Bogotá. The Minister of Foreign Affairs under Las Heras was Manuel José García, formerly Alvear's agent on the questionable mission to Río de Janeiro during the General's brief Directorate. Under later governments García had served again at Río de Janeiro, and in the Rodríguez-Rivadavia administration had been a faithful Secretary of Treasury. Alvear's rejection had been addressed to García, and it may be that this functionary did not feel competent to take his former chief to task. Señor Correa Luna observes that García "with his customary prudence acknowledged receipt."

Las Heras, who had assumed the executive leadership upon the departure of Rivadavia, received the mission, but he made no reference whatever to its work and asked no question about the affairs of Europe or of America. Apparently he had no interest in the outside world: instead he conducted a dreary monologue on the recent material prosperity of Buenos Aires.

García, in the foreign office, welcomed the mission home without mentioning the rejection of the Colombian assignment. Iriarte remembered that he was commended for the complete and orderly files of the mission. For this favorable comment the secretary felt that no credit was due to Alvear. He had found his chief a difficult man to work with; he had broken with him personally; and always he was plagued with the incomplete and ill-written notes which Alvear jotted down so carelessly and then tossed over to him to decipher and to draft into acceptable form (Tomás de Iriarte, *Memorias*, III, 91-101, 110-11, 126-29, 210-11).

31. *Asembleas Constituyentes Argentinas*, Instituto de Investigaciones Históricas de la Facultad de Filosofía y Letras, Emilio Ravignani, ed. (Buenos Aires, 1937), I, (1813-1833), 1001.

32. Some of Alvear's numbered dispatches from his mission are missing. Rivadavia had instructed him to require his Secretary to keep a daily journal of current events relating to South American problems. This journal was to be dispatched every six months. There is no journal of any sort in the archival collection on the *Missión Alvear*.

33. Correspondence between H. R. Nixon and Alvear, AGN, S1, A1, A1, núm. 4.

34. Tomás de Iriarte, *Memorias*, III, 213, 225.

Footnotes to Chapter III

1. Vicente G. Quesada, *Historia diplomática Latino-Americana* (2 vols.; Buenos Aires, 1918), I, 290-91.

2. Argentine accounts of General Arenales gloss over his career after 1824 as governor of Salta with a few vacuous observations of an uncritical nature. For example, see Carlos I. Salas, *Bibliografía del General don José de San Martín* (5 vols.; Buenos Aires, 1910), I, 200.

3. For documentary materials relative to the decrees of Arenales and Sucre, see Vicente Lecuna, *Documentos referentes a la creación de Bolivia* (2 vols.; Caracas, 1924), I, chap. iii. Also, note the comments by the Argentine historian, Carlos Correa Luna, *Carlos de Alvear y la diplomacía de 1824-1825* (Buenos Aires, 1926), pp. 100-105.

4. Text of the act is found in Ernesto Restelli, *La gestión diplomática del General Alvear en el Alto Perú* (Buenos Aires, 1927), pp. 1-2.

5. *Ibid.*, pp. 3-7. The ministers were to receive 8,000 pesos per year, their secretary 2,000 pesos annually.

6. Instructions to the Legation, delivered June 10, 1825. The ministers asked for and received very extensive explanations of ambiguities in the original draft. See Alvear and Díaz Vélez to García, June 14, 1825; García to Alvear and Díaz Vélez, June 16, 1825 (*ibid.*, pp. 13-18).

7. For accounts of this episode from the viewpoint of the liberating army of Peru, see General William Miller, *Memoirs* (2 vols.; London, 1829), II, 300-301; Daniel F. O'Leary, *Memorias* (28 vols.; Caracas, 1884), XXVIII, 414-19.

8. Supplementary Instructions, June 25, 1825 (Restelli, *La gestión diplomática*, pp. 22-23). Having recently floated a loan in London, the United Provinces could make expansive offers to underwrite the costs of war.

9. *Ibid.*, pp. 121-29. News releases which General Alvear sent to Buenos Aires are found in Gregorio F. Rodríguez, *Contribución histórica y documental* (3 vols.; Buenos Aires, 1921), II, 95.

10. Report of the two conferences with His Excellency, the Liberator, held October 8 and 9, 1825, in Restelli, *La gestión diplomática*, pp. 121-32.

11. For non-Argentine reports of these meetings, see Santiago Estenos' report in Vicente Lecuna, *Documentos*, I, 517; O'Leary's summary, based in part on Estenós, in his *Memorias*, XXVIII, 421-30; Bolívar's letters to Tomás de Heres of Peru, Oct. 12, 1825, to Santander of Colombia, Oct. 10 and 11, 1825 (Vicente Lecuna, *Cartas del Liberator*, 10 vols.; Caracas, 1929, V, 114-15, 107-13); Sucre to Santander, Oct. 11, 1825 (*Archivo Santander*, 24 vols.; Bogotá, 1918, XIII, 220-21).

12. Bolívar himself says that Alvear and Díaz Vélez proposed the invasion (Bolívar to Santander, Oct. 10, 1825, in Vicente Lecuna, *Cartas*, V, 110).

13. Later Bolívar developed this plea in greater detail (Bolívar to Santander, Nov. 11, 1825, in Vicente Lecuna, *Cartas*, V, 168).

14. Alvear to García, Oct. 23, 1825 (Rodríguez, *Contribución*, II, 140-41).

15. Alvear and Díaz Vélez to García, Oct. 24; and García to Alvear and Díaz Vélez, Nov. 19, 1825 (Restelli, *La gestión diplomática*, pp. 136-38). Also Estenós to Alvear and Díaz Vélez, nos. 1 and 2, Oct. 9, 1825 (*ibid.*, pp. 162-63).

16. Texts of the addresses, not given in Restelli's compilation, may be found in Rodríguez, *Contribución*, II, 95-97.

17. Díaz Vélez, for some reason, did not attend. He received only one short and perfunctory toast. In such a gathering General Alvear always bore himself well. For accounts of the banquet, see Odriozola, *Documentos históricos del Perú* (10 vols.; Lima, 1874) VI, 316; and Rodríguez, *Contribución*, II, 97-99.

18. O'Leary, *Memorias*, XXVIII, 431 ff. For a charming description of a banquet on the Liberator's birthday, Oct. 28, see Rey de Castro, *Recuerdos del tiempo heróico* (Guayaquil, 1883), pp. 145-52.

19. O'Leary, *Memorias*, XXVIII, 434-35.

20. Díaz Vélez, native of the area, had led its first movements for independence, but as his ties with Buenos Aires tightened he had lost contact with his homeland.

21. Responsible men in the governments that Bolívar had left behind him counseled against such a move. See Santander's advice against a march into La Plata, *Archivo Santander*, XII, 350; XIII, 23, 198, 270, 293.

22. Bolívar to Santander, Nov. 11, 1825 (Vicente Lecuna, *Cartas*, V, 168).

23. Bolívar to Santander, March 20, May 7, 1826 (*ibid.*, V, 257, 288).

24. Alvear and Díaz Vélez to Bolívar, Oct. 21, 1825 (Restelli, *La gestión diplomática*, pp. 155-57).

25. García to Alvear and Díaz Vélez, Sept. 21, Oct. 23, 1825 (*ibid.*, pp. 70-71, 91); Alvear and Díaz Vélez to Bolívar, Nov. 10, Dec. 3, 1825 (*ibid.*, pp. 170, 181-82). Summary of the Fourth Conference held with Bolívar, Dec. 6, 1825 (*ibid.*, pp. 203-5).

26. O'Leary, *Memorias*, XI, contains the letters of Dean Funes to Bolívar: forty communications written between April, 1824, and Oct., 1826. Vicente Lecuna's collection, *Cartas del Libertador*, gives no letters from Bolivar to Funes. See particularly Funes to Bolívar, Aug. 26, Nov. 26, 1825 (O'Leary, *Memorias*, XI, 141-42, 153). For evidence of Bolívar's trust in Funes, besides Alvear's reports, see Bolivar to Santander, Aug. 19, Oct. 27, 1825 (Vicente Lecuna, *Cartas*, V, 75, 156), or to Tomás de Heres, Oct. 27, 1825 (*ibid.*, V, 150); to Santa Cruz, Sept. 25, 1825 (*ibid.*, V, 93).

General Sucre also placed great trust in the judgment of the Dean. See the Marshal's correspondence with Bolivar, July 11, 1825, Feb. 12, 28, April 12, June 6, 1826 (O'Leary *Memorias*, I). Santander of Colombia naturally accepted his leader's interpretation, and so the results of Funes's correspondence spread far. See Santander to Bolívar, Nov. 6, 1825 (*Archivo Santander*, XIII, 273). O'Leary, himself a recipient of a few Funes letters, crystallized this hostile attitude toward the United Provinces in his *Narración*.

27. Funes had written that England would not permit a war in the La Plata estuary because of the damage which would result to British goods and commerce. He said that Canning had so informed Alvear when that minister was in London. Alvear declared that Funes had misinterpreted his report on that issue. See the summary of the Fourth Conference, Restelli, *La gestión diplomática*, pp. 203-5.

28. Alvear and Díaz Vélez to García, Oct. 21, 1825, and García to Alvear and Díaz Vélez, Nov. 19, 1825 (*ibid.*, 117-19); Bolívar to Alvear, Dec. 5, 1825 (Vicente Lecuna, *Cartas* V, 183-86).

29. García to Alvear and Díaz Vélez, Oct. 26, 1825 (Restelli, *La gestión diplomática*, pp. 104-5).

30. De las Heras to the Government of Peru, Sept. 9, 1825, and Garcia to Alvear and Díaz Vélez, Sept. 10, 1825 (*ibid.*, pp. 67-69).

31. Alvear and Díaz Vélez to García, Oct. 24, 1825 (*ibid.*, p. 137); and Alvear (privately) to García, Oct. 23, 1825 (Rodríguez, *Contribución*, II, 141).

32. Summary of Bolívar's ideas on the American Congress at Panama, Dec. 30, 1825 (Restelli, *La gestión diplomática*, p. 227).

33. García to Alvear and Díaz Vélez, Dec. 3, 1825 (*ibid.*, p. 149).

34. The Brazilian Empire, alarmed at the likely prospects of having the Liberating Army invading its ill-defended provinces, repudiated the acts of the provincial governor and made complete satisfaction for outrages committed on persons and property.

35. Funes to Bolívar, Jan. 26, 1826 (O'Leary, *Memorias*, XI, 166).

36. Alvear and Díaz Vélez to García, Jan. 18, 1826 (Restelli, *La gestión diplomática*, pp. 150-51).

37. Bolívar to Alvear, March 13, 1826 (Rodríguez, *Contribución*, II, 166-67).

38. García to Alvear and Díaz Vélez, July 28, 1825, and related documents on Tarija, in Restelli, *La gestión diplomática*, pp. 34-40. Papers relative to the restoration of Tarija bulk larger in the files of the mission than any other subject.

39. An abstract of all matters related to Tarija as discussed in the first two conferences with the Liberator and General Sucre is given in Restelli, *La gestión diplomática*, pp. 132-33, 199-202.

40. Privately he confessed that such was not his real opinion, but he had advanced it as rebuttal.

41. The Argentine ministers were doubly zealous in urging the Liberator to accept their doctrine of no secession without consent of the parent country. Once he had restored Tarija in defiance of popular will, they intended to ask for the Chichas area (somewhat to the northwest of Tarija) as well. Yet when Bolivar asked them about claims for additional territory, they denied having any further demands. They advised Buenos Aires not to worry: their denials were couched in terms sufficiently equivocal to admit revival of the Chichas claims at any time (Estenós to Alvear and Díaz Vélez, Nov. 6, 17, 1825, and Alvear and Díaz Vélez to Bolívar, Nov. 10, 1825 (*ibid.*, p. 165, p. 207, pp. 208-9); Alvear and Díaz Vélez to García, Jan. 18, 1825 (*ibid.*, p. 151).

42. Report of the Third Conference held with the Liberator, Oct. 27, 1825; Bolívar to Alvear and Díaz Vélez, Nov. 6, 1825 (Restelli, *La gestión diplomática*, pp. 165, 200).

43. Resolution of the Bolivian Assembly (Vicente Lecuna, *Documentos*, I, 415); Bolívar to Ciriaco Díaz Vélez, Nov. 17, 1825 (Restelli, *La gestión diplomática*, p. 209).

44. Estenós to Alvear and Díaz Vélez, Nov. 17, 1825, and Alvear and Díaz Vélez to Bolívar, Nov. 10, 1825 (*ibid.*, pp. 207-9).

45. Bolívar to Santander, Oct. 21, 1825 (Vicente Lecuna, *Cartas*, V, 137), and Bolívar to Unanúe, Nov. 10, 1825 (*ibid.*, V, 161).

46. Alvear and Díaz Vélez to García, Dec. 3, 1825 (Restelli, *La gestión diplomática*, p. 183).

47. First conference with Bolívar (Restelli, *La gestión diplomática*, p. 129); Bolívar to Alvear and Díaz Vélez, Nov. 14, 1825 (*ibid.*, pp. 168-69). Bolívar to Tomás de Heres, Oct. 12, 1825, Bolívar to Santander, Nov. 11, 1825 (Vicente Lecuna, *Cartas*, V, 114-15, 168-69).

48. Alvear and Díaz Vélez to García, Dec. 3, 1825 (Restelli, *La gestion diplomática*, pp. 184-85).

49. Alvear and Díaz Vélez to García, Jan. 18, 1826 (Rodríguez, *Contribución*, II, 150). This document, though signed by both members of the Legation, is not found in Restelli's compilation.

50. Alvear and Díaz Vélez to Bolívar, Nov. 10, 1825 (Restelli, *La gestión diplomática*, p. 207); Bolívar to Alvear, March 6, 1827 (Vicente Lecuna, *Cartas*, VI, 215); Sucre to Alvear, Sept. 9, 1826 (Rodríguez, *Contribución*, II, 182); Sucre to Bolívar, May 11, 1826 (O'Leary, *Memorias*, I, 321).

But the Bolivian envoy conducted himself poorly while in Buenos Aires. "They write from below that our envoy to Buenos Aires, Dr. Serrano, is behaving so badly as to discredit the country. I have asked for information from Dr. Funes and am waiting to see if it is necessary to suspend his commission. Everyone says that he is a scamp" (Sucre to Bolívar, April 12, 1826, *ibid.*, I, 312).

51. Alvear to García, Dec. 21, 1825 (private) (Rodríguez, *Contribución*, II, 143); Alvear and Díaz Vélez to García, Dec. 22, 1825 (official) (Restelli, *La gestión diplomática*, pp. 220-21).

52. *Ibid.*

53. Alvear to García, Oct. 23, 1825 (Rodríguez, *Contribución*, II, 141-42).

54. García to Alvear, Nov. 15, 1825 (*ibid.*, II, 151).

55. Alvear to García, Jan. 5, 1826 (*ibid.*, II, 147).

56. García to Alvear, Feb. 15, 1826 (*ibid.*, II, 151).

57. For two generations the impasse continued: Tarija was administered by Bolivian officials, while Argentines periodically revived claims to the territory.

In successive treaties between the two republics the question was always postponed for future agreement. Finally, however, in 1889-1892 definitive treaties awarded the province to Bolivia (*Colección de tratados celebrados por la república Argentina con las naciones estranjeras* II, 215; Infante to Arenales, Sept. 9, 1829, Rodríguez, *Contribución*, II, 133-35; Declaration of the Cabildo of Tarija, Oct. 25, 1826, *ibid.*, II, 136).

58. Díaz Vélez was first ordered to return on Jan. 26, 1826; his last dispatch from Chuquisaca was dated Aug. 16, 1826 (Restelli, *La gestión diplomática*, pp. 248, 336).

Footnotes to Chapter IV, Part I

1. Minute of Forbes's conference with García, March 24, 1825, National Archives, State Department, Argentine Republic, Dispatches, II.

2. "Whether they send a diplomatic agent, even of the third class, to the United States is quite uncertain, but daily evidences are given of their perfect indifference to us" (Forbes to Clay, March 30, 1825, *ibid.*).

3. In that era the United Provinces regularly imported flour from the United States, and American merchants wished to see the import tax removed. But a commercial treaty had never been signed. Rivadavia's instructions to Alvear had stated the position of Buenos Aires: that the administration would have been willing to sign a commercial treaty with the United States if Forbes had indicated that his country desired one. Instead, through conferences with him both nations had reached a satisfactory understanding "on commerce between the two countries." Since that time neither side had made real efforts to conclude a treaty. See also Watt Stewart, "United States-Argentine Commercial Negotiations of 1825," *Hispanic American Historical Review*, XIII (1933), 367-71.

4. Minute of Forbes's conference with García, Sept. 12, 1825, National Archives, State Department, Argentine Republic, Dispatches, II.

5. Forbes to Clay, Nov. 29, 1825, *ibid.*

6. Correspondence on this affair is found in AGN, S1, A2, A4, núm. 9.

7. See Mariano de Vedia y Mitre, *De Rivadavia a Rosas* (Buenos Aires, 1930), pp. 42-103.

8. For a brief survey of Alvear's military career, see Carlos I. Salas, *Bibliografía del coronel Brandsen* (Buenos Aires, 1910), pp. 36-46. This bibliography contains many citations to the Brazilian campaign and to the battle of Ituzaingó, where Colonel Brandsen was killed.

A new governor of Buenos Aires, Manuel Dorrego, made some slighting remarks about Alvear's handling of troops at Ituzaingó. The General's spirited replies fanned party hatred, which ultimately resulted in an attempt to assassinate the victor of the battle.

Criticism of Alvear's generalship was widespread, and increased rather than declined after victory over the Brazilians. Tomás de Iriarte, who served in that campaign as general in the artillery, devotes a long section to Alvear's work as Secretary of Army and Navy, and as commanding General. See Iriarte's *Memorias*, III, 301-504.

9. Forbes to Clay, March 28, 1826, National Archives, State Department, Argentine Republic, Dispatches, II.

10. Those who favored a centralizing, unifying program were called Unitarians. Supporters of a decentralized, confederate form of government chose the name of Federalists. Federalists emphasized the independence of local governments, which—in practice—meant that local chieftains should be unimpeded in their control. Geographically, Unitarians found their greatest support in the city of Buenos Aires and environs, while the rural areas and back provinces generally supported Federalism. Socially the upper classes, professional men, and educated,

city-bred people called themselves Unitarians, while the cowboys and small-town folk embraced the cause of Federalism.

11. Reliable English accounts of this controversial period in Argentine history may be found in such works as W. S. Robertson, "Foreign Estimates of the Argentine Dictator," *Hispanic American Historical Review,* X (1930), 125-37; F. A. Kirkpatrick, *A History of the Argentine Republic* (Cambridge, 1931); C. A. Haring, *South American Progress* (Cambridge, Mass., 1934); J. F. Rippy, P. A. Martin, and I. J. Cox, *Argentina, Brazil, and Chile since Independence* (Washington, 1935); W. A. Robertson, *A History of Argentina* (translation of Ricardo Levene, *Lecciones de historia Argentina*); L. W. Bealer, "Juan Manuel de Rosas," in A. C. Wilgus, ed., *South American Dictators;* J. F. Rippy, *Historical Evolution of Hispanic-America* (New York, 1940).

12. Tomás de Iriarte, *Memorias,* IV, 87, 104, 147-50, 185-86.

13. For a detailed study of the basic disagreement, see John F. Cady, *Foreign Intervention in the Río de la Plata* (Philadelphia, 1929), chap. ii.

14. Julius Goebel, *The Falkland Islands* (New Haven, Conn., 1927), presents a lengthy and definitive study of the legal title to the Islands. He concludes that the islands belonged to Spain, and that Argentina after the Revolution inherited the rights of the mother country.

15. Archival records include no instructions for Alvear in 1832. Vicente de Maza notified the Department of State of the appointment on Dec. 20, 1832. This nomination, which remained in effect until 1835, was recorded in Hasse's *Index,* and thus mistakenly reports the presence of Carlos de Alvear in the United States until the cancellation of his commission in 1835.

16. Aaron Vail, United States chargé in London, found Moreno in 1835 pressing his demands against England. Vail observed, "Due perhaps to our dispute with his country over the Malvinas [Falkland] Islands, my association with the Argentine minister has been rather distant and embarrassed" (Vail to Forsyth, March 4, 1835, in Manning, *Diplomatic Correspondence of the United States: Inter-American Affairs, 1831-1860,* 12 vols.; Washington, 1932-1939, VII, 230).

17. Arana to Forsyth, July 14, 1835 (*ibid.,* I, 189-91). About the same time Carlos de Alvear was voicing to his own government his private regrets over the delay. He declared that in June, 1833, he had been notified of his appointment and had immediately set himself in readiness to depart. Month after month the administration had temporized. He had concluded his private affairs, and since that time had been dependent on his salary. Because he had not departed on his mission, no salary had been forthcoming, and on this matter he grievously complained (MS without heading or date, AGN, S1, A1, A1, núm. 6, Manuscript number 247).

18. Arana to Moreno, Sept. 19, 1835, AGN, S1, A2, A4, núm. 9.

19. Vail to Forsyth, March 4, 1835 (Manning, *Inter-American* Affairs, VII, 230).

20. James D. Richardson, *Messages and Papers of the Presidents, 1789-1897* (20 vols.; Washington, 1897), III, 1246, 1319; IV, 1370.

21. Forsyth to Arana, March 19, 1835 (Manning, *Inter-American Affairs,* I, 17).

22. Dorr to Forsyth, Sept. 24, 1837, National Archives, State Department, Consular Reports, Buenos Aires, V.

23. Alvear to Rosas, Jan. 24, 1838, Archivo del Ministro de Relaciones y Culto (AMREC), Caja 12.

24. In Alvear's last years two younger sons lived with him. La Señora Carmen Quintanilla de Alvear remained with the family. She survived her husband and died in Buenos Aires on March 31, 1867 (Rodríguez, *Historia de Alvear,* I, 66).

25. Alvear to Arana, May 25, 1838, AGN, S1, A2, A4, núm. 13.

26. In his annual message of Jan., 1837, Rosas explained the reason for Al-

vear's long-delayed departure: he blamed it on a misunderstanding with Moreno. On this occasion the Dictator also declared that the purpose of the mission was to settle Argentine claims for the atrocious *Lexington* seizure. In recounting the unhappy fate of the Falkland Islands, Rosas used more bitter words on the *Lexington* episode than he employed in describing the capture and possession of the islands by Great Britain. A copy of his message is found in the National Archives, State Department, Consular Reports, Buenos Aires, V.

27. The instructions relative to the Falkland Islands will be set forth in the following chapter, where the United States-Argentine phases of the controversy will be presented in detail.

28 Arana used "Argentine Confederation" or "Argentine Republic" interchangeably.

29. Rosas had turned upon the French while Santa Cruz was fighting enemies from Chile and Peru. They soon overthrew him and sent him into exile. Years later, activities of Santa Cruz agitated Arana for fear the dictator would find resources abroad to re-establish himself. Copyists in Arana's office prepared extremely lengthy dispatches for Brazil, Chile, and Peru, but the flurry blew itself out before Alvear could take action.

30. Instructions to Carlos de Alvear, AGN, S1, A1, A1, núm. 5.

31. Alvear to Arana, Aug. 4, Sept. 13, 1838, AGN, S1, A2, A4, núm. 13.

32. The first official with whom Alvear talked was Joel R. Poinsett, then Secretary of War, whom he called "an old and close friend." Poinsett greeted him with great kindness and the two men spent some time in reminiscing—presumably of those days when Poinsett, as Consul-General of the United States in Buenos Aires, witnessed Alvear's eager leadership of the Revolution (Alvear to Arana, Oct. 19, 1838, AMREC, Caja 12).

33. Vail to Alvear, Sept. 28, 1838, National Archives, State Department, Notes to the Argentine Republic, VI. Alvear's letter of credentials declared that his appointment was to make effective the nomination of July 14, 1835, which had been made "with the sincere desire of settling the difficulties which unfortunately had interrupted the good understanding between the two republics" (Notes from the Argentine Republic, I, pt. 1). This letter carried no mention of British seizure of the Falkland Islands subsequently nor of the French blockade. The tenor of the letter conformed strictly to Alvear's instructions without the significant additions which relegated the Falkland controversy to second place.

34. Alvear to Arana, Oct. 18, 1838, AMREC, Caja 12.

35 In his dispatch to Arana, Alvear added the curious note that Vail spoke neither French nor Spanish, so that all discussions were conducted through an interpreter. Alvear spoke English; Vail was born in France and lived there for long periods of his life (Alvear to Arana, Oct. 19, 1838, AMREC, Caja 12).

36. National Archives, State Department, Notes from the Argentine Republic, I, pt. 1.

Footnotes to Chapter IV, Part 2 .

1. Julius Goebel, *The Struggle for the Falkland Islands*, pp. 433 *et seq.*; and Ricardo Calliet-Bois, *Una tierra Argentina: Las Islas Malvinas*, chaps. xiv-xvi.

2. Vernet to the Secretary of Government, Dec. 24, 1829, AGN, Sala 10, C3, A4, núm. 5, as cited by Señor Rolando Dorcas Berro, "El 10 de junio de 1829 fué consagrada la soberanía Argentina," *La Nación*, Buenos Aires, June 10, 1947.

3. Slacum to Livingston, Dec. 9, 1831 (Manning, *Inter-American Affairs*, I, 75-78). Unless otherwise cited, the diplomatic correspondence for this chapter will be found in this volume.

Only rarely did Lavalle presume to speak for the nation. Rosas, who repealed so much of Lavalle's work, supported this decree, however.

4. *Ibid.*, I, 109-10, notes.

5. Affidavits presented by Alvear in 1839 (*ibid.*, I, 211-22); Goebel, *The Struggle for the Falkland Islands*, chap. ix.

6. Manning, *Inter-American Affairs*, I, 95-96 n. According to the contract the men presumably did not expect Vernet to keep the skins in trust for them, but would return to them an equal number out of his share of their season's catch. By setting a value on the whalebone they obviously expected a cash consideration, not a return of the merchandise. Vernet may have intended to market it himself and to keep as his commission any amount over twenty-four cents per pound. Certainly the *Bellville* sailors had no use for 3,000 pounds of whalebone on the Falkland Islands.

American complaints later charged Vernet with dishonesty for selling to homeward-bound Englishmen the skins taken from the *Superior* and the *Bellville.* These charges must have arisen as a misunderstanding of what Vernet was to do with the material he was holding as "security." Vernet apparently felt that once he had assumed responsibility for a certain sum, he was free to return its equivalent, not bound to keep the identical merchandise.

7. A copy of Captain Davison's depositions as taken by Consul Slacum is found in Manning, *op. cit.*, I, 66-68, 96-98. Davison sailed with Duncan on the "Lexington" when that captain broke up the colony on Dec. 31, 1832. On Jan. 2 and 3, 1833, Davison swore to further particulars before Captain Duncan. These relations identify certain men whom Duncan arrested and put in chains. The later statements look as if Davison was trying to build up a case for himself.

Vernet published his defense in a supplement of an English language newspaper of Buenos Aires, the *British Packet*, Feb. 25, 1832.

8. Captain Davison, in his affidavits before Slacum and Captain Duncan, says nothing about a commercial agreement for use of the ship on its voyage to Tierra del Fuego nor of Vernet's payment of wages and passage money. Slacum frankly accused Vernet of using uncondemned property for private purposes.

9. Slacum's correspondence with Buenos Aires and Washington vividly details a hostile interpretation of events. See his correspondence in Manning, *Inter-American Affairs*, I, 65-98.

10. Richardson, *Messages*, III, 1116.

11. Van Buren to Forbes, Feb. 10, 1831.

12. Slacum to Livingston, Nov. 23, 1831; Slacum to Anchorena, Nov. 25, 1831; Anchorena to Slacum, Nov. 29, 1831. Slacum was not clear in his own mind whether Argentina had title to the islands or not, although Anchorena received no clue to that uncertainty. Writing to Secretary Livingston on Dec. 9, he particularly denied Argentine title to the islands, and declared that England had never abandoned claim to them. Two weeks later he "supposed" that Argentina possessed title to Patagonian shores and to the Falklands (Slacum to Livingston, Dec. 9, 20, 1831).

Paul D. Dickens, "The Falkland Islands Dispute with the United States," *Hispanic American Historical Review*, IX (1929), 471-87, details the dispute in which Slacum and Francis Baylies sought to nail their propositions to the diplomatic table.

13. Duncan to Slacum, Nov. 29, Dec. 1, 1831.

14. Slacum to Anchorena, Dec. 6, 1831.

15. Anchorena to Slacum, Dec. 9, 1831.

16. Goebel found that Captain Duncan included no report of his seizures in his logbook. The American version comes from Captain Davison and Slacum, who talked with Duncan and other participants in the raid. No American source mentions the use of the French flag, on which all the others insisted. A majority of the witnesses testified that the ship was flying an American flag when it entered the harbor, although some stated that they did not see the flag until later.

17. Manning, *Inter-American Affairs*, I, 216.

18. The Argentine prisoners who finally arrived in Buenos Aires did not charge the Americans with stealing property, nor Captain Davison with claiming items which had not been taken from his ship. For their testimony on the whole period, see Manning, *Inter-American Affairs*, I, 211-22.

19. García to Slacum, Feb. 15, 1832. During the course of the Falkland Islands dispute with the United States, several men occupied the Argentine Ministry of Foreign Affairs. Slacum corresponded with Tomás Manuel de Anchorena and with Manuel José García. Francis Baylies negotiated with Manuel Vicente de Maza. During the whole priod of Alvear's second mission to the United States, Felipe Arana held the portfolio.

20. García to Slacum, Feb. 14, 1832; Slacum to García, Feb. 16, 1832; Vicente de Maza to Livingston, Aug. 8, 1832.

21. Livingston to Baylies, Jan. 26 and Feb. 14, 1832.

22. Baylies to Livingston, May 18, July 24, 1832.

23. Vicente de Maza to Baylies, Aug. 14, 1832. All Argentine claims arising from this event totalled $227,000 (Manning, *Inter-American Affairs*, I, 228). The longer Vernet had to wait for his money, the higher became his claims. When he first published his *Brief Observations* on the damages suffered as a result of Duncan's raid, he claimed no more than 70,000 "pesos fuertes."

24. Baylies to de Maza, Aug. 18, and to Livingston, Aug. 19, 1832.

Baylies explained to de Maza that he was returning the account because he could not consent to let the Argentine government stand as arbitrator between the United States and a private citizen. De Maza declared that he had no such intention. Vernet's account represented, he said, the facts upon which the Argentine government had made its decision, and such facts should be known to the United States.

De Maza sent Vernet's statements to the Secretary of State. When the Secretary of State asked Baylies if this was the same given to him in Buenos Aires, the former chargé answered that he had not retained a copy, nor had he read the original before returning it. Such hot-headed action scarcely comports with responsible statesmanship.

25. Baylies to Livingston, Sept. 26, 1832.

26. Baylies' confidence in British intentions was not misplaced. Two English warships sailed into the Falkland Islands harbor on Dec. 20, 1832, almost exactly a year after Captain Duncan had entered the same port, and took possession. This force encountered small opposition, for the settlement had just undergone a revolution or a mutiny of its own. The old inhabitants had rebelled against the new Argentine governor, and had killed him. Yet when faced with a British invasion, all the colonists united to reject indignantly the demand that they strike their national colors. The captain of the Argentine man-of-war, *Sarandi*, could do nothing to prevent the British themselves from lowering the flag. After receiving the flag from the British, the Argentine commander sailed to Buenos Aires with bad news of loss of the islands.

27. Vicente de Maza to Livingston, Oct. 13, 1832. A rough draft of Alvear's instructions which is undated and unsigned is found in the archival collection S1, A2, A4, núm. 13. Apparently the Secretary of Foreign Affairs abandoned the project while it was yet half done.

28. Protests against the deep offense which Slacum had committed against national dignity were presently abandoned except for diplomatic purposes. Alvear received from the Argentine minister to Brazil the following notice: "The objection which has occurred to you in respect to Mr. Slacum is removed because later events have predisposed the mind of our government in favor of the gentleman, thus forgetting past occurrences as if they had not taken place" (Sarratea to Alvear, June 18, 1840, in Rodríguez, *Contribución*, III, 531).

Still another matter was quietly settled: the schooner *Harriet*, seized by Vernet, was sold in Buenos Aires in Sept., 1833 (*British Packet*, Sept. 28, 1833).

29. Instructions to Carlos de Alvear, AGN, S1, A1, A1, núm. 5. This old claim had been in agitation for years. Halsey had supplied arms and ammunition to Buenos Aires during the latter years of the War for Independence and had never been paid. The Legislature of Buenos Aires had agreed on the amount due, but had not appropriated the money. After leaving his documents with the Assembly for several years, Halsey had directed his attorney to withdraw them. Halsey then presented his papers to the Department of State and sought its aid in collection of the $108,831 due him. Settlement was eventually made in 1851 for $110,000 to be paid in eleven annual installments.

30. Alvear was repeating here the old newspaper charge made by the *Gaceta Mercantil* after British occupation of the islands. He overlooked Slacum's earlier denials of Argentine sovereignty, and he forgot, too, that the English had filed their protest immediately after Lavalle's decree of 1829. There are no grounds whatsoever for supposing that Baylies induced the British to occupy the Falklands.

31. Memorandum of a conference between Carlos de Alvear and John Forsyth, Jan. 14, 1839, AGN, S1, A1, A1, núm. 5.

32. Attached to the paper were depositions of the seven prisoners whom Duncan had taken, including the report of Matthew Brisbane, Vernet's military leader. These are reproduced in Manning, *Inter-American Affairs*, I, 211-22.

33. Alvear to Rosas, Feb. 4, 1839, AGN, S1, A1, A1, núm. 5. Rodríguez, *Contribución*, III, 571 ff., carries a long extract from this letter, but gives no indication of omitted portions.

34. Alvear to Arana, April 30, 1839, AGN, S1, A2, A4, núm. 13.

35. Alvear omitted reference to the fact that Spain had never enforced her fishing regulations. Americans had long fished in those waters with the complete knowledge of Spain and of all the world. Certainly Spain never attempted to secure observance of her regulations by seizures in Vernet's brusque manner.

36. Alvear to Forsyth, March 21, 1839.

37. Arana to Alvear, June 13, 1839, AGN, S1, A1, A1, núm. 5.

38. Forsyth to Alvear, April 6, 1839, National Archives, State Department, *Notes to the Argentine Republic*, VI; also Alvear to Forsyth, April 8, 1839, AGN, S1, A1, A1, núm. 5. "Although this answer did not fulfill Forsyth's purpose, it was not possible to give any other reply for lack of orders on this point (Alvear to Arana, May 1, 1839, *ibid.*).

When Secretary of State John Q. Adams dispatched Caesar Rodney as the first minister to Buenos Aires, he gave him a twenty-three-volume set of laws of the United States and a twelve-volume set of State Papers. This material was to form a part of the legation library. Alvear possessed no copies of the Spanish laws of the Viceroyalty nor did he bring copies of Argentine statutes when he came to the United States.

39. Alvear to Arana, Oct. 30, 1839, AGN, S1, A1, A1, núm. 5.

40. Alvear to Arana, Feb. 15, 1840, AGN, S1, A2, A4, núm. 13.

41. Webster to Alvear, Dec. 4, 1841. At the same time, Webster privately concluded to drop all American claims for damages by Vernet, for the United States could not hold the Argentine government accountable for his acts without recognizing Argentine sovereignty. Secretary Clayton ignored this conclusion in 1849 when he instructed the chargé to Buenos Aires to press for settlement the claims of two fishermen of the wrecked *Bellville* (Webster to Brent, July 15, 1844; Clayton to Harris, Dec. 27, 1849).

42. Alvear to Webster, Dec. 30, 1841. There is no record that Alvear went to Washington during that winter or that he ever conferred with Webster thereafter about the matter. Judging from Upshur's instructions to Watterson, almost certainly Alvear did not meet Webster again.

43. Upshur to Watterson, Dec. 26, 1843; Ewards to Upshur, Nov. 20, 1843.

44. While studying the Falkland problem Webster wrote to a former sea captain, Thomas H. Williams, for later information on the islands. Williams relayed the request to a fellow captain, Thomas P. Trott. These men provided the Secretary of State with an interesting account of the islands under English administration. Their letters may be found in the National Archives, State Department, Miscellaneous Correspondence, under the dates of Dec. 26, 1841, and Jan. 6, 1842.

45. When it was rumored that England was about to seize Cuba, abolish slavery, and set up a free republic, Webster had the American consul in Havana investigate the matter. He assured the consul that any attempt to employ force in Cuba would bring on war with England and that Spain could rely on the military resources of the United States.

The great difference between tolerance of English seizure of the Falklands and assured resistance to similar action in Cuba obviously lay in Cuba's proximity to the United States.

46. Although Rosas refrained from answering Webster's proposal, he did not ignore it. He ordered Manuel Moreno to forward to Alvear from London all materials relating to the Falkland Islands episode. These Alvear received long after they might have been of any use to him (Moreno to Alvear, Jan. 13, 1842, AGN, S1, A1, A1, núm. 5).

47. Calhoun to Brent, July 15, 1844.

48. Bayard to Quesada, March 18, 1886 (John B. Moore, *Digest of International Law*, 8 vols.; Washington, D. C., 1900, VI, 435).

49. W. M. Malloy, (ed.), *Treaties and Conventions . . . between the United States of America and Other Powers, 1776-1909* (2 vols.; Washigton, 1910), I, 777.

At the Río de Janeiro Conference of 1947 and the Bogotá Conference of 1948, Argentina again made specific exception to English control of the islands and asserted her own rights to sovereignty.

Footnotes to Chapter IV, Part 3

1. John F. Cady, *Foreign Intervention in the Río de la Plata, 1838-1850* (Philadelphia, 1929), chap. ii. It is necessary to remember that France had undertaken a simultaneous blockade of Vera Cruz in an attempt to win concessions from Mexico after that country refused to negotiate on certain debts to French citizens. For the Mexican phase of the intervention, see Guillermo Prieto, *Memorias de mis tiempos, 1828-1840* (2 vols.; Mexico, 1906); G. L. Rives, *United States and Mexico, 1821-1848* (2 vols.; New York, 1918), I; and W. H. Callcott, *Santa Anna* (Norman, Oklahoma, 1936).

2. In this account I have followed the sequence given in Professor Cady's work cited previously.

3. *British Packet*, Sept. 29, 1839.

4 Sarratea to Alvear, Río de Janeiro, June 18, 1840, and Arana to Alvear, Nov. 22, 1843 (Rodríguez, *Contribución*, III, 517-18, 530). Alvear normally received a note within five months after its dispatch. Delivery within three months was worthy of comment. Correspondence between Buenos Aires and the United States went by way of Río de Janeiro, where Tomás Guido was stationed. This official was able to forward dispatches through such reliable channels that very few were lost. Arana, in Buenos Aires, was less fortunate. Alvear complained that sometimes he went for a year without news or funds. Most of the instructions from Buenos Aires which went astray were lost between that city and Río de Janeiro.

5. Alvear to Secretary of State, Oct. 24 and 25, 1838; National Archives, State

Department, Notes from the Argentine Republic, I, pt. 1; and Manning, *Inter-American Affairs*, I, 18.

6. Alvear to Arana, Oct. 18 and 30, 1838, AMREC, Caja 12.

7. *Ibid.*

8. French diplomatic service during General Alvear's residence in the United States: 1837-39, Ed. Pontois; 1835-1840, A. Pageot, Secretary of Legation, and from 1842-1850 as Minister Plenipotentiary.

9. Alvear to Arana, Oct. 30, 1838, AMREC, Caja 12.

10. Memorandum of a conference at the State Department with Carlos de Alvear, October 27, 1838 (Manning, *Inter-American Affairs*, I, 208 ff.).

11. Arana to Alvear, Nov. 16, 1838, and Jan. 25, 1839, AGN, S1, A1, A1, núm. 5.

12. *Journal of Commerce*, New York, May 22, 1839.

13. Conference of June 4, as reported in Alvear's dispatch to his government, June 6, 1839, AGN, S1, A1, A1, núm. 13.

14. Alvear to Arana, Feb. 5, 1839, AGN, S1, A1, A1, núm. 5.

15. *Congressional Globe*, 25th Congress, Third Session, p. 86. Pickens of South Carolina, characterizing the intervention in Mexico as especially important to the southwestern states, endorsed the resolution and withheld his own of similar import.

16. Alvear to Arana, Feb. 5, 1839, AGN, S1, A1, A1, núm. 5.

17. *Ibid.*

18. Arana to Alvear, June 13, 1839, AGN, S1, A1, A1, núm. 5.

19. Correspondence on this well-meant gesture may be found in AGN, S1, A2, A4, núm. 9. See also Cady, *Foreign Intervention in the Río de la Plata*, pp. 58-61.

20. In a secret letter from Enrique Lafuente to Félix Farías, April 18, 1839 (Rodríguez, *Contribución*, II, 467).

21. Alvear inquired later of the generous Bodisco what Forsyth had replied to the complaint of "grievous and singular conduct." "He laughed, and gave me a vague answer, saying 'this government today has no other object in view than the election of a President.' "

22. Alvear to Arana, Jan. 10, 1840, AGN, S1, A2, A4, núm. 13.

23. Alvear to Arana, Jan. 15, 1840, *ibid.*

24. Alvear to Arana, Jan. 16, 1840. Arana particularly commended Alvear for his response to M. Pageot and hoped that he would continue to use such dignified language (Arana to Alvear, May 16, 1840, *ibid.*).

25. Arana to Alvear, May 16, 1840 (*ibid.*).

26. Sarratea to Alvear, July 18, 1840 (Rodríguez, *Contribución*, III, 531); MSS, AGN, S1, A1, A1, núm. 4.

Bodisco apparently aroused Argentine hopes heedlessly, for nothing came from his byplay. In July, 1841, Arana directed Alvear to make inquiry if Bodisco had received any word from his government on the subject of recognition (Arana to Alvear, July 19, 1841—Rodríguez, *Contribución*, III, 505-6).

27. Alvear to Arana, Feb. 14, 1841, AGN, S1, A2, A4, núm. 13.

28 Arana to Secretary of State, March 5, 1842, AGN, S1, A2, A4, núm. 9. This communication is not in the files of the State Department.

29. J. D. Richardson, *Messages and Papers of the Presidents*, V, 2050.

30. W. S. Robertson, "Foreign Estimates of the Argentine Dictator," *Hispanic American Historical Review*, X (1930), 130.

31. Alvear to Arana, Dec. 16, 1842, AMREC, Caja 12.

32. Guizot to Lurde, June 26, 1843, as quoted in Robertson, *op. cit.* Guizot's opponents could not force him to take a public stand until the summer of 1845.

33. *El Defensador Americano*, a decree of the General Legislative Assembly, published as a broadside, which Brent enclosed in his dispatches to Washington (National Archives, State Department, Argentine Republic, V).

34. Reports of these conferences are missing from the files of the Ministry of Foreign Affairs. Apparently the editor of the *Gaceta Mercantil* used them in the issue of Feb. 25, 1846, for propaganda purposes and never returned the documents.

35. Alvear to Arana, Nov. 4, 6, and 29, 1845, AGN, S1, A1, A1, núm. 5. One manuscript is missing, but Arana's acknowledgment of Feb. 19, 1846, summarized the minister's report.

36. Alvear to Buchanan, Nov. 1, 1845 (Manning, *Inter-American Affairs*, I, 301).

37. This speech is translated in Dexter Perkins, *The Monroe Doctrine*, II, 71-72. See this work also for the circumstances which forced Guizot to make his declaration.

38. Richardson, *Messages and Papers of the Presidents*, V, 2248-49.

39. Alvear to Arana, Aug. 11, 1845, AGN, S1, A1, A1, núm. 5.

40. Alvear to Arana, Dec. 4, 1845, AMREC, Caja 12.

41. Buchanan to McLane, Sept. 15 and Oct. 14, 1845, *Polk Papers*, First Series, Library of Congress.

42. McKeon to Polk, Oct. 23, 1845, *Polk Papers*, Second Series, Library of Congress.

43. Buchanan to Harris, March 30, 1846 (Manning, *Inter-American Affairs*, I, 31).

44. President Polk had not inadvertently omitted South America from the scope of his remarks. A public letter he wrote in 1844 had been much more expansive: "Let the fixed principle of our government be not to permit Great Britain or any other foreign power to plant a colony or hold a dominion over any portion of the people or territory of either continent." As a hopeful Presidential candidate, and with no prospect of a European blockade, he spoke more boldly than he did after the moderating hand of full responsibility was laid upon him.

45. See Perkins, *The Monroe Doctrine*, II, 76 ff. Senator Allen's remarks on his resolution, as given on Jan. 26, are reported in the *Journal of Commerce*, Jan. 31, 1846.

46. Dexter Perkins, *op. cit.*, II, 87-97.

47. *Daily Union*, Dec. 3, 8, 1845.

48. Alvear to Arana, Aug. 19, Nov. 11, 1845, June 18, 1846, AGN, S1, A1, A1, núm. 5; editorial in the *Gaceta Mercantil*, Feb. 25, 1846; *British Packet*, March 7, 1846.

49. Alvear to Arana, May 10, 1847, AGN, S1, A1, A1, núm. 5; and AMREC, Caja 41. To this glowing dispatch Arana gave no heed except a bare acknowledgment of its receipt.

50. Arana to Alvear, May 8, 1846, AGN, S1, A1, A1, núm. 5.

51. An article of similar import appeared in the English-language newspaper, *British Packet*, March 7, 1846, and July 31, 1847.

52. See Webster's *Speeches and Writings*, V, 205.

53. Harris to Clayton, May 14, 1850 (Manning, *Inter-America Affairs*, I, 496).

54. Buchanan to Harris, March 30, 1846 (*ibid.*, I, 29-32).

55. Graham to Buchanan, July 30, 1847, National Archives, State Department, *Consular Letters*, *Buenos Aires*, VII.

56. Harris to Buchanan, July 15, 1847 (Manning, *Inter-American Affairs*, I, 431-34).

57. Buchanan to Harris, March 30, 1846. I have found no correspondence from Arana authorizing Alvear to make this promise, nor letters from Alvear stating that he had done so.

In order to emphasize the nonterritorial intentions of his government, the British minister, Pakenham, had passed to the Secretary of State a copy of the instructions from Lord Aberdeen authorizing him to make this unequivocal statement.

58. English version of the address in the *British Packet*, Jan. 22 and Feb. 3, 1848.

Footnotes to Chapter IV, Part 4

1. Instructions to Carlos de Alvear, AGN, S1, A1, A1, núm. 5.

2. Arana to Alvear, Aug. 10, 1843, AGN, S1, A1, A1, núm. 5.

3. Alvear to Arana, Dec. 10, 1843, AGN, S1, A2, A4, núm. 13.

4. See the final chapter for a more detailed discussion of Alvear's relation to the Rosas administration.

5 Alvear to Arana, Dec. 18, 1843, and Arana's reply, May 13, 1844, AMREC, Caja 12.

6. Buchanan to Alvear, March 24, 1845, Notes to Argentine Republic, VI; Alvear to Secretary of State, Feb. 13, 1847, Notes from Argentine Republic, I, pt. 2, National Archives, State Department.

Argentine consular correspondence with Buenos Aires is found in AGN, S1, A1, A2, núm. 9; and S1, A2, A4, núms. 9 and 13.

7. Alvear to Arana, Dec. 18, 1843, AMREC, Caja 12. This memorial, published by that House in honor of the Dictator's birthday, included all the extravagant eulogy which a book of that kind could yield.

8. Alvear to Arana, March 10, Sept. 12, 1844, AMREC, Caja 12.

9. Alvear to Arana, March 10, Dec. 15, 1844, AMREC, Caja 12.

10. Alvear to Arana, Nov. 15, 1844, *ibid.*

11. Alvear to Arana, n.d., fragment of manuscript, AGN, S1, A1, A1, núm. 6.

12. Alvear to Arana, June 2, 1845, AMREC, Caja 12.

13. Alvear to Arana, Aug. 19, 1845, AGN, S1, A1, A1, núm. 5.

14. Alvear to Arana, Dec. 8, 1843, Dec. 3, 1845, AMREC, Caja 12.

15. By Alvear's system "Henry Clay" became "Enriclei"; and "Whig" he spelled "Waiage."

16. Alvear to Arana, Aug. 13, 1845, AMREC, Caja 12; Dec. 3, 1845, AGN, S1, A1, A1, núm. 5.

17. Alvear to Arana, n.d., fragment of a manuscript written after Nov. 27, 1845; also to Arana, Jan. 30, 1846, AGN, S1, A1, A1, núm. 6.

18. So well did the editors interpret Alvear's commentaries that the general reader would presume that they were of American authorship. Contrast the various styles in the *Evening Post*, May 1, 1845, the *Journal of Commerce*, Nov. 26, Dec. 3, 1845, the *Evening Post*, Dec. 1, 1845.

19. Alvear to Arana, n.d., fragment of a manuscript cited above.

20. Alvear to Arana, Nov. 6, 1845, AMREC, Caja 12.

21. Alvear to Arana, Nov. 6, Dec. 3, 11, 1845, AMREC, Caja 12.

22. See below a list of articles which Alvear sponsored in the American newspapers, as based on his reports to the Argentine Ministry of Foreign Affairs. Since some of his dispatches are now missing, the list is probably incomplete.

Daily Union (Washington)

February 18, March 20, May 1, 19, June 5, 24, July 25, 1846. A series of seven articles from April 1-28, 1846, in the weekly and triweekly *Union.*

Journal of Commerce (New York)

Nov. 27, Dec. 1, 3, 10, 16, 1845.

Evening Post (New York)

May 1, Dec. 1, 12, 16, 1845; Oct. 21, 24, Nov. 11, 24, 1851.

Sun (New York)
Feb. 4, 5; Aug. 13; Nov. 27, 1845.
Commercial Advertiser (New York)
Nov. 20, 1844; Feb. 1, 4, 1846.
Morning News (New York)
Dec. 2, 1845.
Herald (New York)
Nov. 14, 1844; Dec. 8, 10, 22, 1845.
Register (Salem, Massachusetts)
No. 841 (Fall, 1845)
Courier and Enquirer (New York)
Nov. 9, 1844.
La Patria (New Orleans)
Nov., 1850.
Noticias de Ambos Mundos (New York)
No. 462 (Nov., 1844)
Democratic Review (Magazine)
May, 1846. The author interviewed Alvear for information on Argentina, but the publication was not at his suggestion nor did he see the manuscript before publication.

23. Alvear to Arana, Aug. 19, 1845, AMREC, Caja 12. Captain Voorhees was courtmartialed for disregarding his instructions while on duty in La Plata. He refused to recognize Argentine blockade of Montevideo and attacked the investing squadron. For this offense he was suspended from the service for a period. This incident is discussed in a later chapter.

24. Dodge to Alvear, March 8, 1846; Alvear to Arana, Dec. 26, 1845; Arana to Alvear, April 30, 1846, AMREC, Caja 12.

25. Dodge to Alvear, Dec. 17, 1845 (Rodríguez, *Contribución*, III, 582).

26. *Ibid.*

27. The resolution, in part, read: "That Congress . . . do hereby solemnly declare to the civilized world the unalterable resolution of the United States to adhere to and enforce the principle that any effort of Europe to intermeddle in the social organization or the political arrangements of the independent nations of America, or further to extend the European system of government upon this continent by the establishment of new colonies would be incompatible with the independent existence of the nations, and dangerous to the liberties of the people of America, and therefore would incur . . . the prompt resistance of the United States" (*Congressional Globe*, XV, Jan. 14, 1846, 197-98). The resolution lost by the close vote of twenty-three to twenty-eight.

28. Dodge to Alvear, March 8, 1846 (Rodríguez, *Contribución*, II, 582). I found no indication that either Alvear or Dodge at any time interviewed or corresponded with Caleb Cushing, ablest advocate of strong action by the United States in the Western Hemisphere. It seems improbable, however, that Alvear omitted him from his mailing list.

29. The *National Intelligencer* had previously shown itself hostile to Dodge's blandishments.

30. Dodge to Alvear, March 8, 1846. The editor declared that he had been instructed to express himself strongly against the intervention, but he hesitated to go too far (Alvear to Arana, Feb. 12, 1846, AGN, S1, A1, A1, núm. 6).

31. Dodge to Alvear, March 8, 1846; Alvear to Arana, Feb. 12, March 20, 1846, AGN, S1, A1, A1, núm. 6.

32. Alvear to Arana, n.d., fragment; also to Arana, Dec. 23, 1845, and Jan. 30, 1846, AGN, S1, A1, A1, núm. 6. Moreno acknowledged receipt of Alvear's newspapers and commended him for pointing out "in true American Spirit, the

aggressions in our continent of two of the most powerful and ambitious European powers" (Moreno to Alvear, May 2, 1846, in Rodríguez, *Contribución,* III, 543).

33. A flotilla of French, English, and neutral merchantmen followed the men-of-war in an attempt to open the Paraná River to traffic and thus break Rosas control of the upper provinces. Although the convoy reached Asunción and returned, the attempt was not repeated, and Rosas remained supreme. The allied forces hailed the initial passage as a definitive triumph.

34. The *Sun* was a popular New York daily, and widely read in Europe. Alvear was certain that the English and French would see anything he published there. The editor promised full publicity in his weekly issue of the following Saturday (Alvear to Arana, Feb. 12, 1846, AGN, S1, A1, A1, núm. 6).

35. Alvear to Arana, Feb. 6, 1846, AGN, S1, A1, núm. 5. Rosas was pleased with either the prompt use of news for nationalistic purposes or by the flattery with which Alvear had closed his dispatch—perhaps both. In reply he sent one of his rare notes of approval for Alvear's work.

36. Alvear to Arana, Feb. 20, 1846, AGN, S1, A1, A1, núm. 5. The article took up the usual refrain against Rosas: Twelve years ago Rosas set up a government based on ignorance, falsehood, corruption, spoilation, outrage, imprisonment, torture, banishment, and death. In the midst of Godlike adoration he had let institutions of culture die. Standards of living had declined, importation of firearms had increased, and 12,000 men had met death for opposing him. Frightful tortures and massacres occurred regularly and bodies of the dead were indecently mutilated. Rosas desired to take the territory of Uruguay and was using ex-President Oribe as a screen for his efforts. Since that scheme was being blocked, the Dictator protested that he was defending Uruguayan independence when everyone knew that only French and English intervention had saved the country from his grasp.

37. Alvear to Arana, Feb. 20, May 20, Sept. 14, 1846, AGN, S1, A1, A1, núm. 5.

38. "Alfred Mallalieu" is supposed to have been the pen name under which Manuel Moreno was defending Rosas in London. (See Cady, *Foreign Intervention in the Río de La Plata,* p. 118.) Alvear gives no inkling that he suspected the origin of the "Alfred Mallalieu" articles.

39. A précis of this article is as follows: The United States citizens, after the original burst for independence by the Spanish colonies, have been disappointed at the frequent revolutions in the south. After thirty years they see that the struggle to create new institutions was much more difficult than destroying old ones. Particularly has this struggle been acute in Argentina, a nation of pure Spanish descent, where the people are handsome and stalwart.

During post-Revolutionary days murder, disorder, and Indian attacks broke out. The only man who could defeat the Indians and restore domestic peace was Rosas. This man is fitted for his time and his people. As the Jackson of the South, he is honest, fearless, and thorough in suppressing the Indians. He has brought civil peace and order, has eliminated public graft, and has encouraged immigration. The swarms of defeated, disappointed, criminal, restless, and riotous have fled to other countries and there they compose horrible tales of his cruelty: he adorns his parlor with the pickled ears of his enemies!

The people of Buenos Aires are truly republicans, and Rosas' philosophy is republican; but in this crisis he cannot put his program into effect. As a man of the people he wins his support from the multitude who love him.

40. Alvear to Arana, Sept. 24, 1846, AGN, S1, A1, A1, núm. 5. Paul Harro-Harring, *Dolores, A Novel of South America* (New York, 1846).

41. Alvear to Arana, Aug. 17, 1846, AGN, S1, A1, A1, núm. 5. J. Anthony King, *Twenty-four Years in the Argentine Republic* (New York, 1846). Thomas R. Whitney prepared the text from Colonel King's account. The Colonel's pre-

occupation with military matters, his innocence of Argentine politics, and his unschooled Spanish lend credence to his adventurous tale.

42. Alvear to Arana, Nov. 6, 1845, April 8, 1846, AGN, S1, A1, A1, núm. 5.

43. Alvear to Arana, May 20, 1846, AGN, S1, A1, A1, núm. 5

44. Arana to Alvear, May 20, June 24, Sept. 12, 1846, AGN, S1, A1, A1, núm. 6.

45. Alvear to Arana, n.d. (*circa* 1850), AMREC, Caja 41.

46 Alvear to Arana, Nov. 23, 1850, AMREC, Caja 41. Alvear, translating, identified the French publication as the *Abeja* (Bee).

47. Alvear to Arana, Aug. 13, 1845, AMREC, Caja 41.

48. W. S. Robertson, "Foreign Estimates of the Argentine Dictator," *Hispanic American Historical Review*, X (1930), 136.

49. During his most active period of newspaper campaigning, Alvear subscribed to the following newspapers: the Washington *Daily Union* and *Tri-Weekly Union*, *National Intelligencer;* the New York *Journal of Commerce*, *Commercial Advertiser*, *Evening Post*, *Herald*, *Morning Express*, *Sun*, *Courrier des États-Unis;* the Philadelphia *National Gazette;* the Boston *Post*, *Daily Tatler*, *Daily Advertiser*, *Courier;* the Baltimore *Advertiser;* the Richmond (Va.) *Daily* (Alvear to Arana, Aug. 13, 1845, AMREC, Caja 41). These newspapers Alvear forwarded to Rosas, who used them as news sources for the English-language *British Packet* and for the *Gaceta Mercantil.*

50. Alvear complained at the relatively high cost of living in the United States. Books, newspapers, and postage were out of all proportion to the prevailing prices in Argentina. Frequently he had to lay out extra sums as a tip or bribe in order to assure the integrity of some of the captains who accepted his dispatches for delivery in Buenos Aires or Río de Janeiro. During his first year in the United States, Alvear sent dispatches to Buenos Aires by way of England, and sought by liberal payments to secure passage beyond the blockade (Alvear to Arana, Aug. 22, 1845, AGN, S1, A1, A1, núm. 5).

51. Alvear to Arana, Aug. 13, 1845, AMREC, Caja 12.

52. *Ibid.* Bills of expenditures for 1846 are missing from the files preserved either in the *Archivo Nacional* or in the *Archivo del Ministro de Relaciones Exteriores y Culto.* In February Alvear entered a claim for postage for the past seven years, only to have Rosas reject it as unjustified, nor would Rosas listen to his repeated appeals for more funds in order that he could continue to urge resistance to the blockade (Alvear to Arana, Dec. 11, 12, 1845, and Feb. 27, 1846, AMREC, Caja 12).

53. Rosas' only grounds of complaint with Alvear's work in his last years were irregularity of the delivery of dispatches, a factor beyond Alvear's control, and the envoy's persistent use of the incorrect heading "Excelentísimo Señor" instead of the proper form "Vuestro Señor."

Footnotes to Chapter IV, Part 5

1. Alvear to Arana, Feb. 18, 1843 (Rodríguez, *Contribución*, III, 573-74).

2. Alvear to Arana, n.d. (*ca.* Jan., 1849), AGN, S1, A1, A1, núm. 6, enclosure number 237.

3. In the round of banquets given in honor of Lord Ashburton, Alvear renewed his acquaintance of 1823 when he had known the British envoy as one of the Baring Brothers, whose firm was considering a loan to the United Provinces. Lord Ashburton had not forgotten the occasion or the loan, since defaulted, and recommended to Alvear that his nation should resume payment and establish once again a favorable financial rating (Alvear to Arana, June 23, 1842, AMREC, Caja 12).

4. Alvear to Arana, April 12, May 26, 1839; March 30, 1840; March 29, June 23, Sept. 5, 1842; AGN, S1, A1, A1, núm. 5; and S1, A2, A4, núm. 13; AMREC, Caja).

5. Alvear to Webster, Aug. 29, 1842, National Archives, State Department, Notes from the Argentine Republic, I, pt. 2.

6. Alvear to Arana, Sept. 12, 1842, AMREC, Caja 12.

7. Alvear to Rosas, Feb. 18, 1843 (Rodríguez, *Contribución*, III, 574). Alvear's citation is more indignant than specific. Presumably he was referring to the Linn Bill, which passed the Senate in Feb., 1843, but failed in the House. He wrote as if the proposal had been enacted into law already.

8. See Arana's acknowledgment of Alvear's dispatches of March 19, June 24, 1846, AGN, S1, A1, A1, núm. 5.

9. Alvear to Arana, n.d. (*ca.* Jan., 1849), AGN, S1, A1, A1, núm. 6.

10. Alvear to Arana, Sept. 5, 1842, AMREC, Caja 12.

11. Alvear's concept of the term "race" was extremely loose. The English-speaking peoples he called the Saxon or, sometimes, the Anglo-Saxon race. On other occasions he referred to the "Texas" race.

12. Alvear to Arana, June 23, 1842; March 12, April 18, July 19, 1843, AMREC, Caja 12, and AGN, S1, A1, A1, núm. 5.

13. Strong sympathy caused Alvear to observe that President Bustamente of Mexico sought to revive the Pan-American Congress "after the manner of the glorious Colombian President" (Alvear to Arana, March 13, 1839, AMREC, Caja 12).

14. The Mexican representative to the United States, Juan N. Almonte, told Alvear that Colombia, Peru, and Ecuador had agreed to attend, and invitations were being dispatched to Chile and Argentina. The other countries which had accepted wanted to name Lima as the meeting place, but Mexico thought her capital the logical site (Alvear to Arana, Oct. 27, 1842, AMREC, Caja 12).

A conference of South American states met at Lima in 1848, but its proposals were never ratified by the participating states. Its deliberations came to nothing (Enrique Gil, *Evolución del Panamericanismo*, Buenos Aires, 1933, pp. 30-32).

15. Alvear to Arana, July 19, 1843, AMREC, Caja 12.

16. "This discourse is worthy of being read and meditated upon by all men in the new republics of America, not only for the high concept of probity and knowledge which is revealed by this illustrious author, but also for what he says on the means taken to foment insurrection in Texas and the conduct observed by the American government in this business with Mexico" (Alvear to Arana, Dec. 4, 1842, AMREC, Caja 12).

17. Alvear to Arana, June 22, 1844, AMREC, Caja 12. In this dispatch the minister refers to previous estimates of expansion which, he said, would increase as the United States advanced in "civilization and industrial development." Sometimes he makes the word "civilization" synonymous with "industrial development" and on other occasions it indicates simply a praiseworthy state of vague import.

18. Alvear to Arana, Dec. 6, 1844; March 11, 13, 1845, AMREC, Caja 12.

19. In 1849, with better perspective, Alvear set the beginning of territorial expansion at the acquisition of "Salvatierra" (presumably he referred to Amelia Island), and said that this success gave birth to the seizure of the two Spanish Floridas (Alvear to Arana, n.d. [*ca.* Jan., 1849], AGN, S1, A1, A1, núm. 6).

20. Alvear to Arana, March 13, 1845, AMREC, Caja 12.

21. Alvear to Arana, March 17, 1845, AMREC, Caja 12. Calderón de la Barca also gave to Alvear another communication which regretted the action of the United States as disturbing to harmony between friendly nations.

22. Alvear to Arana, Feb. 5, Nov. 19, 1839, AGN, S1, A2, A4, núm. 13; March 13, 1839, AMREC, Caja 12. In 1849 his opinion was still unchanged: "It is painful to see that the government of a powerful nation should sink to the point

of employing perfidy and bad faith in order to repress a neighboring republic which, rather, ought to be entitled to its protection; but the conduct of the past two administrations and especially the last one has been marked by a series of unjust acts all directed with the object of taking over a large part of its territory . . . for which end it has not hesitated to employ either injustice of acts or falsity of motives" (Alvear to Arana, April 23, 1849, AMREC, Caja 41).

23. Alvear to Arana, March 13, 1839, Aug. 11, 1845, June 15, 1848, AMREC, Cajas 12 and 41. Alvear reported that all people of Spanish origin shared his fears for the ultimate fate of Mexico. Perhaps so, for in 1846 there appeared in the Spanish court a scheme to establish a monarchy in Mexico in order to save it from national extinction. The language of this proposition shows an attitude toward the United States which is identical with that of Alvear. At no time, however, did he prescribe for Mexican salvation any remedy except "to change her ways" or "induce more white men to immigrate." Apparently he had ceased thinking that salvation lay in the royal courts of Europe. For an account of the Mexican plot, see Perkins, *The Monroe Doctrine*, II, 142-44.

24. Alvear to Arana, Aug. 11, 1845, AGN, S1, A1, A1, núm. 5; Alvear to Arana, n.d. (*ca.* Jan., 1839), AGN, S1, A1, A1, núm. 6; Alvear to Arana, Feb. 25, April 25, 1849, AGN, S1, A2, A4, núm. 13.

25. Alvear to Arana, June 15, 1848, AMREC, Caja 41.

26. Alvear to Arana, April 25, 1849, AGN, S1, A2, A4, núm. 13.

27. Alvear to Arana, Feb. 25, 1849, AGN, S1, A2, A4, núm. 13.

28. Alvear to Arana, Aug. 23, Nov. 2, 1849, AMREC, Caja 41.

29. *Archivo Americano*, II (1847), 299.

30. Alvear to Arana, Oct 29, 1849, AMREC, Caja 41. For other references to the amazing growth of the "Anglo-American Confederation" through immigration, see also a rough draft of an undated manuscript presumably written about Jan., 1849, in AGN, S1, A1, A1, núm. 6; and also Alvear to Arana, Nov. 28, 1847, Feb. 25, 1849, AMREC, Caja 41; and Alvear to Arana, Feb. 8, 1851, AGN, S1, A1, A1, núm. 6.

31. Alvear to Arana, n.d. (*ca.* Jan., 1849), AGN, S1, A1, A1, núm. 6.

32. Alvear to Arana, March 17, 1845, AMREC, Caja 12. By omission of Paraguay, Alvear presumed Argentine sovereignty over that country.

33. Alvear to Rosas, Feb. 18, 1843 (Rodríguez, *Contribución*, III, 573-75).

34. *Ibid.*

35. Alvear to Arana, April 18, 1843; March 13, 1845, AMREC, Caja 12.

36. Alvear to Arana, n.d. (*ca.* Jan., 1849), AGN, S1, A1, A1, núm. 6; Alvear to Arana, March 13, 1845, AMREC, Caja 12.

France would never fight to save Cuba for England, Alvear predicted. The United States with Cuba would outdistance England in the Western Hemisphere. He saw no hope of preventing acquisition of Cuba, nor of stopping the expansion of the United States thereafter.

37. Alvear to Arana, Aug. 23, 1849, Aug. 15, 1850, AMREC, Caja 41.

38. Alvear to Arana, Oct. 18, 1849, AMREC, Caja 41; March 18, 1851, AGN, S1, A1, A1, núm. 5.

39. "Spain has made great progress recently in agriculture, manufacturing and trade. Due to the energetic effort of General Narváez its government seems well consolidated. After losing the Americas, emigration ceased and its population has grown to sixteen millions. Its geographic position in Europe and its possession of the Antilles, Philippines, coast of Africa, Majorca and Minorca in the Mediterranean all place her in a position to wreak fearful havoc on North American commerce by privateering" (Alvear to Arana, May 26, 1850, AMREC, Caja 41). Less than a year before Alvear had written that American privateers would fight "with bitterness and success" against English and French navies.

40. Alvear to Arana, Aug. 15, 1850, AMREC, Caja 41; January 22, 1851,

AGN, S1, A1, A1, núm. 6; April 30, 1851, AGN, S1, A1, A1, núm. 5; Aug. 19, 1851, AMREC, Caja 41. He complained that this "good faith" was exerted to punish participants after failure of the expedition, when reasonable care would have prevented the departure of the expedition in the first place.

41. Alvear to Arana, Aug. 23, 1851, AMREC, Caja 41. Reports of the meeting may be found in the New York *Morning Express*, Aug. 23, 1851.

42. Alvear to Arana, Dec. 10, 1849, AMREC, Caja 41.

43. Alvear to Arana, Dec. 4, 1842, AMREC, Caja 12.

44. See Mary Williams, *Anglo-American Isthmanian Diplomacy, 1815-1915* (Washington, 1916), for a background of the trans-Isthmanian diplomacy.

45. "The chargé of Nicaragua, who to his lack of talents adds the charm of bad manners, was persuaded that England would never declare war against the United States because she would starve. He supposed, mistakenly, that without the United States, England would not be able to exist" (Alvear to Arana, Jan. 22, 1850, AMREC, Caja 41).

46. Alvear to Arana, June 15, 1850, AMREC, Caja 41.

47. Alvear to Arana, Dec. 10, 1849, AMREC, Caja 41; Jan. 30, May 15, 1851, AGN, S1, A1, A1, núm. 5.

Footnotes to Chapter IV, Part 6

1. Documents relating to this affair are found in Manning, *Inter-American Affairs*, I, 25-29, 237 n.; and in John B. Moore, *Digest of International Law*, I, 178-82.

2. Alvear to Arana, June 15, Aug. 13, 21, 1845, AGN, S1, A1, A1, núm. 5. Other routine correspondence on various phases of this trial are given in this packet. Rosas responded to Alvear's congratulation on the favorable outcome of the case by declaring that the prompt decision was due to the magnanimity and justice of the United States (Arana to Alvear, Aug. 19, Nov. 11, 1845, *ibid.*). Rosas, using material which Alvear had sent, gave the case great publicity in the Argentine press. See the *Archivo Americano*, II, 159-76.

3. Alvear to Arana, Aug. 20, 1845, AGN, S1, A1, A1, núm. 5. Alvear was not authorized to bid for such an agreement, and it was against such independent proposals that Rosas solemnly warned him before he left home in 1838.

4. Memorandum of a cabinet meeting, Aug. 26, 1845, *Polk Papers*, First Series, Library of Congress.

5. Alvear to Arana, fragment, n.d., AGN, S1, A1, A1, núm. 6, and also his dispatch of April 30, 1839, A1, A2, A4, núm. 13.

6. Alvear to Arana, Dec. 3, 1845, AGN, S1, A1, A1, núm. 5. Alvear was reasonably correct in his interpretation of the American attitude toward the Spanish people. Often this feeling was revealed unconsciously. When war talk prevailed during the Oregon controversy, the New York *Daily Globe* dared England to start trouble, declaring, "after all, we are no Mosecho Nation, Argentine Republic, or poor Asiatic. . . ."

As a preface to an article on La Plata politics, the editors of the *American Review* III (1846), 160, expressed deep suspicion of English or French territorial aspirations "whenever they come into contact with half-civilized or savage nations too weak to take possession of their country by force and too uncultivated to diplomatize with skill."

7. Alvear to Arana, Nov. 26, 1850, AMREC, Caja 41.

8. Alvear to Arana, Feb. 11, 1846, AGN, S1, A1, A1, núm. 6.

9. Alvear to Arana, Oct. 26 and Dec. 5, 1851, AMREC, Caja 41.

10. Alvear to Arana, Feb. 5, March 18, 1849, AMREC, Caja 41.

11. Alvear to Arana, Sept. 21, 1846, AGN, S1, A1, A1, núm. 5.

12. Rough draft of manuscript without date, AGN, S1, A1, A1, núm. 4, packet number 194; Alvear to Arana, April 28, 1841, AGN, S1, A2, A4, núm. 13; also his dispatches of June 15, Nov. 2, 1848, and Dec. 9, 1849, AMREC, Caja 41.

13. Alvear to Arana, March 5, 1841, AGN, S1, A2, A4, núm. 13.

14. Alvear to Arana, May 13, 18, 1844, AMREC, Caja 12.

15. Alvear to Arana, July 13, 1844, *ibid.*

16. Alvear to Arana, May 13, 1849, AGN, S1, A2, A4, núm. 13.

17. Alvear to Arana, Sept. 15, 1851, AMREC, Caja 41.

18. *Journal of Commerce* (New York), July 19, 1845.

19. Although Alvear had regularly complained to Rosas of a total lack of funds, he had by 1845 established quarters in a good hotel, with his own furniture, library, and pictures. His official correspondence for the first three years of his ambassadorship he had left in Washington, and this material escaped loss. Some of his current material which was being copied elsewhere was saved. All his personal and official correspondence from 1842 to 1845 was burned. Alvear explained the rather impressive list of personal losses by saying that he was trying to keep a residence worthy of his country and appealed to Rosas for some remuneration to cover the damage, but his requests were totally ignored (Alvear to Arana, Aug. 3, 1845, AGN, S1, A1, A1, núm. 5).

20. The motion failed. When the Austrian Emperor heard of the proposal, he started to recall Baron Bodisco, then changed his mind, saying that only what passed the chamber was important. Owing to the democratic form of government, he could ignore the rest. When Stoeckl, the Russian minister, saw how narrowly the United States had avoided a break of relations with Austria, he observed, "This country is in luck; everything comes out right" (Alvear to Arana, May 19, Aug. 19, 1850, AMREC, Caja 41).

21. Alvear to Arana, Aug. 28, 1850, AMREC, Caja 41.

22. Alvear to Arana, Dec. 28, 1848, *ibid.*

23. Alvear to Arana, Dec. 11, 1845; April 8, 1846, AGN, S1, A1, A1, núm. 5.

24. Alvear to Arana, Oct. 29, 1849, AMREC, Caja 41.

25. *Ibid.*

26. Alvear to Arana, April 20, Sept. 19, Oct. 29, 1850, AMREC, Caja 41.

27. Domingo Faustino Sarmiento, *Obras* (Santiago de Chile, 1886), tomo V, "Viajes por Europa, Africa, y America," pp. 333 ff. Also, *A Sarmiento Anthology*, ed. Allison W. Bunkley (Princeton University Press, 1948) gives extensive translations in the chapter entitled "Travels in the United States in 1847," pp. 191-266.

28. A fragment of this manuscript is in the Donación de Alvear, Archivo General de la Nación, S1, A1, A1, núm. 4, packet 194. The text was first published in *El Diario*, a Buenos Aires newspaper, on Nov. 5, 1889, at the centenary of Alvear's birth, and was reprinted in a book recording the services at the time, as edited and prepared for publication by Juan E. de Alvear, under the title *Corona Fúnebre*, pp. 125-37.

29. Alvear considered Quiroga, Rosas, and Artigas unworthy of public honors. The mention of this latter name aroused his hatred of the chieftain who had driven him from the Directorate. The old feeling flared up, and the final paragraph castigates the sins of Artigas: using the brutish imbecility of the lowest classes for private ends, enslaving the upper classes, assassination, throat-cutting, exile, confiscation of property, robbery, and unchecked exercise of a monstrous savage without religion and without conscience. Alvear confessed that the great majority of the Argentine people, following this barbarous system, had cast him out of office and made "the revolution of April 15, 1815, the great triumph of Artigas."

Footnotes to Chapter IV, Part 7

1. Alvear to Rosas, Feb. 4, 1839, AGN, S1, A1, A1, núm. 5; and reprinted in Rodríguez, *Contribución*, III, 572; Tomás de Iriarte, *Memorias*, III, 315; V, 83.

2. Arana to Alvear, July 9, 1841 (Rodríguez, Contribución, III, 505-507). Guido wrote in 1849 of the death of Sarratea in Paris and of the temporary assignment there of Mariano Balcarce. This opening gave Alvear the opportunity he long had wanted, but Rosas overlooked him.

3. Felix Castro of Buenos Aires served as business agent for Alvear. He received the checks from the government and after distributing sums to creditors and to the family, would send the remainder to Alvear. Generally a firm doing business in Baltimore and Philadelphia accepted the money and ordered its North American agents to honor the drafts General Alvear should make on them. Neither the General nor the associates in North America could know when the government had failed to make payment to his agent. The firm frequently found that it had accepted drafts from Alvear when his agent had made no deposits in Buenos Aires. Alvear was subjected to long and embarrassing delays if he had to wait for word of the deposit to reach him before filing his draft. Since Rosas never had enough funds except for war, Castro was in a difficult position. He was unwilling to make any protest over nonpayment for fear that the government officials would call him a Unitarian—the usual title given to any objector. Ultimately this reproach was laid against him, and he escaped only by fleeing the city for a time. His personal correspondence with Alvear is found in AGN, S1, A1, A1, núm. 4.

4. Alvear's initial annual salary amounted to 500 *pesos metálicos* (or gold). In Nov., 1843, the Secretary of Foreign Affairs stated that the minister's salary amounted to 7,000 pesos of an unspecified sort, with an additional 500 *pesos metálicos* for a departmental scribe.

In 1851, under the new Urquiza regime, Alvear received 690 gold pesos per month. This sum he divided as follows: 370 pesos for himself, 120 for Emilio, 170 for the family in Buenos Aires, and 30 pesos to an agent who was accumulating a trust fund for his wife (Zimmerman and Frazier [an Argentine business firm] to Alvear, Dec. 17, 1851, AGN, S1, A1, A1, núm. 5).

5. Alvear to Rosas, March 13, 1839, AGN, S1, A1, A1, núm. 5; and another undated (about 1840), AGN, S1, A2, A4, núm. 13; and Alvear to Arana, Feb. 14, 1841, April 18, 1843, AMREC, Caja 12; Sept. 2, 1844, May 14, Aug. 10, Feb. 6, 1846, AGN, S1, A1, A1, núm. 5.

Neutral contemporaries considered Alvear an opponent of Rosas whom the Dictator mercifully sentenced to exile rather than to assassination. This is the traditional explanation of Alvear's relationship to Rosas. See Dorr to Forsyth, Sept. 14, 1835, Consular Letters, Buenos Aires, IV; and Pendleton to Webster, Sept. 23, 1852, National Archives, State Department, Argentine Republic, Dispatches, VIII.

6. Alvear to Arana, May 10, 1841, AMREC, Caja 12.

7. Alvear to Arana, Dec. 10, 1843, AGN, S1, A1, A4, núm. 13.

8. New York *Evening Post*, May 1, 1845.

9. Arana to Alvear, Feb. 19, March 27, 1846, AGN, S1, A1, A1, núm. 5; also Rosas' annual message to the Twenty-second Legislature, 1842.

10. Tomás de Iriarte, *Memorias*, IV, 185-86; V, 110-11, 150.

11. For some of the decoded letters, see Rodríguez, *Contribución*, II, 447-519.

12. Alberdi to Alvear, April 4, 1846 (*ibid.*, III, 590); manuscript of this and letters immediately following are found in AGN, S1, A1, A1, núm. 4.

13. General D. Z. Benavente, a native Chilean, had been an old companion of Alvear during the days of exile in Montevideo when both men fought as allies of

the Chilean Carrera brothers. By 1846 Benavente had forgotten conveniently that he had fought for anything beyond independence. See Tomás de Iriarte, *Memorias*, I. 170 ff.

14. Benavente to Alvear, April 16, 1846.

15. Madariaga to Alvear, April 25, 1846.

16. Pirán to Alvear, July 19, 1846.

17. "The noble and happy resistance that my government has given to two of the most powerful nations of the earth has raised to an eminent height the reputation and credit of the Illustrious General, the Very Excellent Senor Don Juan Manuel de Rosas, to whom the Argentine Confederation is the debtor for the credit and reputation she enjoys and to see herself the first among the Spanish-American nations . . . for which, as sons of that soil, the individuals that compose this legation send to you the most sincere recognition, and ask that you will be pleased to present these sentiments to the Governor and Captain-General as well as the most cordial congratulations and best wishes for the good outcome which have attended the wisdom of his acts, projects, and resolutions" (Alvear to Arana, Sept. 24, 1848, AMREC, Caja 41). See also in this file Alvear's dispatch of April 21, 1850, which expresses parallel if less fulsome praises.

18. Alvear to Ferrero, Sept. 19, 1851 (Adolfo Saldías, *Papeles de Rosas*, II, 197). As Rosas began to lose his hold in Argentina, official correspondence carried increasingly bitter headings or "aspirations." Alvear, by 1851, was beginning his dispatches: "Death to the crazy traitor, savage Unitarian Urquiza."

19. Discourse of Don Valentín Alsina at the tomb of Alvear, 1854. Draft in AGN, S1, A1, A1, núm. 4. Reprinted by Juan E. de Alvear (ed.), *Corona Fúnebre*, p. 85.

20. Arena to Alvear, Dec. 31, 1851, AGN, S1, A1, A1, núm. 5.

21. Peña to Alvear, Feb. 25, 1852, AGN, S1, A1, A1, núm. 5.

22. Alvear to Peña, June 4, 1852, *ibid.*

23. López to Alvear, May 11, 1852; López to the President of the United States, May, 1852, *ibid.* The two older sons, Emilio and Diego, returned to Buenos Aires, while a younger son, León, assumed the duties of secretary.

24. Alvear to Urquiza, July 13, 1852, AGN, S1, A1, A1, núm. 4. As a postscript Alvear gave his permission to Urquiza to publish the letter if he should desire to do so.

25. Alvear to Urquiza, July 13, 1852, *ibid.*

26. Guido to Alvear, June 8, 1852, *ibid.*

27. Alvear to Urquiza, Oct. 28, 1852, *ibid.*

28. Carlos de Alvear to his son, Emilio, n.d. (1852) (Rodríguez, *Contribución*, III, 595-96). The original draft is in AGN, S1, A1, A1, núm. 4, packet 194.

29. López forgot that Alvear was living in exile until Rivadavia secured the passage of the Law of Oblivion. After his return to Buenos Aires, Alvear was on trial during Rivadavia's administration, not one of its directors. In the last months of this government Alvear had been absent on his mission to England and the United States. During Rivadavia's second administration Alvear was then often considered a rival of the government.

30. López to Alvear, Oct. 5, 1852 (Rodríguez, *Contribución*, III, 596).

31. Peña to Alvear, Aug. 23, 1852, AGN, S1, A1, A1, núm. 5. The revolt of the province of Buenos Aires in 1852 against the administration of Urquiza did not affect Alvear's position in the United States. The seceding province notified Washington and Alvear that it would not be bound by his acts. No foreign recognition was accorded this rump government and Alvear ignored the decree (Alvear to Peña, Oct. 27, 1852; Peña to Alvear, July 1, 1852; Alsina to Alvear, Sept. 29, 1852, AGN, S1, A1, A1, núm. 5; Alsina to Alvear, July 7, 10, 1852, AGN, S1, A2, A4, núm. 13; Pendleton to Webster, July 9, 1852, National Ar-

chives, State Department, Argentine Republic, Dispatches, VIII; decree of Alsina, Sept. 22, 1852, AGN, S1, A1, A1, núm. 6.

32. Alvear to Webster, April 22, 1841, Aug. 30, 1842; Alvear to Legaré, May 2, 1842; Alvear to Upshur, Dec. 28, 1842, Notes from the Argentine Republic, I, pt. 2, National Archives, State Department; Castro to Alvear, April 24, 1841, AGN, S1, A1, A1, núm. 4. Also, the State Department circular to the Diplomatic Corps, Aug. 27, 1842, AGN, S1, A1, A1, núm. 5.

33. Alvear to Webster, January 5, Feb. 6, 1851, National Archives, State Department, Notes from the Argentine Republic, I, pt. 2; Webster to Alvear, Jan. 11, Feb. 5, 1851, *ibid.*, Notes to the Argentine Republic, VI.

34. Alvear to Peña, Oct. 28, 1852, AGN, S1, A1, A1, núm. 5.

35. Don Diego was regarded as one of the most promising young men of his generation. Education and residence abroad had given him a better training than most of his contemporaries. He ranked high in Urquiza's favor and for a time edited his official organ, *El Progreso*. The United States chargé in Buenos Aires, Pendleton, mentioned him to Webster as one who had contributed greatly to the success of the revolution. "I mention him particularly since his father has been so long and favorably known at Washington" (Pendleton to Webster, March, 1852, National Archives, State Department, Argentine Republic, Dispatches, VIII).

36. Manuscripts, AGN, S1, A1, A1, núm. 5.

37. León de Alvear to Peña, Nov. 5, 1852, AGN, S1, A1, A1, núm. 5; and circulars to the Diplomatic Corps, AGN, S1, A1, A1, núm. 4.

38. León de Alvear to Tomkinson, Nov. 5, 1852, AGN, S1, A1, A1, núm. 4.

39. See the funeral orations in the collections by Juan E. de Alvear, *Corona Fúnebre*. Also, AGN, S1, A1, A1, núm. 4, the section marked "no date" for accounts of the funeral.

Notes to Appendix

1. Archivo General de la Nación, Buenos Aires, AGN, S1, A1, A1, no. 10. A special search of the British archives reveals no documentary proof of this conference. There are copies neither of Canning's invitation and questionnaire nor of the written replies which Alvear says that he left with the British minister.

Notes to Translation

1. AGN, S1, A2, A4, no. 10. Apparently Alvear composed his report in great haste; certainly his secretary gave little heed to punctuation. With a semicolon and a *que* he rushes from one thought to the next. It has seemed advisable to pay greater attention to customary punctuation in order that subjects and predicates may not be too deeply obscured.

Notes to Diplomatic Comment

1. Tomás de Iriarte, "Cuarenta Anos Antes," *Revista de Buenos Aires*, X (1866), 193-224.

2. Tomás de Iriarte, *Memorias*, III, 162-63.

He did not reproduce all of the second interview, but veered away from it by a transparent strategem: "The rest of the conference I have mislaid but it continued to the end in this same vein." Yet it didn't! Iriarte stopped the transcription at the place where the President was complaining about the privateering which persisted among the Latin-American nations. And Iriarte had no use for the official account of Monroe's remarks on Brazil since in the memoirs he had garbled these with those of Adams and then presented the whole as the "first" interview with Monroe. Conscious omission of relevant facts for an ulterior purpose was a trait in Alvear which Iriarte disliked very much.

3. John B. Moore, *Digest of International Law*, V, 507-9.

INDEX